"This great book [*A Christian Philosophy of Education*] with its commendable candor, rugged vigor, and transparent honesty, deserves to get the attention of a vast audience."
—*The Southern Presbyterian Journal*

"Gordon Clark is one of the profoundest evangelical Protestant philosophers of our time. . . . Those who have not yet read his works have a rewarding opportunity awaiting them."

—Carl F.H. Henry

"Clark's thinking is . . . a magnificent and earnest effort to bring all things into captivity to Christ and his word. . . . Clark [is] one of the most distinguished Christian thinkers of our time."
—*Westminster Theological Journal*

WITHDRAWN

WITHDRAWN

A CHRISTIAN PHILOSOPHY
of
EDUCATION

A CHRISTIAN PHILOSOPHY
of
EDUCATION

Gordon H. Clark

The Trinity Foundation
Jefferson, Maryland

Cover: *Titian's Schoolmaster*
Giovanni Battista Moroni
National Gallery of Art, Washington; Widener Collection

A Christian Philosophy of Education
© 1946 Lois A. Zeller and Elizabeth Clark George
Second revised edition © 1988 The Trinity Foundation
Post Office Box 169
Jefferson, Maryland 21755
Printed in the United States of America.
ISBN: 0-940931-20-6

Contents

Books by Gordon H. Clark

Readings in Ethics (1931)
Selections from Hellenistic Philosophy (1940)
A History of Philosophy (coauthor, 1941)
A Christian Philosophy of Education (1946, 1988)
A Christian View of Men and Things (1952)
What Presbyterians Believe (1956)[1]
Thales to Dewey (1957)
Dewey (1960)
Religion, Reason and Revelation (1961, 1986)
William James (1963)
Karl Barth's Theological Method (1963)
The Philosophy of Science and Belief in God (1964, 1987)
What Do Presbyterians Believe? (1965, 1985)
Peter Speaks Today (1967)[2]
The Philosophy of Gordon H. Clark (1968)
Biblical Predestination (1969)[3]
Historiography: Secular and Religious (1971)
II Peter (1972)[2]
The Johannine Logos (1972)
Three Types of Religious Philosophy (1973)
First Corinthians (1975)
Colossians (1979)
Predestination in the Old Testament (1979)[3]
I and II Peter (1980)
Language and Theology (1980)
First John (1980)
God's Hammer: The Bible and Its Critics (1982, 1987)
Behaviorism and Christianity (1982)
Faith and Saving Faith (1983)
In Defense of Theology (1984)
The Pastoral Epistles (1984)
The Biblical Doctrine of Man (1984)
The Trinity (1985)
Logic (1985)
Ephesians (1985)
Clark Speaks From the Grave (1986)
Logical Criticisms of Textual Criticism (1986)
First and Second Thessalonians (1986)
Predestination (1987)
The Atonement (1987)

[1] Revised in 1965 as *What Do Presbyterians Believe?*
[2] Combined in 1980 as *I & II Peter.*
[3] Combined in 1987 as *Predestination.*

Foreword

Americans spend, collectively and severally, voluntarily and involuntarily, $300 billion on education each year; federal, state and local governments appoint commissions to discover why public education has failed; and books analyzing and lamenting the state of American education become runaway best-sellers. Yet with all this expenditure and activity American education continues to worsen, for not one American in a thousand understands the proper purpose of education.

"The end of learning," wrote John Milton, "is to repair the ruin of our first parents by regaining to know God aright, and out of that knowledge to love him, to imitate him, to be like him. . . ." If this be so—and the Bible says it is so—then the aims of education in America are all wrong.

The purpose of education is not to enable the student to earn a good income.

The purpose of education is not to preserve our American system of government and political freedom.

The purpose of education is not world unification.

The purpose of education is not to teach young people a trade.

The purpose of education is not to encourage the never-ending search for truth.

The purpose of education is not to put the student in

harmony with the cosmos.

The purpose of education is not to raise the consciousness of students and train them for world revolution.

The purpose of education is not to prepare students for productive careers.

The purpose of education is not to integrate the races.

The purpose of education is not the social adjustment of the child.

The purpose of education is not to stay ahead of the Russians (or the Japanese) in technology.

The purpose of education is not to create good citizens.[1]

No, the purpose of education is far different, far more noble than any of these things. The purpose of education is to make Christian men, men transformed by the renewing of their minds after the image of Him who created them.

Yet the educational system in the United States is hostile to such education. It regards men as trousered apes, and its products, understandably enough, behave like untamed ani-

---

1. Those libertarians who are fond of blaming government involvement in education on Martin Luther and the Reformation should read their mentor, Aristotle. In the *Politics* he wrote: "No one will doubt that the legislator should direct his attention above all to the education of youth, or that the neglect of education does harm to states. The citizen should be molded to suit the form of government under which he lives. . . . And since the whole city has one end, it is manifest that education should be one and the same for all, and that it should be public, and not private—not as at present, when everyone looks after his own children separately, and gives them separate instruction of the sort which he thinks best; the training in things which are of common interest should be the same for all. Neither must we suppose that any one of the citizens belongs to himself, for they all belong to the state, and are each of them a part of the state, and the care of each part is inseparable from the care of the whole. . . . That education should be regulated by law and should be an affair of state is not to be denied. . . ."

It was precisely the Biblically-based Reformation that denied the totalitarianism of Plato and Aristotle. Men are creatures of God, and the authority of governments is limited, severely limited, by the Bible. The punishment of evil-doers, not the education of the young, is the function of government. I can explain the failure of libertarians to quote Aristotle and the Bible only on the basis of their anti-Christian bias.

mals. The focus of American education, if one can speak of it having a focus, is not merely on this world, but on the most unimportant things in this world. The various educational philosophies in vogue in the last half of the twentieth century agree in only one thing: their opposition to Christianity.

The anti-Christian origins of our anti-Christian public school system were explained more than a century ago by a Unitarian turned Roman Catholic, Orestes Brownson. Describing a movement of which he was a part in the early nineteenth century, the utopian socialism of Robert Owen, the Scottish industrialist, Brownson wrote:

The great object was to get rid of Christianity, and to convert our churches into halls of science. The plan was not to make open attacks on religion, although we might belabor the clergy and bring them into contempt where we could; but to establish a system of state,—we said *national*—schools, from which all religion was to be excluded, in which nothing was to be taught but such knowledge as is verifiable by the senses, and to which all parents were to be compelled by law to send their children. . . . The first thing to be done was to get this system of schools established. For this purpose, a secret society was formed, and the whole country was to be organized somewhat on the plan of the *carbonari* of Italy, or as were the revolutionists throughout Europe by Bazard preparatory to the revolutions of 1820 and 1830. . . . [T]he plan has been successfully pursued, the views we put forth have gained great popularity, and the whole action of the country on the subject has taken the direction we sought to give it. . . .[2]

2. Orestes A. Brownson, *The Works of Orestes A. Brownson*, Henry F. Brownson, collector (New York: AMS Press, 1966), volume XIX, pp. 442-443; as quoted in *Is Public Education Necessary?* Samuel L. Blumenfeld (Phoenix: The Paradigm Company, 1985), pp. 95-96.

Now, after more than a century of government education, the effects of this anti-Christian educational system are becoming clear even to some non-Christians. But while the non-Christians see the problems—the crime, the drugs, the promiscuity, the diseases, the illiteracy, the ignorance, the disbelief in truth—they do not see the solution. A University of Chicago Professor, Allan Bloom, published a best-selling book on education last year, *The Closing of the American Mind.* In his book, Professor Bloom, who is not a Christian, offers a brilliant analysis of the moral and epistemological relativism that now controls our entire culture, including education, the view that all values are relative, and there is no truth, but only various "truths." But while his analysis is acute and, at times, brilliant, Bloom is like the doctor who diagnoses the disease but never prescribes a cure. Or worse, the doctor prescribes a treatment that will exacerbate, not meliorate, the disease.

Bloom criticizes the modern American university because it is not a *uni*versity, but a *multi*versity: "The university now offers no distinctive visage to the young person. He finds a democracy of the disciplines. . . . This democracy is really an anarchy. . . . There is no vision, nor is there a competing set of visions, of what an educated human being is. . . . There is no organization of the sciences, no tree of knowledge. . . . Thus, when a student arrives at the university, he finds a bewildering variety of departments and a bewildering variety of courses. And there is no official guidance, no university-wide agreement, about what he should study. . . . So the student must navigate among a collection of carnival barkers, each trying to lure him into a particular sideshow."

Professor Bloom recalls that the first student rebels at the University of California at Berkeley in the 1960s were objecting to this very phenomenon: competing carnival barkers, each trying to lure them into a sideshow. The students wanted then, as students want today, a comprehensive and unified view of things. That is precisely what American education cannot give them.

Nearly twenty years ago another critic of American education outlined the problem this way:

> Directly or indirectly, the influence of philosophy sets the epistemological standards and methods of teaching for all departments, in the physical sciences as well as in the humanities. The consequence, today, is a chaos of subjective whims setting the criteria of logic, of communication, demonstration, evidence, proof, which differs from class to class, from teacher to teacher. . . . It is as if each course were given in a different language, each requiring that one think exclusively in that language, none providing a dictionary. The result—to the extent that one would attempt to comply—is intellectual disintegration.
>
> Add to this: the opposition to "system-building," i.e., to the integration of knowledge, with the result that the material taught in one class contradicts the material taught in the others, each subject hanging in a vacuum and to be accepted out of context, while any questions on how to integrate it are rejected, discredited and discouraged.
>
> Add to this: the arbitrary, senseless, haphazard conglomeration of most curricula, the absence of any hierarchical structure of knowledge, any order, continuity or rationale—the jumble of courses on out-of-context minutiae and out-of-focus surveys—the all-pervading unintelligibility—the arrogantly self-confessed irrationality—and consequently, the necessity to memorize, rather than learn, to recite, rather than understand, to hold in one's mind a cacophony of undefined jargon long enough to pass the next exam.[3]

---

3. Ayn Rand, "The Cashing-in: The Student Rebellion," in *The New Left: The Anti-Industrial Revolution* (New York: New American Library, 1971), pp. 31-32.

What is Professor Bloom's solution to this anarchy in higher education? After nearly 350 pages of analysis and criticism he writes: "Of course, the only serious solution is the one that is almost universally rejected: the good old Great Books approach, in which a liberal education means reading certain generally recognized classic texts, just reading them, letting them dictate what the questions are and the method of approaching them. . . ."

But this, of course, and I emphasize the *of course*, is not a solution at all, still less a serious solution, and it is certainly not the only solution. For the "bewildering variety of courses" offered by contemporary universities, Bloom would substitute a bewildering variety of philosophies. "Just reading" Plato, Aristotle, Hegel, Kant, Augustine, Aquinas, Rousseau, Calvin, Darwin, Descartes, Bacon, Hobbes, Locke, Leibniz, Anselm, Marx, Spinoza, Berkeley, Kierkegaard, Nietzsche, Hume, Machiavelli, Ockham, Spencer, Plotinus, Pascal, Freud, Shakespeare, Moses, the Apostle Paul, Lucretius, Swift, Smith, Homer, Scotus, Bonaventure, Luther, Russell, James, Montesquieu, Aristophanes, Bossuet, and Dewey is simply substituting one carnival of sideshows for another. Professor Bloom's solution, spread before the world in several hundred thousand books, is no solution at all. What is needed is a comprehensive unifying philosophy of education, and he offers none. Could anything speak more eloquently of the intellectual bankruptcy of humanism than this?

Where Professor Bloom fails, Gordon Clark succeeds, and brilliantly. Clark presents a coherent philosophy of education, a philosophy that can guide not only the university, but the kindergarten as well. The end of education is not the creation of carpenters, engineers, and plumbers, nor even doctors, lawyers, good citizens, and scientists, but *men*. Christian men. Guided by Christian philosophy, all of education, from kindergarten to university (Bloom does not discuss the first 13 years of education at all) can aim at instilling the love of truth and of God in the minds of the young.

Solomon explained the purpose of education long ago:

To know wisdom and instruction,
To perceive the words of understanding,
To receive the instruction of wisdom, justice, judgment, and equity:
To give prudence to the simple, to the young man knowledge and discretion, (a wise man will hear and increase learning, and a man of understanding will attain wise counsel),
To understand a proverb and an enigma, the words of the wise and their riddles.
The fear of the Lord is the beginning of knowledge, but fools despise wisdom and instruction. If you cry out for discernment, and lift up your voice for understanding, if you seek her as silver, and search for her as for hidden treasures, then you will understand the fear of the Lord, and find the knowledge of God. For the Lord gives wisdom; from his mouth come knowledge and understanding. Happy is the man who finds wisdom, and the man who gains understanding; for her proceeds are better than the profits of silver, and her gain than fine gold. She is more precious than rubies, and all the things you may desire cannot compare with her.

John W. Robbins
December 23, 1987

Preface

The large variety of religious books to which the public has been treated during the last one hundred years has in the main represented two points of view. First, the Roman Catholics have efficiently resurrected Thomas Aquinas and have applied his principles to the major phases of human life. By an increasing volume of scholarly works they have made Neo-scholasticism a force in the present day world. The second religious viewpoint is that of liberalism or modernism. But though the amount of publication has been tremendous, and though this type of religion has come to dominate most of the large Protestant denominations, modernism, in contrast with the fortunes of scholastic philosophy, has suffered serious reverses. The liberals of some decades ago were on the verge of ushering in the millennium. Evolution and the doctrine of man's inevitable perfection had almost made us angels, and Utopia was just around the corner. This easy optimism was shaken by World War I, and World War II was its *coup de grâce.* But if the rude facts of history have shaken its complacency, the calmer methods of philosophy have been equally damaging. The attempt to conserve Christian values without basing them on orthodox theology is seen to result in an unstable position. Rejecting revelation in favor of experience, the modernist today must choose between acknowledging an anti-christian experience or retracing his steps to some sort of normative revelation.

He must become humanistic or orthodox.

In an endeavor to meet this need, a third type of religious philosophy has come to the fore. It is the neo-orthodoxy or neo-supernaturalism of Karl Barth and his associates. Insofar as this development is a witness to the instability of liberalism, it serves a useful function. But the claim that Barthianism is a return to Calvinism cannot be sustained. The more one examines this neo-orthodoxy, the less orthodox it is seen to be. Then, too, the theories of paradox and the Wholly-Other God seem to be philosophically untenable. For these reasons Barthianism is not an escape from the religious dilemma that demands either humanism or a real orthodoxy without any neo.*

Though sufficient argument to justify the force of this dilemma cannot be inserted in an introduction, the inherent seriousness of the problem places upon every individual, and especially upon the liberals, the obligation of considering the two possible choices. Humanism is receiving attention and adherents. The historic position of Protestantism ought also to be studied. But instead of being a welcome subject of study, Protestantism faces constant attempts to prevent its being heard; and the impression is sedulously cultivated that the problems have all been settled, and Calvinism has nothing worthwhile to say. The result naturally is that historic Protestantism is dismissed thoughtlessly. Let it be granted that some of the blame falls on the orthodox Protestants themselves. For one reason or another they have not done as the Roman Catholics have done: They have not developed a philosophy and applied its principles to contemporary problems. Nor does this present book attempt to supply this deficiency.† With the exception of

---

* See Gordon H. Clark, *Karl Barth's Theological Method* (Nutley, New Jersey: Presbyterian and Reformed Publishing Company, 1963).

† See however, Gordon H. Clark, *A Christian View of Men and Things; Religion, Reason*

Chapter 8, the treatment is almost purely popular and makes no claim of being an ambitious scheme to expound a Protestant system of philosophy. Furthermore, it is limited to the one field of education, and even in this field its formulations are far less comprehensive than the conventional title, if taken literally, would indicate. Yet while the subject is but one among many, education is important in its own right. And not only so; for in addition, the one is a test case for the many. The study of education presumably will show that conservative Protestantism has certain definite philosophical principles, and that these principles are applicable both to education and to other problems as well. And if perchance more capable writers are stimulated to publication on these many subjects, there may grow a body of literature sorely needed by orthodox Christians, and still more sorely needed by those who wander in this dark world without a light to guide them.

Almost forty years have passed since the first edition of this book appeared, and it is now dated. This second edition is also dated. Many of the old references remain. New data have been added. But the subject matter is never out-dated. On the contrary, more than ever the Christian people of America need to be impressed with the necessity for Christian education.

The present book is about three halves the length of the earlier one. It is useless to burden a Preface with a list of deletions and additions. Perhaps the most important improvement is the clearer indications of the logical connections between the parts of the argument.

May God, partly through this argument, save our young people from this present world.

Gordon H. Clark

and Revelation; The Philosophy of Gordon H. Clark, and the other books of Dr. Clark.—Editor.

Chapter 1
The Need for a World-View

"Those who can, do; those who cannot, teach; those who cannot teach, teach Education." From the testimony of a large number of students who have been required to take courses in Education, not only does there seem to be some truth in this harsh, popular judgment on their professors, but one also gains the impression that the courses the professors teach are of even less value. What there is of value, according to common student opinion, has been diluted, padded, and stretched to make several courses instead of being assembled into a single one the equal of courses in mathematics or history. It is not surprising, therefore, that Departments of Education must depend on legislative compulsion rather than on intrinsic merit to obtain students. In all the curriculum no other subject is so widely condemned as is Education.

This situation indicates that professors of Education and courses in Education are two important problems in educational philosophy. Other professors and other courses are also problems. No author can write very fully on education without giving some space to questions of curriculum. And if not much attention is paid to the person of a college professor, the teachers in the elementary grades are objects of study. Nor does educational theory slight the pupil. The prospective teacher must study child psychology. A school can operate satisfactorily only if the teachers understand children. Then, too, schools and school systems have administrators. These higher officials perforce develop policies, and the problems involved are usually perplexing.

Although this listing of the problems of education may not be complete, it is sufficient to produce a striking contrast between the obvious importance of these matters and the widespread condemnation of courses in Education. When one stops to think, this condemnation is a remarkable phenomenon. The secular society of our day would do well to remember that Plato considered the training of children to be exceedingly important. For people who respect the Hebrew and Christian traditions the Bible can be quoted: "Gather the people together, men, women and children . . . that they may learn . . . and observe to do all the words of this law; and that their children, which have not known anything, may hear . . . ."* Proverbs 22:6 is a more familiar passage: "Train up a child in the way he should go; and when he is old he will not depart from it." Other verses, both of precept and example, could be added. Not only have great leaders, like Plato and Moses, emphasized education, but large numbers of parents, to varying degrees no doubt, have followed their recommendations. Schools of many types in all lands at all times have exerted great influence. Surely then their aims, their methods, and their results are worthy of serious study: Education is a possible topic of investigation as truly as physics or literature. To have it condemned so widely by its own students is indeed a curious phenomenon.

Perhaps the phenomenon contains its own explanation. If education is as worthy a field of investigation as physics and history, and if it is taught by incompetent professors, the disparity between the possibilities of the subject and its actual

---

* Deuteronomy 31:12-13

teaching could easily produce acute disappointment and harsh judgment. But this cannot be the complete explanation. There are poor teachers of physics and history also. The reasons for failure must be sought in the methods used, unsuccessfully, to assemble valuable contents for the courses. Education is a respectable subject for study because it is an important human activity having vital relationships with many, if not all, other human activities. It is an essential component of the world. And if it is to be treated adequately, its place in relation to the rest of the world must be accurately located. Education cannot be properly considered in a state of isolation. As an important part of the world, its understanding requires a general view of the world of which it is so important a part. The professor of Education therefore ought to have a developed and consistent philosophy. Of course, in any mediocre School of Education there are courses with the title, The Philosophy of Education. But it is a fact, another curious fact, that few philosophers in this country have bothered with education, and few professors of Education know much general philosophy. This divorce between Education and philosophy, particularly in the case of those who teach the philosophy of Education, seems the best explanation of Education's discredit. The courses are vague, they are confused, they lack unity and direction; the textbooks are inflated with an inelegant disproportion of pontifical quotations; and these things are true because no comprehensive world-view governs their development. If education as a subject is to achieve the respect its inherent worth demands, its professors must produce a basic world-view into which their educational theories fit and on which they depend. Doubtless every professor of Education has some sort of philosophy underlying his views of education, but it is ordinarily an unconscious philosophy, unexpressed and unacknowledged, or at best poorly formulated.

If criticism has been too severely centered on professors in Departments of Education up to this point, a pertinent and perhaps aggravated illustration of the deficiency may be seen in the policy of American colleges and universities in general. Let us extend our examination beyond Departments of Education and consider the schools and colleges. Are the universities, either collectively or as separate wholes, superior to their Departments of Education?

When attention is directed to the educational policy of the American universities, a difficulty appears at once. Should one even suggest that there is a collective educational policy? Or is it not true that every institution has its own philosophy and that there are few agreements? One college emphasizes golf and the social graces, a second is known throughout the country for nothing but its football, and a third in one of the north-central states has the largest proportion of Phi Beta Kappa members on its faculty. Some colleges offer typing and home economics; others say that training the fingers does not constitute a liberal education. Some colleges make swimming a requirement for education; others are more impressed with a student's ability to read German. It is therefore more than doubtful that one can legitimately speak of *the* philosophy of *the* American university.

If there is no uniform philosophy for all American universities, can it be said that each one singly has its philosophy? Does not the large proportion of Phi Beta Kappas show that the college referred to has a liberal arts rather than a vocational philosophy? No doubt it does. But "liberal arts" is neither a very extensive nor a very strict philosophy. Emphasis on liberal arts does not make a college Hegelian or Pragmatic. On the faculty of such a college there are doubtless representatives of several philosophical schools. Accordingly the philosophy of that college does not extend very far into details, nor is there strict enforcement of any one view.

When attention turns from "the American university," and from any single college regarded as a unit, a more uniform philosophy may be discovered within some departments. In one college all the teaching of psychology is directed to convince the student of the truth of one particular theory, be it behaviorism or parallelism; while in another laboratory experimentation is so stressed, as scientific method, that theory and interpretation are eschewed. Their philosophy is to have no philosophy: Each experiment emphatically is significant, but no one answers the question, Significant of what? The Philosophy Department of the University of Minnesota has been one hundred per cent Logical-Positivistic. But other philosophy departments deliberately select their professors so as to have exponents of many views.

At any rate—however it may be with some departmental exceptions—American colleges have no philosophy of education. They may have some vague ideals or aims. The school that stresses golf has the aim of producing young gentlemen. When typing and home economics are included in the curriculum, the aim is mildly vocational, or perhaps the idea is "preparation for life." Of course, strictly vocational schools have the most definite aims of all—and the least philosophy. The aims of the liberal arts schools are more general and vague. Catalogues state them in impressive language with little content. They strive for "excellence in education"; but there seems to be no clear-cut, definite, all embracing philosophy—just an aggregate of disjointed, cultural ideas.

Someone may, however, attempt to reply that these are differences of detail only. It is impossible for two universities to be exactly alike, and the various curricula are just the means which different administrators think are most efficient to reach what is essentially the same end. Are they not all trying to give to students an "education"?

Thus to cover all the various procedures of a hundred different institutions under the name *education* is not exactly conducive to clarity. A training of the fingers does not seem to be the equivalent of a training of the mind. The excellent typist cannot ordinarily solve problems of physics or understand the course of history, and ordinarily the scholar cannot type in a professional manner. In fact, the situation is worse than this. The schools of Education have long discussed the aims of education, and while most of their work concerns elementary education, it is instructive to note that they generally speak of *aims* in the plural rather than of *the aim* of education. This is a tacit admission of failure to find any one comprehensive aim. It is a failure to provide any criterion by which one subject should be included and another excluded from the curriculum.

More recently the departments of Education have begun to speak of *citizenship* as the one comprehensive aim of education. By its various programs the school is to produce good citizens. But again comes the question of clarity: Is good citizenship any clearer a term than education itself? In pre-war Japan, in Hitler's Germany, and in all Communist countries, good citizenship means subservience to the ruling Party; and good education may be a governmentally controlled procedure for inculcating the thoughts of Chairman Mao.

We hope that citizenship means and will continue to mean something very different in the United States. But even in the United States there is little agreement on the meaning of good citizenship. In 1933 when the National Recovery Administration came into existence, some people argued that, although they would not have initiated that particular plan, yet since the President had demanded it, everyone ought to obey its provisions and help it to succeed, for otherwise there would be no cure for the depression. But some argued that it was unconstitutional, that it violated fundamental American liberties, and that its success would be worse than any depression. They were in the minority, but they happened to be right, so right that the non-packed Supreme Court agreed with them. Though despised by the majority, they were good citizens.

Or again, in those early thirties many people spoke of the Supreme Court as thwarting the will of the majority of the people. Especially the labor unions called for majority rule, and anyone who opposed majority rule would be in their eyes a bad citizen. American tradition, however, has never favored simple majority rule. Among all the governments of the world the United States has been foremost in protecting the right of minorities, and the smallest minority is the individual, and these rights are not regarded as gratuities from the government in power, but as God-given. It is clear then that good citizenship is an ambiguous term, and to use it as the comprehensive aim of education is merely an attempt to hide a deep confusion. The confusion is deep because the substituting of unrelated aims for a single comprehensive aim in education is both the result and the example of the absence of any ultimate aim for human life as a whole. If the educators had any view of the chief end of man, they would find it easier to locate the proper place of a liberal education. Whether it be the views of an individual professor or the policy of a faculty, all will be confusion unless founded on an unambiguous world-view. But this is what modern education does not have.

Since the majority of professors of Education have no extended and definite philosophy, since also common opinion supports them in thinking that the details of Logical Positivism, Hegelianism, and Existentialism are irrelevant to the teaching of children and even to the administration of a university, it is necessary to show why this loose view is mistaken. Nor is it hard to do so. The most obvious starting point is the fact that teachers teach children. There is a subsidiary discussion as to whether teachers teach children or whether they teach arithmetic. That is to say, educators sometimes debate whether the classroom should be subject-centered or pupil-centered. Since the present writer wishes to emphasize content and subject matter, and delights in the quip about the progressives who teach children and do not teach arithmetic, and the other quip about the third grade pupil who proudly told his old-fashioned parents that he did not need to learn arithmetic because he was developing a social consciousness, he cannot be accused of unwarranted bias when he insists that teachers do and must teach children. At least they (should) teach arithmetic to children.

No doubt a teacher can teach some arithmetic to third grade pupils—or calculus to college sophomores—without knowing much about philosophy or about pupils either. But his teaching is better if he does. Those educators in particular who teach children and not arithmetic are strong for child psychology. The teacher must know children.

But now we have fallen into an "ocean of arguments" no less deep and wide than Plato's *Parmenides*. Suppose the child, the human being, is an evolutionary product, simply a more complicated animal, without a soul, especially without an immortal soul. The late Supreme Court Justice, Oliver Wendell Holmes, said, "I can see no reason for attributing to man a significant difference in kind from that which belongs to a baboon or to a grain of sand. . . . I wonder if cosmically an idea is any more important than the bowels."* Bertrand Russell's famous passage, quoted in chapter three, builds life and therefore education "only on the firm foundation of unyielding despair." The end of man is a doom, pitiless and dark. All the labor of the ages is destined to extinction and must inevitably be buried beneath the debris of a universe in ruins. Suppose on the

---

* As quoted in Ben W. Palmer, "Hobbes, Holmes, and Hitler," *The American Bar Association Journal* (31:569), November 1945.

other hand that God created man in His own image and breathed into him the breath of life, with the result that those redeemed by Christ shall glorify God and enjoy him forever.

Teachers teach pupils. But whereas a teacher with the first view of what a pupil is teaches despair along with arithmetic or social consciousness; the teacher with the second view teaches hope.

In these two views, naturalism and theism, are intertwined all the strands of philosophy. Even the question whether the government should control education for its own ends and ban God from the schools, or whether the church, home, or private corporations should do the educating, depends on what man is. Once admit that the teacher teaches pupils, it is impossible to rule out any part of philosophy as irrelevant.

Among the considerations that have come under review, some mention has been made of the effect of government on education. Mention should also be made of the effect, or alleged effect, of education on government. Americans often speak of public education as if it were the main support of democracy. Without an educated populace all sorts of evils would proliferate, and the professional educators claim that unless the legislatures appropriate almost unlimited amounts of tax money for the schools, the nation will shortly collapse. The fact of the matter is that with hundreds of billions already appropriated for public education, all sorts of evils have proliferated and the nation is already collapsing. A Justice of the United States Supreme Court was forced to resign in the 1960's because of suspicious financial arrangements. The 1970's and 1980's have seen a series of national scandals in all three branches of government. No wonder America raises its crime rate faster than it inflates its money.

And education? Far from being the bulwark of democracy and the savior of civilization, public education cannot protect itself. Its products are its enemies. Fifteen years ago the United States Office of Education estimated that damage by vandals to public schools ran as high as one hundred million dollars yearly. Window breakage in Chicago alone cost about one million dollars a year. In New York City in one year 243,652 windows were broken, at a cost of $1,218,260. Arson cost Los Angeles $850,000 in two years. This means arson on school property: not general arson as in the Watts riots. Does this widespread damage, caused by the schools' pupils, give the impression that civilization can be protected by public education? Rather, civilization must be protected from public education.

On a broader scale one notes that educated nations cause more evil than uneducated nations. The American Indians went on the war path, and the cannibals of the Congo fought and killed; but the really important wars were initiated and executed by England, France, Germany, and the United States. Note too that the first three nations did not wage such terrible wars during the unenlightened Middle Ages as they have done since acquiring higher academic standards.

Another, but not so violent effect of education is hedonism. In the summer of 1969 over 300,000 young people—one estimate by televison reporters was 500,000—gathered for a music festival in a small New York town. Nearly all smoked marijuana, some used heroin, and at least one died there from an overdose; fornication was widespread. What is wrong with American education that it results in such a group gathering in one place at an assigned time? How many more such irresponsible social parasites were there who could not attend that gathering?

In the past twenty years several similar but smaller gatherings have occurred and drug use and fornication have become permanent American institutions. Public schools have become centers for both activities.

One must therefore ask whether educators have any good reason for supposing that education, American public education, can influence government and society for good instead of for evil. If there is any possibility that education can be productive of good, that possibility depends on the inclusion of morality in the curriculum. But what is morality? How are moral norms discovered and known? Do they or do they not require a theological foundation? The present volume, as its title suggests, asserts the need of a theological basis for morality; but the sole point intended at this juncture is that a knowledge of child psychology, including of necessity a view of the origin and nature of man, the relation between education and government, and the inclusion or exclusion of morals and theology, requires an intelligent educator to have a rather well-developed philosophy or world-view.

Most educators, unfortunately, have little philosophy and oscillate among aggregates of discordant opinions. Yet, while public elementary schools and private, as well as state, universities usually have no definitely elaborated world-view, there may be something that can be called the philosophy of modern American education. In spite of the fact that one is Hegelian, another realistic, and another pragmatic, there is a certain unity observable. It is however, a negative unity. It is the unity of opposition to Christianity. The Hegelian may be and often is very religious; he speaks with evident piety of the Absolute God; and collectively he writes a large number of volumes on religion. The pragmatists are more frequently irreligious, though William James, before he became a behaviorist and repudiated consciousness, held to some sort of a god. But whether they speak of a god or not, they do not believe in a transcendent, personal Creator; they do not believe in a Sovereign God; and they most emphatically do not believe in sovereign grace. This rejection of the very basis of Christianity pervades all their teaching. Suppose they are teaching history: In this case they may give certain economic causes of a war, but they would never think of considering a war as a punishment sent by God on account of national sin. The effect of this naturalistic view on the explanation of the destruction of Jerusalem in 586 B.C. is obvious and disastrous. Or, in teaching sociology, the cure for crime appears to them to be the removal of slums and other external changes. Murder may be something to be discouraged and even punished, but that there is an inherited evil character and that capital punishment for murder is divinely ordained are matters only for more or less polite rebuttal. Despite the fact that here and there a professorial chair is held by a true Christian, those illustrations are sufficient to justify the statement that modern education is unified, though negatively, by an anti-Christian philosophy.

The first choice, therefore, among world-views on which to base a theory of education is a choice between Christian theism and some non-Christian view that reduces ultimately to a form of humanism. That these are the only two alternatives may require a little explanation, but that the educational theory appropriate to a godless world-view must differ *toto coelo* from that of Christian theism ought to be immediately evident.

Before any attempt is made to justify a theistic world-view as a basis for educational theory, it might be wise to show more definitely and in greater detail the trends in modern American schools. While the majority of educators have maintained that metaphysics, philosophy and religion have little to do with education, not all the educators in the country have so ignored the need of a guiding philosophy, and some justice ought to be done to them. Then, further, an examination of conditions is all the more imperative because they reflect and gain significance from the present sad but crucial state of the world.

For long periods of time human history moves placidly

along, troubled only by minor disturbances. Then in a short span of years everything seems to happen at once. A storm overtakes the race, breaking up all the fountains of the great deep; and when the waters subside, the course of history has been set for the next epoch. The sixteenth century was such an age of storm. Henry VIII, Martin Luther, John Calvin, Francis I, Ignatius Loyola, Caraffa; and a little later Philip II, Queen Elizabeth, Henry IV, the Duke of Alva, and John Knox all lived in the fifteen hundreds. During this period it was settled that Germany should be Lutheran, Scotland Presbyterian, England Episcopal; the Inquisition determined by murder that Italy and Spain should remain Romish; the mass murder of some seventy-five thousand Calvinists on St. Bartholomew's Eve in 1572 made France half Romish and half infidel. These results have endured for four hundred years.

Not only did the sixteenth century witness the Reformation, it also saw in the Renaissance the birth of the modern scientific mind. While inventions and detailed scientific applications have been multiplied in more recent years, the general scientific world-view, based on the application of mathematics to problems of physics, was fixed for the coming centuries even before Descartes was born.

The twentieth century bids fair to rival the sixteenth. Two world wars have already occurred and with a third a constant threat, this century will truly be one of upheaval. Hitler wished to set the direction of history for the next thousand years. He may well have done so—aided, of course, by Roosevelt, Churchill, and Stalin. The twentieth century, so far, lacks indications of impending religious cataclysms. Its changes, therefore, may parallel more closely the social and educational revolution of the Renaissance, or, more likely, the break-down of the Roman Empire, than the spiritual quickening of the Reformation. From all that can be seen now, humanism and

Communist hatred of Christianity will be the prevailing philosophy of the coming age.

While the political situation that makes newspaper headlines occupies popular attention, the use which dictators have made of the means of education shows clearly that the role of schools and universities is of more profound significance. Educational policy in the new society, whether for good or evil, will be a basic factor. For this reason it is important to know what are the recent trends in American universities and to anticipate, so far as is possible, at least the immediate future.

First, let us examine the educational interests of American colleges before December 7, 1941. If a generalization be permitted—a generalization, however, with happy though infrequent exceptions—educational discussion was bogged down in a morass of triviality. Primary educators discussed whether grammar schools should end at the sixth grade instead of the eighth and whether a junior high school should be inserted before the senior high school. College educators repeated the same theme with respect to junior colleges. Faculties spent hours discussing comprehensive examinations, junior-senior hours, and one-half grade point for some extracurricular activity. They gave earnest attention to how they were doing things, but little reflection was given to the things they were doing. Perhaps the faculties thought they knew what an education was, but their lowering of graduation requirements gave little evidence of it.

The liberal arts requirements were altered to cater to a group of students who, having found German and mathematics too difficult for them, thought they were competent to reform economics and sociology. On the other hand, the requirements on students intending to enter professional schools were raised so far as their technical subjects were concerned. There were pre-law, pre-medical, pre-engineering, pre-dental courses.

These courses on the whole provided excellent technical training, and with the crowding out of the liberal arts they produced expert ignoramuses, efficient cogs in somebody's machine. William Clyde Devane in the Autumn 1943 issue of *The Yale Review* repeated what a few clear-sighted people had known for some time. Students, he said, now graduate from high school—he might have said college—unable to write, read, or speak English; unable to cope with mathematical problems which require algebra and trigonometry; unable to use any foreign language—and at a time of international upheaval when all these things are very much needed.

Some educators glorified this condition. One remarkable statement, almost requiring no comment, is that of Edward Lee Thorndike, in an address "Human Resources," published in *The University and the Future of America*, by the Stanford University Press in 1941.

> The welfare of a community, that is, the goodness of life for good people in that community, can be measured by a composite index made up of thirty-seven items of fact, such as the infrequency of death in infancy, the infrequency of death from typhoid . . . the frequency of ownership of homes, of automobiles, and of radios, the frequency of domestic installations of telephones, electricity, and gas . . . .

It is true that our best-trained men can invent radios and radar; it is true that they can reduce typhoid and infant mortality—more power to them; it is true that they can produce bigger submarines and better explosives; but it ought to be as clear as a flare and as emphatic as a bomb that *who* uses these for *what* is a tremendously more important matter than their invention. In fact, the impact of Pearl Harbor, Korea, and Vietnam ought to have focused educational attention on this basic question. Thorndike's telephones will multiply, but their wires may carry commands to massacre Jews and Christians; radio and television will be greatly developed, but it may be used for totalitarian propaganda; and young men who have not died of typhoid may make excellent KGB agents. Every mechanical aid, by which Thorndike judges that a society is good, can be used by bureaucrat or dictator to make his society bad.

How can the people of the United States become competent to judge and therefore withstand the barrage of propaganda? The barrage has come. *Time, Newsweek*, and the news programs on television are supposed to be news media. They are actually propaganda outlets. For example, on Friday, August 15, 1969, Chet Huntley ended his news program with a vicious denunciation of Protestants. There was no news in it at all. It was unadulterated invective. He stopped just short of saying that the Roman Catholics of Eire should invade Ulster and massacre the Protestants. And of course the news is slanted, too. How slanted must the populace already be that such interpretation should be allowed on television? If some form of education prepares people to detect slanted news and thereby prevent a social climate where hate propaganda is accepted, it is not the present form of American education. Least of all is it a narrow technical training that produces expert ignoramuses. This is not to deprecate engineering, much less to oppose physics and chemistry. But something additional, something more important is needed. What is it?

These questions are far more basic than those of extracurricular grade points and the length in hours of a comprehensive examination. Though unanimity is not achieved among the educators, it is fortunate that their attention is somewhat withdrawn from trivialities to really important problems. Unanimity is too much to expect—far too much when the questions are so essential. Instead of reaching unanimity, educational discussion has developed two radically antagonistic positions.

The one stresses vocational education. On this side there are probably only a few university men. The former president of Antioch College, Algo D. Henderson, seems to be in this camp. His article in *The American Scholar* of Autumn 1943, called for more rather than less vocational instruction and practice for the regular college student; he looked for the extinction of the American middle class and foresaw a nation of workers and of government clerks. In such a society a rigid or common curriculum must be abolished, and education must be geared into the work of the world by a system of apprenticeships at jobs.

This does not seem to be the view of most university men; it accentuates the defects of the previous educational set-up; but it has the backing of bureaucrats and has been aided, perhaps unintentionally, by Army and Navy programs. The Army and Navy bought education on contract. Industry in peace time can conceivably do the same thing. But in both cases they pay for what they want and they want nothing else. While industry has ordinarily assigned specific problems to its research men and has been interested only in applied science, it is just possible that a very large corporation might support a little pure science; but it is less conceivable that it would support an archaeological expedition; and only if it could be turned into patronage, could one think of the Tammany delegation in Congress voting for research in Hellenistic philosophy. The question should be put pointedly and insistently: Who can best judge the content of an education—a bureaucrat, a labor racketeer, or (with all their failings) a college faculty?

The second group of educators, apparently including the majority of university people, rejects the vocational view. Robert Hutchins, former president of the University of Chicago, spoke earlier, but World War II brought others to his general position as they saw the result of Germany's repudiation of the liberal arts in favor of government-propagandized technical education.

No one denies that applied science can be worthwhile; no one denies that great inventions have been made; but Western civilization, as it became mechanically unified by telegraph, telephone, radio, and television, has disintegrated socially, morally, and religiously. Physical means of living have been multiplied, but the purpose and end of life, which alone make the means worthwhile, have faded from view.

It is not only the factories that have inaugurated the piece-work system; the universities have done the same thing, and people in general have adopted the piece-work method of living. A chemical formula is valuable because it makes varnish; an animated cartoon is valuable because during the show one can forget one's worries; a job is a good thing because we like to eat. These fragments of civilization, Thorndike's thirty-seven fragments, are accepted as valuable in themselves alone without a suspicion that a life of detached fragments has no value at all. Why not commit suicide and save so much bother? Seriously, why not?

To remedy the defect of modern civilization, the defect of having no chief purpose and accomplishing it efficiently, this second group of educators points to the broader basis of judgment provided by a liberal arts education. An able exponent of this demand for a unifying life purpose was Lewis Mumford in "Unified Approach to Knowledge and Life," happily included in the same volume that contains Thorndike's vacuum cleaner philosophy. The article is to be highly recommended. Mumford stresses the need of orientation, of seeing the relationships between chemistry and aesthetics, economics and Greek grammar, literature and mathematics. That is, he wants us to see life as one whole. He has a keen sense of the need of a criterion by which to judge the conflicting voices of television, press, and movies. And if these voices, instead of conflicting, all speak a centrally controlled ideology, there is still more urgent need of calm criteria. A narrow technical training provides no safeguard against being deceived. Only a liberal arts education that uncovers three thousand years of human motives, foibles, reflections, and devices offers hope. Only a knowlege of how one science or one part of a science is related to all other knowledge can give one the needed perspective on life. Chemistry is undoubtedly important and worthwhile, but only if it is integrated with morality. Greek grammar has value, but only if it contributes to the chief end of man. Now the study of the relationships among chemistry, Greek, and anthropology is not just another subject among many. While it is so listed for convenience' sake in college catalogs, philosophy is rather the subject that underlies our approach to and use of all other subject matter. Philosophy is the study not of a part but of the whole. And for the lack of serious study of the whole, American education has lowered its standards, compromised with commercialism, and distinguished itself by mediocrity.

There are, then, two discernible trends in American education today: First, some want government-propagandized vocational training and aim to crush private institutions by high taxes; second, the large majority of university men desire free schools committed to the wisdom of the liberal arts. Perhaps ambiguously committed. These men insist on freedom, academic freedom; some even speak of the autonomy of the university and wish to evade responsibility to the nation's courts of law in criminal cases, like the clergy in medieval times. But nonetheless they are eager for tax appropriations and they organize marches on the legislatures. One must now ask, Are these attitudes consistent? Latin American universities are autonomous. They have just about the poorest academic standards in the world. Free from criminal prosecution, armed militants are in control; they terrorize the less radical students, hire and fire professors to suit their likings, and hope to overthrow the government. So much for autonomy. Accepting tax money is not so obviously destructive of academic freedom. But tax money brings government control, in degrees, more and more, until it ends in a Nazi, feminist, Marxist, or other statist theory of education. How can professors whose salaries come from the State fail to slant their teaching in favor of State subsidies? How can they fail to oppose, to counteract, to ridicule a theory of true freedom, and to harass and finally eliminate professors with conservative views? This has already been done on a large scale, for most faculties have few conservatives. Nevertheless, between 1945 and 1985 there has been a growing emphasis on liberal arts.

President Hutchins before World War II was the first to bring public attention to the need for a basic philosophy to unify education. Against the prevailing tide he struggled to convict education of a fragmentary, disjointed approach and to urge a unified approach governed by basic principles. Now he has many educators to echo his demands. They have sounded a needed note and deserve our gratitude. But they seem to have failed in one very important point. It will, I trust, not be construed as a lack of appreciation if a single criticism is offered in conclusion.

The one great flaw in the work of President Hutchins is that while he emphasized the need for a basic philosophy to unify education, he failed to supply the philosophy. For the contents of his ideal curriculum he proposed a series of great books. This program is one of considerable excellence, and it has enjoyed wide popularity. It not only reintroduced some of the great books into college courses, but from 1945 to 1955 adults formed clubs to discuss them. There must have been a dozen, possibly twenty, such discussion groups in the medium-sized city of Indianapolis. Even some of President Hutchins' opponents conceded that these books had been unwisely neglected for many years. Their study and discussion was a great improvement. But, note well, the books proposed do not present a single, unified philosophical system, nor have I been able to discover that President Hutchins provided for their explication on the basis of a definite philosophy. In other words, Hutchins analyzed modern education, diagnosed its disease, said that a remedy is needed, but he failed to write the prescription. Now, if someone wishes to unify education, it is not enough to say that a philosophical basis is necessary. To accomplish such a result, it is essential to provide the philosophy.

Mumford, too, it seems, also failed at this crucial point. In fact, to speak clearly, his conclusion makes success impossible. The reasons for this assertion must be deferred to the following chapters. Here, as a conclusion to this first chapter, what they aim to show can be stated only in the form of a thesis, to wit:

There is only one philosophy that can really unify education and life. That philosophy is the philosophy of Christian theism. What is needed is an educational system based on the sovereignty of God, for in such a system man as well as chemistry will be given his proper place, neither too high nor too low. In such a system there will be a chief end of man to unify, and to serve as a criterion for, all his activities. What is needed therefore is a philosophy consonant with the greatest creed of Christendom, the Westminster Confession of Faith. In such a system, God, as well as man, will have his proper place. This alone will make education successful, for the social, moral, political, and economic disintegration of a civilization is nothing other than the symptom and result of a religious breakdown. The abominations of war, pestilence, and economic collapse are punishment for the crime, better, the *sin*, of forgetting God.

But Mumford, excellent as his article is, with an allusion to the phraseology of Augustine, aims to found the new City of Man. Let us, on the other hand, contemplate the more solid foundations and the greater splendor of the City of God.

Chapter 2
The Christian World-View

Christianity is a supernatural religion; it is through and through the contradictory of naturalism and humanism. Christians believe in a God who is distinct from and independent of the natural world. The natural world is God's creation and is in all respects without exception entirely and wholly subject to him. There are other things also that might very well be said of Christian theism, for though Christianity is theistic, not everything called theism is Christian. No doubt Islam is properly called theistic, and in one sense of the word English Deism also, and Unitarianism. Christianity therefore is not just a belief in the existence of God, of some sort of God, even of a God who created the world. Aside from the other particular doctrines summarized in the creed mentioned at the end of the last chapter, Christianity teaches a Triune God, and this is entirely different from Islam and Unitarianism. Not only so: Christianity also teaches that God revealed himself in Holy Scripture and controlled the events therein recorded. For a Christian, therefore, a discussion of theism cannot completely exclude these matters. The present chapter must mention some of them. But nevertheless a defense of the theistic world-view has to consider the arguments for the existence of God. At any rate theism means that the world and all its contents, education included, cannot be understood apart from the existence of a God of some sort.

The humanist denies the existence of God. True it is that some modern humanists want to retain the term God for emotional or symbolic purposes. One humanist defines "God" as those characters of nature that enable us to enjoy life. No lengthy arguments are needed to prove the existence of this "God." Everyone, and particularly the atheists, acknowledge that some events are enjoyable. But this god is no God at all. The more honest humanists admit it. The humanist denies the existence of God because he views the world as a self-contained and self-explaining fact. There is nothing beyond, behind, around, or before it. He proceeds on the first principle so clearly enunciated by Lucretius long ago in *De Rerum Natura* I, 149-150:

> *Principium cuius hinc nobis exordia sumet,*
> *Nullam rem e nihilo gigni divinitus umquam.*

The basic principle that we shall assume as our starting point is that nothing has ever been created by divine power.

The question to be answered therefore is, Who was right, Epicurus or Jesus Christ?

In recent years the magnificent development of archaeology has been claimed by Christians as demonstrative of their position. For example the now antiquated Wellhausen theory affirmed that the Pentateuch, instead of having been written by Moses, was a production of the Babylonian captivity and contained nothing of historical value relative to the time of the patriarchs. Genesis was an historical novel, uncritically composed, and could throw light, an indirect light, only on the age of the prophets in which it was written. In particular, the war of the five kings recorded in the fourteenth chapter of Genesis is pure myth, as is seen by the fact that the east side of the Jordan, down which the armies are said to have marched, was never of any military importance; all the invasions of Palestine from the north and east came down the west side of the Jordan. So argued the proponents of the Wellhausen criticism. But in 1929, in the buried cities of Ham and Ashteroth, on the east side of the Jordan, archaeologists discovered military fortifications dating from the time of Abraham. This and countless other fragments of information, when pieced together, have effectually disposed of the contention that Genesis reflects Palestine from the viewpoint of a Babylonian captive. Where the narrative has been tested, it has been found true; and Christians have the right to cast into the teeth of their adversaries the challenge to produce some definite and tangible evidence of the falsity of any historical statement in the Bible.

On the other hand, while it is true that non-Christian critics have made sweeping claims without evidence, even denying that the Hittite nation ever existed, Christians too have sometimes used arguments that cannot strictly be justified. The fallacy of some Christian applications of archaeological data becomes apparent when all the detail is summed up in a single premise and the form of the inference is bared to examination. Because the Bible has been shown to be true in these hundred and one cases, as some unwary Christians like to state the general argument, it follows that the Bible is therefore true in a thousand other cases not yet tested. Obviously this does not follow; and the fallacy is all the more glaring in that the points examined are matters of history where shards, weapons, and artifacts are legitimate evidence, whereas the other thousand contain a great deal of doctrinal or theoretical material which is not susceptible of archaeological verification. How can pieces of pottery prove the doctrine of justification by faith alone?

As in war the most fatal blunder is to underestimate the enemy's strength, so in the battle for truth careless argumentation is not conducive to progress. Sadly enough, the particular type of fallacy mentioned above is inexcusably frequent among Christians. Not that they alone are guilty, for it is a common human failing. When a cheap politician is addressing a party rally, the inexperienced listener may fail to note that the speaker is listing as his premises the party policies which at least are doubtful. Then drawing the inference from these premises the admitted fact that this party is the best of all parties, the speaker can be confident that the loyal audience will uncritically accept the premises and admit the validity of the argument. In logic books this is called the fallacy of asserting the consequent. Of course it is not fair to say that whenever the fallacy occurs it was intentionally prepared by the speaker. The speaker himself may be sincerely deceived, or the fault may lie wholly with the listener who misunderstands. One may wonder, for example, what goes on when Jehovah's Witnesses attack the Deity of Christ. As is well known, they vigorously attack the Roman church, and then claim that the Deity of Christ is a Roman invention. The housewife to whose door the Witness has come may think in her own mind: The Romanists believe in the Deity of Christ and their councils have so declared; the Romanists have widely departed from the purity of the Gospel; why of course that is true; so that, though I never thought of it before, it now seems likely that the Bible does not teach the Deity of Christ. Between this housewife's meditation, and the well-meaning Christian who argues that since Wellhausen is wrong, the Bible must be God's Word, there is no logical difference. He has not proved the truth of the Bible; he already believed that the Bible was true, and therefore he erroneously assumed the validity of an inference alleged to prove it.

It is essential, then, in any serious argument never to be deceived by the truth of a conclusion. When facing an opponent, one's conclusion is not a matter of common agreement and he will soon see the invalidity of the argument and reject the conclusion. Hence when a Christian attempts to force the data of archaeology beyond the limits of logical validity, he is playing into the hands of the enemy. Archaeology is extremely valuable and deserves support, but it does not prove that the Bible is true, much less do s it prove the existence of God. It is valuable in refuting the claims of the destructive critics. It shows that they have been persistently and uniformly wrong. This is all to the good. But Christianity has other and more subtle enemies than Wellhausen and the destructive critics.

One of these more subtle enemies is willing to admit that archaeology has confirmed many historical statements in the Bible. If in a good humor and forced to it by historical evidence, he might even admit the occurrence of miracles; and, if in a very good humor, he might go so far as to agree that the resurrection of Christ was at least possible. But he would question the validity of basing Christian truth, or any religion, on historical premises. Spinoza, for example, considered religion to be a system of universal truth, so that the contingent truths of history would be irrelevant. Kierkegaard also refused to base religion on historical propositions. Some of his followers say that the events of Christ's life are of no importance to us. The existentialists go still further. Contradicting Spinoza they discard universal truths also. Religion is not concerned with truth; revelation is not a communication of truth; God can mystically reveal himself through falsehood.

But before getting bogged down or fogged in by mystical falsehood, let us examine a secular view that would remain undoubtedly atheistic even if it were forced, by historical research, to admit many of the miracles and other events recorded in the Bible. Suppose, to be concrete, that Joshua actually did pronounce certain words and that at the same time the sun just happened to stand still. If this is a coincidence of history, it proves nothing as to the existence of the God of Israel. Suppose fire actually did consume Elijah's sacrifice. To be sure it is a wonderful world and many queer things happen. The old uniformitarian philosophy is too narrow, too mechanistic; we who are up to date must admit the infinite diversity, disparity, and unconnectedness of events. William James wrote a book, *The Pluralistic Universe*. In it he chiefly opposed Hegel, who saw the world as one. All its parts were completely unified in, and all its problems were completely solved by, the Absolute. James objected, and he objected to Theism as much as and even more than he objected to Absolutism. The universe is not one, either in itself, or in some omniscient mind. No one thing is related to everything else. There are no universal relations. This is a marvelous, a pluralistic, a miraculous world, and Christians who try to force it into medieval forms of logic are stupidly intellectual. Suppose Jesus did rise from the grave. This only proves that his body resumed its activities for a while after his crucifixion; it does not prove that he died for our sins or that he was the Son of God.

A pluralistic universe, or better, a pluriverse, has lots of room for miracles. Though the arguments against Hegel and in favor of pluralism contain elements a Christian need not admit, the inference that miracles do not establish theism is perfectly valid. Miracles could be used to defend polytheism; or, as in James, simply the disconnectedness of events. The Resurrection, viewed purely as an isolated historical event, does not prove that Christ died for our sins according to the Scriptures, (1) because Lazarus rose from the dead though he did not die for our sins, (2) because sin is a theological concept defined by and not a premise for a particular view of God and man, and (3) because a Christian usage of miracles and history presupposes the falsity of pragmatic pluralism. On such questions as these archaeology and history are utterly incompetent.

It should of course be clear that these considerations do not justify an ignoring of the Resurrection in Christian preaching. Although the Resurrection is not the basis of the Christian faith, it is an important, an essential, part of the message. In the Acts of the Apostles there are several resumés of sermons: Peter's sermons, on the day of Pentecost, at the Beautiful Gate, before Cornelius; Paul's sermons, in the synagogue at Antioch of Pisidia, on the Areopagus; and in all these the Resurrection finds a place. Indeed Christians today may well judge between true and false evangelism, between a Gospel in full strength and a diluted Gospel, by measuring the evangelist's sermon against those summarized in the Acts.

Now while the Resurrection, a statement of which is easily understood, was preached to all sorts of audiences, other material involving an extended knowledge of the Old Testament could not at first be used with the Gentiles. The Jews, naturally, were prepared to understand the Gospel; the Gentiles were not. And as some of the fuller explanation had to be postponed in Gentile preaching, some of the more elementary facts did not need explicit mention in the Jewish mission. For this reason, Peter's sermon at Pentecost and Paul's sermon on Mars Hill were different, both in content and in results. Since faith cometh by hearing, it is not surprising that the prepared audience responded, while the unprepared audience did not.

Likewise today some subjects require immediate attention more than others, depending on the knowledge of the audience. A people saturated with a sentimental notion of the love of God needs to hear about his righteousness and wrath; and, to come to the point in question, when modern philosophy has rejected the type of Greek philosophy prevailing in the first century of our era; when, to make a more recent comparison, the twentieth century has broken with the nineteenth and pragmatically denies that the world is rational, it follows that the Christian, while defending his whole system, must pay special attention to the part immediately attacked. There may have been a time when people would believe in God but not in miracles; there may have been a time when people believed in a rational universe but not in a personal God; now, however, even the rationality of the universe is brought into question, and it requires little insight to realize that historical events are no defense against such an attack.

The Christian view of the world—and this is also true of ancient Greek philosophy and nineteenth century Hegelianism —requires it to be conceived as rational, uniform, and harmonious. But pragmatism does not. While not all pragmatists exhibit the vehemence of the following quotation, yet their general notion is fairly well represented in the words of Bertrand Russell, who, if I mistake not, somewhere wrote concerning the rationality of the universe: "The most fundamental of my intellectual beliefs is that this is rubbish. I think the universe is all spots and jumps, without coherence or orderliness or any of the other properties that governesses love."

When the Christian is faced with such a thorough-going pragmatism, he must admit that the pragmatist is essentially correct in his contention that historical events of themselves do not constitute theism. The miracles of the Bible are clearly incompatible with the type of world uniformity assumed by the ordinary forms of idealism and materialism. But they can find a queer though not logically impossible place in pragmatism as well as in the uniformity of theism. The alleged events, instead of constituting Christian theism, stand themselves in need of philosophic interpretation. In fact this modern enemy of Christianity might conceivably argue that these miracles rather support his own view. They show that there is no uniformity to the world. Things just happen; all sorts of things; that is the way things are; we must accept them as brute facts. Thus the historical events and miracles of the Bible are simply disjointed events and do not lead us to accept the theistic theory which the Bible imposes on them.

In view of this pragmatic dealing with history, its positivistic denial of universal law, of metaphysics, of supernatural interpretation, it may be permitted by way of anticipation to suggest the conclusion that, instead of beginning with facts and later discovering God, unless a thinker begins with God, he can never end with God, or get the facts either.

Therefore the reflective Christian, after he has silenced the criticisms of the philologian and historian, must turn from archaeology to theology in order to answer the pragmatic philosopher. Traditionally, three types of argument have been used to prove the existence of God; if any one of them should prove validly the existence of the God of the Holy Scriptures, the battle would be over and archaeology would be merely the subsequent operation of mopping up. But is any one of these three arguments valid?

It would probably be out of place here to insert a technical disquisition on the classic proofs for the existence of God. A few historical references must suffice. The ontological argument, first published by Anselm, Archbishop of Canterbury, in the eleventh century, and reduced to a syllogism by Descartes, viz., God, by definition, is the being who possesses all perfections; existence is a perfection; therefore God exists; was soon rejected by the Roman Catholic theologians under the influence of Aristotle and Thomas Aquinas; it was severely criticized on logical grounds by Immanuel Kant; and in general is at best looked on with considerable suspicion. None the less, W.G.T. Shedd in his *Dogmatic Theology*, who may be taken as an example of a few Protestant theologians, seems to approve of the ontological argument to the exclusion of the other two. More frequently, however, the theologians attempt a compromise. Admitting that none of the three is conclusive, they claim that together, each helping the other, they are satisfactory. The situation may be compared with a lawyer who puts a witness on the stand. The opposing counsel shows that the witness is an inveterate perjurer and that his testimony cannot be relied upon. But, replies the first lawyer, I shall put three perjurers on the stand and their combined testimony will prove my point. It should be noted that Anselm developed the ontological argument to render all other arguments superfluous. The other two, in Plato's *Laws* and Aristotle's *Physics*, were also supposed to be conclusive. And it would seem that any such argument would have to be either an all sufficient proof of God's existence or a logical fallacy. These arguments cannot be merely half correct; there is no such thing as semi-validity. An alleged demonstration is either valid or invalid. If it be valid, the conclusion is established, and that is the end of it; if it is invalid, that is the end of it, too. Those who think that each argument has some value should learn from plane geometry what is meant by demonstration.

The ontological argument, based as it is on the definition of God, makes no appeal at all to experience. The cosmological argument was framed to make the minimum appeal to experience. In its barest essentials it runs: Since something exists—a contingent being like myself for instance—there must also exist an eternal necessary being. Thomas Aquinas and the Roman Church accept this as conclusive. They also accept the argument which appeals to the greatest possible experience —the teleological argument. It has no lowest terms. From all the order perceived in all the details of astronomy, physics, chemistry, botany, zoology, psychology, and morality, it is inferred that there must be an ordering mind which has so arranged the universe. Among Protestants some early writers give it absolute value; for example, John Locke writes: "But though this [God's existence] be the most obvious truth that reason discovers, and though its evidence be (if I mistake not) equal to mathematical certainty; yet it requires thought and attention . . . ."* Kant himself was tremendously impressed by the teleological argument, but his sober reflection led him to regard as fallacious the cosmological and teleological as well as the ontological. Even if the principle of causality could be applied beyond the world of experience—which Kant denied— the arguments would prove only the existence of a being just logically greater than the world. In other words, they might prove a contingent, or finite god, but they do not demonstrate the absolute, necessary Being, the transcendent Trinity. Hence practically all the later Protestant theologians explicitly repudiate the enthusiasm of Locke and state that the force of the argument is not mathematical, *i.e.*, not rigorous, or strictly logical.

If now all empirical material, such as archaeological investigations, and the classic arguments for the existence of God do not prove Christian theism, it is natural to ask why any one should accept a theistic philosophy. The question taken literally is legitimate, but the insinuation that one should never adopt a world-view except on a demonstrative basis, rests on a confusion which reflection should have little trouble in dissipating. For it should be equally evident that, if theism does not admit of strict proof, the same is not less true of the anti-theistic systems of pragmatism, pantheism, and materialism. In this respect therefore theism is under no greater disadvantage than is any other system: Basic world-views are never demonstrated; they are chosen. William James and Bertrand Russell may believe in a pluralistic universe, but they can offer no demonstration of this, the most fundamental of their intellectual

---

* *Essay Concerning Human Understanding,* IV. v, I.

beliefs. The mechanist believes that all natural phenomena can be reduced to mathematical, quantitative equations, but he never gives a mathematical demonstration of his belief. So it is with every world-view; the first principle cannot be proved— precisely because it is first. It is the first principle that provides the basis for demonstrating subordinate propositions. Now if such be the case, the thoughtful person is forced to make a voluntary choice. As a matter of fact, the thoughtless person as well is forced to choose, though the necessity to make a choice and the particular choice made may not be so obvious. It is obvious, however, that a thoughtful person, one who wishes to understand, one who wants to think and live consistently, must choose one or another first principle. He may choose theism, or he may choose pantheism, or he may prefer to reject these possibilities and claim to be a skeptic. This too is a choice.

The term skepticism, however, needs clarification. Etymologically a skeptic is one who seeks; but philosophically a skeptic is one who does not find. Or, rather, he finds that there is nothing to be found. There is no truth, and knowledge is impossible. Aside from the self-contradiction of asserting the truth that there is no truth, skepticism is not a world-view. In particular no theories or policies of education can be deduced. Neither can objections against naturalism or theism be based on pure ignorance. It is therefore useless to spend further time on skepticism.

For the same reason nothing much need be said about agnosticism either. It does indeed have one advantage over skepticism in that it cannot so easily be convicted of self-contradiction. The agnostic simply does not know. He does not know that there are no truths; he merely does not know which propositions are true. But neither the skeptic nor the agnostic really believes what he says. As Augustine long ago pointed out, when such a man eats his dinner be believes that it is probably better to eat than starve. He does not know that he will escape starvation, but he believes that he has a better chance of survival, if he eats. Neither does he know that survival is better than starvation; but he believes so. More to the point, he may say that he neither asserts nor denies the existence of God. But his actual daily life is lived in conformity with the one postulate or the other.

The Christian believes in God; he believes that God will hold every one to account for the deeds done in the body; and he expects a day of wrath and judgment. He acts in accordance with his belief. By trusting in Christ's finished work, and by giving evidence of that faith in his works in obedience to the injunction, "if ye love me, keep my commandments," the Christian shows to the world which postulate he accepts. But even if the self-styled skeptic or agnostic says nothing at all, it is perfectly clear that he believes there is no final judgment. He may protest in words that this is not true. He will say, "It is not true that I believe there will be no judgment; I merely do not believe there will be a judgment. I do not know whether there will be a judgment or whether there will not. I am an agnostic, I do not know." Now, either there is a God or there is not; either there is a final judgment or there is none. The skeptic *must* live by one or the other of these beliefs. He prays or he does not. But beyond this, if his protestation were sincere, he would have to admit that there was one chance in two that divine judgment would overtake him. If he knows nothing, and if there must be either a judgment or not a judgment, then so far as he knows the chances are even that there will be a judgment. And if a man really believed in the possibility, not to say the probability, of a judgment of God's wrath on sin, he would not adopt the attitude of indifference characteristic of self-styled agnostics. Their indifference is clear evidence that they believe that they are safe, that no judgment awaits them. Their life and action show what they believe. In this case, actions speak louder than words.

Hence, whether one wish it or no, one is forced to adopt this or that theory. And there is no sense in denying in words the regulative principle which controls the life.

Leaving skepticism and drawing the argument closer, one may examine several positive theories which have been advanced in discussions touching on God and the world. Polytheism, henotheism, and deism have had their day and are no longer serious contenders in this debate. Atheism, pantheism, and theism are still chosen as living views. Now if it can be shown that pantheism and atheism are in reality identical, the choice of world-views will be narrowed down to theism and its contradictory, atheism. Nor is this so difficult as at first it may seem.

Atheism is the open and unashamed denial of the existence of God; pantheism is the unctuous affirmation that all is God. Paradoxical as it may appear, all and nothing sometimes mean the same thing. For, in ordinary language, when God and the world are mentioned, the intention is that two distinct entities are meant. Indeed, it is too optimistic to believe that the poverty-stricken, not to say lazy, human intellect would have invented two such words to designate the same object. Certainly they are not synonyms. Therefore when the pantheist affirms that the world is God, he is in reality denying any distinction between the two terms, and since evidently he does not intend to deny the existence of the world, he must intend to deny the existence of a transcendent creator. Pantheism is regularly urbane and cultured; atheism is blatant and unshaven; but their assertions are logically equivalent, for the essence of their message is that there is no creator.

Now this denial results in such curious complications that it is hardly a tenable or choice-worthy theory. For an illustration, suppose that the discoverer of an uninhabited island in some remote ocean should search it to determine whether a particular form of animal life ever existed in that place. It is quite possible for him to search carefully and, discovering no evidence, still remain in ignorance. He could not be sure, however, that the particular animal had never lived on the island, because, even though the search had been diligent, still tomorrow the remains might be discovered. Nor is this an arbitrary illustration. An early Russian cosmonaut concluded that there was no God because he had not seen him when orbiting the earth. This provoked the wry but appropriate comment that if he had stepped out of his capsule, he would have seen him.

But whether much or little evidence is needed to lead one to a belief in God, it is clear that no finite amount of searching could rationally lead one to deny the existence of God. During the time of the atheist's investigation of this earth, it just might be that God was hiding on the other side of the moon, and now that rockets can take the atheist to the moon, there is no reason to hold that God might not go over to Jupiter—for the express purpose of inconveniencing the atheist. "He that sitteth in the heavens shall laugh; the Lord shall have them in derision." Or if the atheist, instead of pursuing his investigations into the far reaches of space, should minutely examine the smallest particles of matter, nothing he could find in this direction would be evidence against the existence of God. The medieval philosophers spoke of the traces or footprints of God in nature and said that God has initialed or put his trade-mark upon his creation. The atheist of course does not believe this, but there is nothing impossible about it; quite the contrary, it is entirely impossible that "No-God" should initial things. In the constitution of the atom there is nothing that an omnipotent creator could not have produced. Whether each atom is a miniature solar system, or whether some other arrangement is a better explanation, God is at least as plausibly its cause as Vortex or Brute Fact. The assertion that there is no God is one which in the nature of the case cannot have evidence. The assertion that there is a God can have evidence in its favor. Not only does the *prima facie* absence of evidence condemn atheism, not only the impossibility of evidence, but equally the significance of the atheistic assertion apart from any question of evidence. The atheist who asserts that there is no God, asserts by the same words that he holds the whole universe in his mind; he asserts that no fact, past, present, future, near, or far, escapes his attention, that no power, however great, can baffle or deceive him. In rejecting God, he claims omniscience and omnipotence. In other words an atheist is one who claims that he himself is God; and the pantheist must be said to join him in the same claim.

It may now begin to appear that theism is a saner choice than its atheistic-pantheistic alternative. And there is no other possibility, for agnosticism is not a theory. Yet even though ignorance is not a solution to any problem, is it not still a possible state of mind? Is it necessary to find a solution? Must one adopt a positive theory? Is not neutrality possible? The explorer on the island was not forced to make a statement before he had the evidence; he suspended judgment; why then cannot judgment be suspended in this? Does not the explorer illustration negate the earlier suggestion that the option between theism and atheism is a forced option? The answer is clarified under a closer examination of the argument by which atheism is rejected. Atheism, in the very nature of the case, can produce no evidence in its favor. None of the events or things in the world can validly support the conclusion that no creator exists. The explorer, too, is asking a question which evidence is incapable of answering in the negative; and this is exactly the point of the illustration; but when a possible affirmative answer is contemplated, further analysis of the situation is needed.

Colloquially we may say that the discovery of a single

fossil, the minimum of evidence, is sufficient to prove the presence of that type of animal life. But from a more technical standpoint this is not true. The discovery of a fossil does not prove the presence of the animal any more than the Resurrection of Christ proves His deity. The fossil is merely a minor premise; the major premise is the whole complex of natural law which connects fossils with extinct animals. Without such a connection no inference from a fossil could validly be drawn. At first sight this seems to strengthen the objection. If the proposition about an extinct animal is an integral part of the universal system; if it is either true or false and skepticism is impossible; then suspension of judgment is impossible. But, the objector insists, suspension of judgment is possible, as every scientist knows, and therefore one may suspend judgment about God also. This objection obviously rests on the assumption that scientists suspend judgment on empirical questions. And apparently they do, for two reasons: Namely, they do not publish assertions until they have discovered the evidence, and they as well as the rest of us go about their daily duties without the fossil making the least bit of difference. Now, these two reasons for assuming that the scientiest suspends judgement are more apparent than real. True, he may not publish a book until he has unearthed the fossil; but neither will he spend time, money, and energy digging for fossils in places where he believes there are none. When he organizes a scientific expedition, he is acting on a definitely adopted belief, and the resources he throws into such an expedition are the measure of his belief. The whole procedure depends altogether on the assumption that fossils are to be found. And this is not suspension of judgment.

In the second place, it was urged that all of us can do most of our work without ever thinking of fossils. True enough, but it does not prove that we can suspend judgment with reference to

God. That there is a fossil and that there is a God may both be equally integral with the universal system; but these two propositions do not occupy the same logical position in the system. The former concerns a very limited portion of reality, so that it is unnecessary to maintain a definite belief, affirmative or negative, in order to get married or to buy groceries. But the latter proposition, God exists, so affects all reality and all life that it is implicated even in the argument by which the scientist infers extinct animals from discovered fossils. If there is no God, if everything is brute fact, then the fossil may be brute fact, also. A blind cosmic evolution, operating mechanically, can produce fossils from inanimate lime as easily as from animals. If things just are, there is no guarantee that a given fossil has in reality come from an extinct animal. The atheist quickly replies that an omnipotent creator can as easily create a fossil as he can produce it from a living animal. Undoubtedly, so far as power is concerned, God could so create a fossil without a genealogy. John the Baptist said that God is able of these stones to raise up children to Abraham. But God did not raise up children. I doubt that he creates fossils independently of previous animals. This doubt is based on the Biblical description of God as wise and immutable. Maybe wisdom and immutability are not sufficient to prove the point. But the atheist has nothing whatever to support a doubt. If he denies that God follows an intelligent plan in controlling the universe, he cannot rely on inanimate matter, point centers of force, or operational Energy to produce fossils always in the same way. Scientific method cannot prove that the past was like the present or that the future will be. Or even that the present is like the present. Some things contract as they cool. Water contracts to 39.2° and then expands. Boyle's law is good enough for most gases within a limited range of temperature. But it does not hold for other gases. Therefore if the atheistic scientist refuses to base his descriptions of the past, his extrapolations of the present, and his predictions of the future on a belief in an immutable divine plan, he cannot object to the theist on the ground that God might create a fossil.

At any rate, apparent suspension of judgment depends on the fact that particular scientific problems determine only a few human activities; but the belief or disbelief in God, since it is logically basic, determines them all, including buying groceries. A man either lives with the fear of God before his eyes, attempting to make his whole life a song of praise to his Creator, or he does not. If he does, he is a theist; if he does not, his life shows that, far from being neutral, his serious belief is that God will not judge him and his actions, that is, there is no God who rules the universe with him in it.

Still it remains true that no demonstration of God is possible; our belief is a voluntary choice; but if one must choose without a strict proof, none the less it is possible to have sane reasons of some sort to justify the choice. Certainly there are sane reasons for rejecting some choices. One most important factor is the principle of consistency. In the case of skepticism inconsistency lies immediately on the surface. Explicit atheism requires only a little analysis before self-contradiction is discovered. Some statements of naturalism more successfully disguise their flaws. But all these choices are alike in that it is not sane, it is not logical, to choose an illogical principle.

Consistency extends further than a first principle narrowly considered, so that it can be shown to be self-contradictory in itself; it extends into the system deduced from the first principle or principles. The basic axiom or axioms must make possible a harmony or system in all our thoughts, words, and actions. Should someone say (misquoting by the omission of an adjective) that consistency is the mark of small minds, that he does not like systems, that he will act on one principle at one time and another at another, that he does not choose to be consistent, there would be no use arguing with him, for he repudiates the rules, the necessary rules of argumentation. Such a person cannot argue against theism, for he cannot argue at all.

There are such people. They are not found so much among naturalists or humanists as among the professedly religious. Karl Barth espouses *paradox*. Emil Brunner's faith *curbs* his logic. Others say life is deeper than logic; and still others disdain *merely human logic* as a mark of sin and secularism. I suppose they also disdain merely human arithmetic when they try to balance their checkbooks.

While consistency is one of the basic reasons for adopting a world-view, from a more proximate standpoint the world-view must function as a practical postulate. This statement is capable of more than one interpretation. Sometimes practical postulates, regulative principles, or ideals are considered as something less than strictly true. For Kant, God, freedom, and immortality were heuristic principles and not constitutive elements of the real world. He is parodied, but not essentially misrepresented, by the summary of his moral theory in the phrase, "We cannot know there is a God, but we ought to act as though there were one." Similarly in science Kant postulates the unity of the world: Though the phenomenal world may not be a unit, the scientist must assume that it is, in order to proceed with his experimentation.

Surely there is something illogical about such a view. Whether science or religion, why should one accept a principle that is not so? We should act as if there is a God, only if there is. If there is no God, no reason can be found for accepting the postulate. And, if you please, think soberly about living as if there were no God, if in fact there is one. When now the theist speaks of theism as a practical postulate, he is not indulging in any "as-if" philosophy. He means that God exists and that one should conduct his daily life by that belief. It is called a postulate because it is an indemonstrable first principle and not a theorem derived from more ultimate premises.

Theism then is the philosophy that acknowledges God as its first principle. This bare statement does not define Christian theism, however. "God" cannot be taken as an empty name. Christian theism has a very particular definition of God. Since Spinoza called nature God, Christianity can be said to be more interested in *what* God is, than in the bare existence of something with that name attached to it. The God of Christianity is the God described in the Bible, not the god of Islam, Unitarianism, or some other religion.

It is better to say that the truth of the Bible is the basic axiom of Christian theism, for it is there alone that one learns what God is. It is there alone that one learns what man is. And what children are. And what college students are. And what education should be. There is still more but this chapter does not aim to give an account of the entire system. In conformity with tradition, the argument has centered on the question of God's existence. As an axiom or first premise it is incapable of *proof* or *demonstration*. Right from the start, at the very beginning, we say, "I believe in God the Father Almighty."

It is the part of wisdom never to claim more for an argument than it can bear; and understatement is recognized as a better error than overstatement. The position here defended is intended to be neither the one nor the other; rather it is intended to express in philosophical language what theological or Biblical language means by the phrases: "We walk by faith and not by sight;" and, "Now we know in part." And if the non-theist claim more than faith in favor of his axiom, he should find a good private secondary school and study geometry.

Chapter 3
The Alternative to Christian Theism

If an observer went into a shoe store and watched half a dozen men buying shoes, he could not tell from their actions which were humanists, idealists, pragmatists, or Christians. One's philosophy seems to make no difference in purchasing shoes. Some devout Christians, whose interest lies in recommending very high spiritual standards rather than in asserting the irrelevance of philosophy to daily life, complain that the actual conduct of Christians in just about every phase of life is so similar to the conduct of non-christians that apparently one's religious or irreligious beliefs have no effect on what people do. This uniformity has of late been disturbed. Christians do not take heroin or snort cocaine. They are not promiscuous, as unbelieving college students blatantly are. Christians do not encourage or take part in riots—though some large denominations do indeed finance terrorism. Christians do not set fire to buildings and then shoot the policemen and firemen who come to the scene. They do not shoot down planes and massacre the survivors. In these matters, at any rate, there is an observable difference between Christians and some non-christians. Of course some non-christians also are not guilty of these crimes; so that even here there seems to be no clear-cut distinction between the effects of two different sets of first principles. This pretty much accords with the widespread common opinion that philosophy and religion are irrelevant in actual living.

But such observations, either in a shoe store or in politics, are limited and therefore defective. If the observer could note how two different men wear their shoes and what purposes they advance by walking on the sidewalk, the observer might see some differences. So, too, the teaching of arithmetic looks uniform in many classrooms, but may well be different in larger contexts. That this is the case, that the first principles of one's philosophy control the general tenor of one's life, receives support from the following samples of evidence.

At a formal occasion a college speaker argued in favor of the thesis that the coming age would be the best in all the world's history. He told the students that they should be glad to live today: The era of the common man, the advent of social equality, and the imminent and still more wonderful discoveries of science will all contribute to the formation of a society happier than we have ever dreamed of. At the same college only a few weeks later the honor day speaker predicted that the coming age would be, or at least was in danger of being, another Dark Age. With the social upheavals and under the threat of a still more devastating war, it might well be the worst age in the world's history.

The choice between a theistic and a humanistic world-view has a direct bearing on one's expectations for the future; and therefore even on the purchase of shoes. Pessimism and optimism result logically from philosophic presuppositions. There are different types of optimism, one derived from one principle, the other derived from another. Of course, a given thinker may blunder and draw fallacious inferences from his own principles. He may believe that his world-view commits him to optimism rather than to pessimism, or to one type of optimism rather than another, when in logic it does not. This complicates the analytical problem for an author who wishes to speak generally of all humanists or of all Christians. But these individual stumbling blocks can be avoided by studying historical developments. The course of a philosophy throughout several generations will ordinarily bring to light what was originally obscure. For purposes of illustration something of interest may be found in three types of philosophy that have successively become popular within the last hundred years.

The temper of the latter part of the nineteenth century was in general optimistic. From 1870 to 1914 there were no great wars; it was during this period also that the rapid advance of science and invention began. Although that earlier progress has been overshadowed by our later age, yet in its time it was breathtaking. In western Europe and particularly in America the standard of living rose rapidly. Under such economic and intellectual conditions it is not surprising that optimism flourished. In turn this optimism is evidence that it was a happy era. Had the times been miserable, unquestioned confidence in continual progress could not have become popular. To be sure, some imperfections remained; but these were quickly to be remedied, and the thinkers of that period anticipated the speedy and certain arrival of Utopia.

Herbert Spencer voiced the prevailing sentiments. In his *Social Statics*, in chapter two entitled "The Evanescence of Evil," he says:

> The inference that as advancement has been hitherto the rule, it will be the rule henceforth, may be called a plausible speculation. But when it is shown that this advancement is due to the working of a universal law; and in virtue of that law it must continue until the state we call perfection is reached, then the advent of such a state is removed out of the region of probability into that of certainty. If anyone demurs to this, let him point out the error .... Progress therefore is not an accident, but a

necessity. . . . As surely as a blacksmith's arm grows large and the skin of a laborer's hand becomes thick; . . . as surely as a passion grows by indulgence and diminishes when restrained; . . . so surely must the things we call evil and immorality disappear; so surely must man become perfect.

This is optimism, to be sure, but one must note what kind of optimism it was; one must note on what principle it was based. It was not based on the ideal economic and political conditions then prevailing, though these added plausibility and force to the conclusion. Nor was Spencer's optimism based on the belief in a beneficent God. One of the poets said, "God's in his heaven; all's right with the world." But Spencer was not that poet. Spencer based his optimism on the theory of evolution. His basic world-view was not theistic. He had rejected the Biblical concept of God and had substituted an Unknowable. With this as a basis he thought it reasonable to expect uninterrupted progress. The goal of perfection was not merely probable but certain and necessary. Immortality and evil would soon disappear. Spencer was an optimist.

It is questionable, however, that a theory of inevitable human progress can be based on a knowledge of the Unknowable. An omnipotent and all wise God can justify optimism, even in ages of tragedy; but even in an epoch of peace and prosperity an Unknowable cannot. Spencer actually relied more on the theory, or on a theory, of evolution. Alfred, Lord Tennyson saw the evolutionary world as "red in tooth and claw," but Spencer saw nothing but uninterrupted improvement. What human being can doubt that human beings are better than mere animals? Universal law therefore assures us that evil will evanesce before A.D. 1900 and the state we call perfection will have been reached. Granted, Spencer did not use the date A.D. 1900; but nevertheless there seems to be a flaw in his inference.

Although Spencer exemplified the temper of the age, not everyone was so wholeheartedly optimistic. Toward the end of the century William James, for example, felt a slight twinge of caution. James, too, had rejected Christian theism; but unlike Spencer he could not, in his examination of the world, find a reasonable basis for asserting that perfection is certain and necessary. When he looked about him, he saw a pluralistic universe in which independent forces of good and evil were struggling for the mastery. Far from the certainty of perfection, the outcome of history was unknown and, to some degree at least, was a matter of pure chance. Ultimate irrational indeterminism had to be admitted because the forces were independent, and because there was no omnipotent Deity to exercise absolute control. He argued that there was no omnipotent Deity on the ground that there were evil forces in the world that such an Almighty Being would not tolerate. No humane God can truly be happy, James says somewhere, so long as a single cockroach suffers from an unrequited love. With this pluralistic view of the universe James urges us to take an active part in the struggle. It is not certain that good will win, and we must enter the fray and perchance swing the balance.

One may wonder whether some brash student ever asked James why he should not enter the fray on the side of evil. The outcome is uncertain, and sometimes it would seem that the forces of evil have the better chance of winning. Since in the pragmatic theory truth is what works and success is the ultimate test, it follows that if we can contribute to the success of evil, we have at least fought in the cause of truth. In any case it is difficult to see why one should engage in a dangerous fight for the purpose of making cockroaches happy.

In 1914 history and philosophy combined to darken still further the cheerful light of optimism. Spencer's doctrine of automatic, inevitable perfection could not survive the shock of war, especially since his nebulous Unknowable was not known to guarantee the outcome. And James's more feeble finite god was just another name, a useless name on the cosmic census. If there were an almighty God who could be known, and who could inform us of His plans, mankind could then have confidence. But if there is no such God, if there is no Unknowable, if even there is no finite god, what can we expect in the future?

It was, and is, the task of humanism to answer this question. Spencer had made the whole universe favorable to human desires. James had offered man at least a fighting chance. But humanism must view the cosmos as indifferent, if not actually hostile, to man's hopes and destiny. Do the sands of the sea worry if war besets the human race? Will algae or mosquitoes be perplexed if a hundred million Americans are atomized in one night? Should the stars in their courses run to man's aid and comfort? Man came from dust; to dust shall he return. In the meantime let man get along as best he can in an indifferent universe.

But how well does such a universe allow him to get along? A quotation from Bertrand Russell gives an answer sufficiently clear:

> That man is the product of causes which had no prevision of the end they were achieving; that his origin, his growth, his hopes and fears, his loves and his beliefs are but the outcome of accidental collocations of atoms; that no fire, no heroism, no intensity of thought and feeling, can preserve an individual life beyond the grave; that all the labors of the ages, all the devotion, all the inspiration, all the noon-day brightness of human genius, are destined to extinction in the vast death of the solar system, and that the whole temple of man's achievement must inevitably be buried beneath the debris of a universe in ruins—all these things, if not quite beyond dispute, are yet nearly so certain that

no philosophy which rejects them can hope to stand. Only within the scaffolding of these truths, only on the firm foundation of unyielding despair, can the soul's habitation henceforth be safely built. . . Brief and powerless is man's life; on him and all his race the slow sure doom falls pitiless and dark. Blind to good and evil, reckless of destruction, omnipotent matter rolls on its relentless way; for man, condemned today to lose his dearest, tomorrow himself to pass through the gate of darkness, it remains only to cherish, ere yet the blow falls, the lofty thoughts that ennoble his little days . . . proudly defiant of the irresistible forces that tolerate for a moment his knowledge and his condemnation, to sustain alone, a weary but unyielding Atlas, the world that his own ideals have fashioned despite the trampling march of unconscious power.*

This sad, infinitely tragic tone is far removed from the blithesome optimism of Spencer. Its pessimism is of the darkest night, and its defiant courage is but the mask of hysterical despair. But there is one thing to be said in favor of this that is called humanism: It is logically consistent. Given a world such as naturalism or humanism describes, how else could one continue to live? Spencer was not consistent. If his god was unknowable, Spencer had no logical right to speak of the certainty of perfection. But if the world is Russell's world, then there is every right to predict certain defeat and destruction in the future. Russell is at least consistent.

It may be interesting to note in passing how such a view affects phases of life not ordinarily called philosophical. The argument to this point has now led us to expect that a general view of the world will affect all phases of life; but in particular it is interesting to see how this view affects, say, the writing of a novel. One may seriously and legitimately ask the question

* Bertrand Russell, *Mysticism and Logic* (London: Longmans, Green and Company, 1925), pp. 47-48, 56-57.

whether or not art can survive in a humanistic world. What sort of novels, for example, could be written by a humanist?

In the writing of Thomas Hardy the best possible answer is seen. The indifference of the universe to the hopes and aspirations of men becomes an almost perverse delight in frustrating their desires. The indifferent world is a tragic world. But more than this, the indifferent world soon becomes an absurd world. As Thomas Hardy develops from one novel to another, the chance occurrence that brings tragedy with admittedly artistic effect is multiplied and multiplied until the world is little more than a ridiculous series of chance events, tragic perhaps, but certainly inartistic. The ridiculous cannot be great art.

Theodore Dreiser also believes that life is without a purpose; it is but a confusion of experience without intelligible emphasis. Its only tolerable moments are those which satisfy the hunger for power, sexual desire, or the desire to collect art objects. Such a humanistic view poses technical problems for the novel as a form of art. Most obvious is the fact that there is no logical stopping point. No doubt the death of an important character furnishes a convenient end, but it does not of itself produce a logical or aesthetic finish. And some of Dreiser's novels, minus even this convenience, just stop. Another problem that humanism imposes on the novel is the selection of material. In a world governed by a divine plan, in a world of clear moral distinctions, material can be selected and arranged for a purpose. But on the basis of a humanistic philosophy incidents cannot have any structural or moral significance. It cannot be fully argued here—it would require a course in Christian aesthetics—but the suggestion is made that true art is possible only on a theistic assumption. Artists may inconsistently be humanists, but a humanistic, atheistic, purposeless universe provides no basis for art.

This philosophy poses problems for art because it poses problems, not only for technical scholars, but for every common man in his everyday life, including the education of his children. Let us ask most seriously whether or not the calamity of war, the pain of the wounded and dying, the brutality of torture and tyranny, famine and disease are justified by hunger for power, by the desire for sexual gratification, or by the collection of art objects. It takes a Stalin and a Goering to answer affirmatively. Many people, like James, have stumbled at the Biblical conception of God because of the problem of evil; but the problem of evil is not peculiar to an academic statement of Christian philosophy. Evil exists as a real factor in the world. And before one rejects Christianity for this reason, one ought to consider clearly what kind of a solution to this problem and what kind of a universe humanism has to offer.

Here exactly lies the stumbling block of humanistic philosophy. Man must get along not only with an indifferent universe,—that would be bad enough—he must also get along with other men; and other men are often not just indifferent— they are definitely hostile. In view of the deliberate perpetration of recent atrocities, Spencer might better have written on the Evanescence of Good, rather than on the Evanescence of Evil. The vileness and cruelty that have devastated Europe, the massacre of sixty million Chinese, thirty million Russians, and several million Tibetans, the terror and torture inflicted on the Vietnamese by Ho Chi Minh, the genocide in Cambodia, and Cuban troops in Africa, make it impossible to think of the world, including humanity, as merely indifferent. If we wish to frame our views on the basis of empirical evidence, as the scientific humanists insist we ought, we must conclude that humanity, and therefore our world, is thoroughly evil.

In the writer's opinion, mistaken and jaundiced though he may be, it requires egregious blindness to see Utopia in the coming age. Perhaps the writer was frightened as a child, and now from the depths of his subconscious he fears the future. But it is also possible that the optimistic psychologist who would thus dispose of the world situation was given a piece of candy when a child, so that now his unconscious tints the future with rosy hues. Of all the truths that are staring us in the face, the most unmistakable one would seem to be the deep rooted savagery and the inherent evil of human nature. Civilization and education put a veneer over man's nature, and the veneer lasts for a time. Then the opportunity to gain power and world domination presents itself, and a nation, a race, the human race, shows its concealed colors.

Even those who are loathe to admit that man is by nature evil have had man's evil so forcibly brought to their attention that they are seeking a remedy. Bombs far more terrible than the two that ended the war with Japan force us to find a remedy for evil or to be annihilated. Civilization cannot survive another world war, and the human race itself can scarcely survive. So clear is this that the discouraged remnant of the army of optimists is fighting a rear-guard action to find a remedy for man's evil nature.

But what remedies can they offer? Education is often acclaimed as such. But in view of the fact that one of the chief culprits of World War II was one of the most highly educated nations in the world, is it unreasonable to question the efficacy of education? Germany had every advantage that education could offer. Yet within a few years Hitler was able to make beasts out of, not just a few, but out of millions of his people. If education is so powerful for good, how can one explain the eruption of vileness of such a large scale? And even if education were as miraculous as its proponents say, what chance is there of educating all the world within the next ten years? In that time every nation will have learned how to manufacture atomic bombs. Can the world be educated so as to remedy man's evil in a decade? And even if the citizens of the United States, Great Britain, and France are so educated, what guarantee is there that some other nation will not try to dominate the world by an undeclared war? Education is a sorry remedy for man's evil. Instead of preventing war in the past, it has served to make war more terrible. Education will make the next war the last.

But perchance the optimists are thinking of a new type of education—something never before tried. Perhaps they do not mean courses in physics and literature. Perhaps they mean courses in ethics, morals, and, could it be, religion? But what religion? The religion of the Unknowable, the finite god, or omnipotent matter? Certainly they do not mean a Christian education, which for its effect depends upon the supernatural regenerating power of the Holy Ghost to change man's evil nature and to implant new habits. But if supernatural Christianity is not what they mean, is not their hope of preventing the next war a forlorn delusion?

Optimism fades. But then pessimism forces one to ask a very disturbing question. If there is no justification for living except lust for power, sex, and art objects, is life worth living at all? If soon we are all to be killed by radioactive poison or AIDS, what is the use of going on? An unknowable deity cannot give us hope and confidence; neither can a finite god; and omnipotent matter rolling on its relentless way brings us only despair. Why then, if we are dust, why should we not voluntarily return to the dust and become unfeeling and indifferent ourselves? Neither Spencer, James, nor Russell can give us a reason to live. The only reasonable reaction to humanism is suicide. Russell and the humanists are more consistent than Spencer, for they are pessimists. But if the humanists wish to be completely consistent, they ought to kill themselves. They cannot consistently even buy a pair of shoes.

This line of thought and its relevance to education need further emphasis. So far Spencer, Russell, and Dreiser have been the examples. Now, probably pessimism is to be expected from exponents of naturalistic science like Bertrand Russell. If Ernest Nagel does not voice such pessimism, it strikes us as strange. For obviously if the constituent elements of the universe are atoms or sub-atomic particles, man has no future. Nagel spoke of:

> spatio-temporally located bodies, whose internal structures and external relations determine and limit the appearance and disappearance of everything that happens. . . . There is no place . . . for an immaterial spirit directing the course of events, no place for the survival of personality after the corruption of the body which exhibits it.*

Russell describes his hopelessness in superb oratory; but nothing could be more grim than Nagel's plain statement. However, if one expects a grim view from humanists, perhaps some author or other has a more religious world-view, not precisely Christian theism, but some sort of "spiritual" view, in which man need not be such a hopeless figure. The existentialists are anti-scientific enough, and some of them are mildly religious; what do they have to say?

First, Heidegger makes man, rather than spatio-temporally located bodies, central in his world-view. He uses such queer phrases as "man alone exists. Rocks are, but they do not exist." Just what this means in detail need not detain us, for it is too complex; but at any rate Heidegger gives man fundamental importance in his philosophy. So much so that he classifies God with rocks, instead of with man. "God is, but he does not exist." The aim or duty of man is to achieve "authentic existence."

---

* Presidential Address, American Philosophical Association, 1954.

Very simply this means more or less to cast aside hypocrisy, mediocrity, and self-deception. It means the acceptance of responsibility. One must squarely face the world as it is, or perhaps, better face himself as he is. Above all this means that one must face death as it is. Death is not to be thought of as a punishment for sin; Adam would have died, even if he had not sinned. The Christian view makes death a logical "accident" to human nature. But for Heidegger death is a part of the human constitution. It is a built-in consequence of man's being a temporal existence, for man's existence is constituted by time.* Not only so, but Heidegger's death is not Christianity's death. The latter promises everlasting life; for Heidegger death liquidates man or *Dasein*. There is no possibility of a man's surviving his demise. Incidentally, Heidegger offers a very unsatisfactory objection to the suggestion that one should commit suicide and escape the troubles of an authentic being's struggle with the world as it is. His objection seems to be nothing more than the observation that suicide deprives a person of the ground of his existence. Of course it does. But is it not better, is it not less painful, so to deprive oneself? Authentic existence is such a frustrating exercise that inauthentic existence seems more comfortable; and no existence at all seems preferable to inauthentic. If a man must crumble to dust and that is the end of it, is it not pitiful to go on courageously?

---

* A number of existential theologians have made use of arguments based on time: *e.g.*, Oscar Cullmann, *Christ and time*, E. Lampert, *The Apocalypse of History; et al.* Running through these arguments is the theme that salvation is (or would be, if there were such a thing as salvation) man's transcendence of time. It is a virtual deification. It follows that if man is essentially temporal, salvation is impossible. The Christian viewpoint is quite different. Man is indeed essentially temporal. He can in no way "transcend time," become eternal, and rise to the level of God. But he can be saved from sin, and from the death that is the penalty of sin. In heaven his ideas will come in temporal succession. The relation of before and after still continue *ad infinitum*; but his existence will conform to divine precept and none of the tragic, painful results of sin will affect him.

Now, second, Sartre, although he is hardly a religious writer, deserves mention because he is the world's outstanding existentialist; and surely he is not an advocate of naturalistic scientism. Yet as clearly as Nagel he has no sympathy with the hope of immortality, and like Heidegger he wishes us to face death as an aspect of our absurd, contingent facticity. Birth and death are both absurdities; and the life between is equally absurd. "Death . . . removes all meaning from life."

In spite of this dismal view Sartre, like Heidegger, repudiates suicide. Suicide is absurd and meaningless; it is a vain and empty gesture. Nevertheless, upon reflection, one may suspect that suicide could be the only meaningful possibility open to man. It is meaningful and of value in that it puts an end to a meaningless life full of anxiety and trouble. It is difficult to sympathize with or consider plausible Sartre's contention that death "does not penetrate me," that it is irrelevant to my actions, and therefore "my freedom remains total and infinite." A life of seventy years is not infinite; nor is a life of absurdity and pain properly characterized as "freedom." Suicide is the only act that makes any sense at all.

Now third, Bultmann is no doubt a religious thinker, and therefore one might expect to find his view of life and death less grim. This expectation, however, is disappointed because he is in essential agreement with Heidegger. Guilt and anxiety are ontological conditions of human life. They can in no way be removed. We must just learn to live with them. "Man must abandon all security and commit himself unreservedly to the future and thus alone achieve his authentic Being." Now, fourth, and last, Tillich may or may not be a religious writer, but at least he is a theologian. He calls for courage. In the face of anxiety and death and meaninglessness, we must have the courage to be. This is the courage of despair. Man must give up all hope of an infinite future life; he must reject the notion that death is due to sin. He must determine not to look beyond himself for help. Tillich's "God," the Ground of Being, is useless.

In these so-called religious writers and theologians, from whom one would naturally expect a word of hope, the tragedy, the meaninglessness, the despair of human life is as clear as it is in Bertrand Russell. Guilt, anxiety, and the finality of death are ontological aspects of human beings and can in no way be removed. There is no God to deliver us. The only voluntary escape is suicide.

Of course the God of the Bible can deliver us. He is omnipotent and he shows his favor to his people. But none of these writers believes the Bible. On their principles the conclusion is inescapable: Man is doomed, he has no hope; he can live in courageous despair, or in inauthentic self-deception, or he can commit suicide.

Obviously these men have not committed suicide. They continued to live and write books. And although as scholars they claim to argue cogently, their refutation of suicide is so flimsy that we accuse them of inauthentic self-deception, or, more plainly put, irrationality. Their conduct is inconsistent with their theory. When such persons, either existentialists or naturalistic humanists, take an interest in education, their state of mind must show through to some extent. Inconsistent though they be to take an interest in education or in anything else, the force of their pessimism and hopelessness cannot be without effect. Even in the teaching of arithmetic a pessimistic education will be distinguishable from a theistic and optimistic education, at least on rainy days. Sooner or later (the present writer raised the question in third grade) the pupil will ask, Why should I learn arithmetic? Then if the teacher is authentic and honest she will say, Arithmetic helps you when you lose faith in God. Or, she will say, with more truth, Arithmetic will help you gain power and dominate other men. Or, with true zoological scholarship she may say, Arithmetic is a phase of the evolutionary process that leads to the extinction of the human species.

There are at least two answers the consistently humanist teacher cannot give. She cannot give Plato's and Aristotle's answer that man is rational and that knowledge is valuable for its own sake. Nor can she say (it is forbidden by judicial decree) that learning arithmetic is a divine command and is therefore one way of glorifying God.

Non-theistic justifications of arithmetic are failures because non-theistic theories of life are failures. The only meaningful or rational act in a meaningless life is suicide. Inconsistently these people go on living; and so do we. In us is a deep urge for life; we do not want to die. But that very urge testifies to a purpose in the universe that humanists deny and that evolution cannot explain. Somehow all men dimly feel that life is worthwhile; and men today, arrested by their view of the frightful future, are wondering what life's purpose is. If they restrict their view to the observable world, if they study nature and politics, they must descend, as they have descended, from optimism to doubt, to pessimism, and despair.

But if they reject such a godless view of the world, if they turn from an empirical study of science and politics and seek the living God who has spoken a more sure word of prophecy, then they may know the purpose of life and of the universe, and they will be enabled to face the next war, the ensuing dark ages, and the evil nature of man at least with equanimity. Indeed they will face it with more than equanimity, for they will know that history is not moving toward utter futility, but toward a glorious reign of righteousness when the kingdoms of this world are becoming the kingdoms of our Lord and of His Christ; and He shall reign forever and ever.

Chapter 4
Neutrality

Those who object to the argument of chapter two may admit that in an abstract philosophic sense neutrality between two highly developed, mutually incompatible systems of thought is impossible. A teacher of Riemannian geometry does not merely remain silent about Euclid's parallel axiom, he operates on the contradictory assumption. Similarly there is no neutral ground between the proposition that God created the world out of nothing and the proposition that the universe is an eternal self-existing entity. But though objectors may admit that there is here a philosophic incompatibility, they may at the same time hold, in contradiction to chapters one and three, that philosophy is so remote from the practical business of teaching children that any concern over anti-religious influence is purely academic. Even the optimism or the pessimism of the teacher does not affect the contents of arithmetic. Philosophically, neutrality is impossible, they grant; but educationally neutrality is a fact.

This seems to be the commonly held opinion about the decisions of the United States Supreme Court banning prayer and Bible reading from public education. Prayer is definitely a religious activity; and the State must not support any kind of religion. Let arithmetic be taught and religion ignored. Now, there is one good point at least in the Court's decision. The case originated in a school system whose officials had written out a prayer and had required the teachers to pray that prayer. The school officials had supposed their prayer to be innocuous and satisfactory to all religions that prayed at all. It was a "non-sectarian" prayer. Since the decision, various amendments to the Constitution have been proposed that would permit non-sectarian prayer. Presumably this would mean a prayer composed by the school board and imposed by them on the teachers. In so far as this was and is the case, a Christian must view the Court's decision with favor. For, in the first place, it forces the teacher to make a prayer with which she disagrees, either because she is irreligious and does not want to pray at all —and compliance makes her a hypocrite, or because she is religious and sees that this non-sectarian prayer is not neutral, but anti-Christian.

The reason these non-sectarian prayers are anti-Christian can very clearly be stated. The Bible teaches that all prayer to God must be based on the merits of Jesus Christ. No one can come to the Father but by Christ. There is no other name by which we can be saved. Hence to pray without including Christ in the prayer is an offense against God. It is far better to have no prayer at all in school than such a non-sectarian prayer. The use of the word sectarian or non-sectarian is itself an offense and insult. Sect has always had a pejorative sense, and to stigmatize a Christian prayer as sectarian is not an exercise in neutrality.

It might seem then that the Supreme Court has maintained neutrality by its prohibition of prayer in the schools, and that only those who want prayer are anti-Christian. Of course, also, any who do not want prayer are anti-Christian; and it was quite a feat for the Court to satisfy devout Christians and loud-mouthed atheists by the same decision. But whether the decision and its results can satisfy the Christian, and whether the schools are neutral, now that the school board theologians can no longer impose their prayers, still requires a little more discussion.

That neutrality is impossible becomes clearer and clearer as the system of Christian theism is further understood. Mention has already been made of the fact that Christianity is not to be identified with and restricted to a bare belief in God. For example, Christianity has a theory of evil; it differs from the humanistic theory; and therefore a secular school cannot adopt the same policies a Christian school adopts in dealing with recalcitrant pupils.

That there are recalcitrant pupils hardly needs to be said. But perhaps it does need to be said to those who conveniently forget what is going on. In addition to the material recounted in chapter one, there was the case of subversive, obscene, Black Panther literature sold to high school students in Indianapolis in 1969 with the approval of at least some of the teachers. But it is illegal for the Gideons to distribute New Testaments on school property. In the first two weeks of the 1969-70 school session, fifty robberies and beatings, including stabbings, were reported to the Indianapolis police. The police believed that these were less than half the crimes committed because children who are victimized are often afraid to report the attack for fear of reprisals. Some parents refuse to send their children to school in order to save them from violence at school. In one of the affluent Indianapolis high schools it is estimated that fifty percent of the pupils are drug addicts. Not all heroin addicts, to be sure; but on their way by means of glue, goof-balls, L.S.D., and similar drugs.

These evil conditions have been encouraged by the liberal, humanistic policy of dealing with lesser forms of student misconduct. Liberalism has ridiculed the Christian notion of punishment. From babyhood children must be spoiled, not spanked, or in any way repressed. As early as 1922 John Dewey in *Human Nature and Conduct* (Part II, Section 2) encouraged youth to rebel against parental discipline. Parents have tamed "the delightful originality of the child;" they instill in him moral habits; and the result is a mass of "irrationalities" and "infantilisms." When Dewey's philosophy is translated into the penal code, with its emphasis on rehabilitation (for the criminal is sick, not wicked; and the community is guilty, not the criminal), twenty thousand people commit murder in a single year in the United States, and not one of them is executed. The following year, naturally, more people commit murder.

Neither John Dewey, nor the liberal penologists, nor the public schools are to be blamed for the origin of these crimes. Liberal theologians and liberal educators are to be blamed for failing to repress evil. The public schools deserve ridicule when they claim to be the saviors of democracy. By their permissiveness they have encouraged arson, drug addiction, and sexual immorality. Even in strictly curricular affairs their permissiveness and their extension of the concept of democracy beyond its proper political meaning often have resulted in the attempt to make all pupils equal by reducing requirements to the minimum so everybody can pass. In such schools, more often in metropolitan areas, a student must not flunk; he must be promoted. In high schools that have come under the present writer's observation, some juniors (no doubt seniors, too, but the following examples are restricted to personal knowledge) cannot read fourth grade material; in a botany lab a student could not read the instruction sheet, and a twenty-year-old boy "graduated" without being able to read—well, without being able to read two paragraphs of anything. This sort of democracy, this permissiveness, these liberal policies encourage and augment evil, but they do not initiate evil. Evil is initiated in what John Dewey calls the delightful originality of the child.

The present argument aims to show that a school system

cannot operate as a neutral between the liberal and the Christian position. A school system must have some policy for delinquent children, or for those who begin to cause trouble, and this policy cannot be both left and right. It cannot be both Christian and humanistic; and there is no middle, neutral ground. The two philosophies and their educational implications differ on what to do, on what evil is, and on how it originates. Something has been said of the prevailing views of public educators; now it is required to show that Christianity has a totally different view of evil and totally different policies for combatting it.

In the first place, Christianity defines evil conduct as a transgression of God's laws. Vandalism is not an evolutionary hang-over from animal ancestry. In fact animals do not vandalize, commit arson, or rape. These are strictly human activities; and they are wrong because God has forbidden them. That they occur is due to Adam's original sin and the depravity that all his natural posterity have inherited. Every child is born with a sinful nature. He just naturally goes wrong. David in Psalm 51 was not referring to illegitimacy when he said, "I was shapen in iniquity and in sin did my mother conceive me." And in Psalm 58:3 it is written, "The wicked are estranged from the womb; they go astray as soon as they are born, speaking lies." Paul in Ephesians 2:3 says: "We . . . were by nature the children of wrath, even as others." And in the *locus classicus*, Romans 5:12-21, Paul makes our connection with Adam abundantly clear. The Bible paints a dark picture of human nature, a picture as dark as the headlines in the morning newspaper.

In the early years of this century, when the modernists would not openly admit that their religion was anti-biblical, they tried to reinterpret and soften the Scriptural expressions in favor of their theory of the inevitable perfectibility of man. Now that most of them have gone over to humanism—by now it should be clear that neo-orthodoxy or the dialectical theology is as humanistic as anything else—and openly reject the Scripture, they are more likely to admit that the orthodox Lutherans and Calvinists correctly exegeted the passages on total depravity. Of course they do not believe that the Scriptural view is true; in spite of the newspaper headlines they think there is little sin, and, as there is no life beyond the grave, salvation is not an issue.

In spite of the humanist's rejection of the Bible, he must give some explanation of the headlines. Very popular at present is the idea that social conditions are the cause of crime. For purposes of argument it makes little difference whether one enumerates a long list of social ills or whether one centers on a single particular. A very frequently mentioned particular is the existence of slums. Granted, slums are undesirable; but their undesirability does not show that they are the cause of crime. Now, aside from the fact that slums do not cause the affluent suburbanites to form clubs for wife swapping, there is good evidence that instead of slums being the cause of bad people, bad people are the cause of slums.

This one piece of evidence is offered. As late as 1950, even 1955, the area in Indianapolis between College Avenue and Meridian Street, north of 20th Street, and even north of 16th Street, was a pleasant, well-kept area of family homes. Some of the homes were even a bit luxurious. But even the less expensive houses were clean, comfortable, and agreeable to look at. They had been built earlier in the century and their garages were at the back of the lots, facing on alleys wide enough for two cars to pass carefully. The slums below 16th Street, and more below 10th Street, grew worse and worse. The city razed about a mile square. There were no slums anymore. But the displaced slum dwellers had to live somewhere, so they moved north to 16th Street. Their front lawns turned to mud that flowed over the sidewalks. Shingles and sidings were not repaired. Debris, including mattresses and broken furniture, clogged the alleys so that no cars could pass. Then came the rats. It was not the rats who brought the people; it was the people who brought the rats. In a few years this area became the city's crime center. On our own church lawn a girl was attacked and in the struggle one of her eyes was gouged out. Evil people changed this lovely neighborhood into a slum. The nice homes did not make the people better, the people made the homes worse.

Of course the Biblical view of sin is not based on empirical observation. The example of Indianapolis was not intended to prove the Bible true; it was intended to illustrate the falsity of the secular view. The Biblical doctrine of original sin, inherited corruption, and total depravity, is a matter of divine revelation. And this revelation explains the headlines better than humanism does.

If anyone thinks that too much is being made of the prevalence of crime, though it is difficult to exaggerate the peril of our national condition, it should also be pointed out that even the so-called lesser sins are offenses against God. If society only is in view, some violations of moral standards are not very important. But if we worship God instead of society, no sin is unimportant. In the Christian view motive is as important as overt act. God has commanded us to love him with all our mind and strength; without this motivation even our apparently good deeds are evil. Therefore, including hardened criminal and respectable socialite, we can echo Shakespeare's thoroughly Christian sentiment, "one taint of nature makes the whole world kin."

This all shows that Christianity does not attribute the origin of sin to the public schools; it also shows that the more Christian theism is explained in detail, the less can humanistic education be regarded as neutral; and consequently it becomes clear that education founded on one of these philosophies will differ from the other in its academic policies and procedures.

For example, some obstreperous college students are demanding seats on the boards of directors, with a voice in controlling the curricula. Some college administrators agree, in the hope that this will reduce rioting on campus. In one college a new president was elected with the help of a student's vote, while some of the directors were denied the vote. Now, the Biblical directions on how to manage a church, with emphasis on elders, on authority, and against giving control to the inexperienced and unlearned, can be extended to schools. In addition to the fact that a student spends only four years at college, and would therefore be present only two years, or at most three, before being seated on the Board; and would therefore know next to nothing at the beginning of his official duties, nor stay long enough to be of any substantial service; in addition to this, I say, it is ludicrous to give students control over the curriculum. They come to learn, not to control. Granted, a student has the right to choose an engineering school or a school of pharmacy, instead of liberal arts. Even in this case he may choose unwisely, for his inclinations at twenty-two are often different from his expectations at eighteen. How much less does he know of what the engineering curriculum or the liberal arts curriculum should contain! I have seen even elected faculty committees propose seriously defective alterations of the curriculum.

When liberal permissiveness occurs in the lower grades, education ceases. The idea that the child should choose a project and the teacher give a little help has produced the story, true or not, of the child who complained, Must we always do what we want? Children need self-control and parental control more than they need self-expression. Why should there be any teacher at all, if the pupil is competent to control the courses? A popular liberal slogan has been, "learning by doing." So the ten year old smokes pot, tries out sex, and sticks a knife into another kid's ribs. He learns by doing. Apparently some educators never suspected that some things should not be done and not be learned. But the pupil is not competent to decide such matters. Thus the theological doctrine of human depravity, while and because it applies beyond the sphere of formal education, has a definite bearing on the methods and aims of schools.

Perhaps the non-Christian educator may now grant that the educational views of a Christian are affected by philosophy or theology. Yet the non-Christian may still wish to deny that his own professional theories are determined by a prior rejection of the Christian view of God and man. But even though he disclaims any such prior controlling choice, his denial rests on a mistaken analysis of his own mind. It cannot be too strongly emphasized that the educational policies of any educator or school system derive their character from an underlying philosophy. Let the directors, the superintendents, and the principals of a school system claim that they base their views only on neutral experiment and observation, apart from any *a priori* philosophy, and their claim is untrue. Experimentation itself, as the philosophy of science shows, is based on philosophic principles.* The choice of methods of experimentation is directed by the experimenter's view of what the world is like. This point can be successfully argued with an abundance of reasons. But for the present purpose just one consideration will suffice. Experimentation in psychology and pedagogy may indeed improve the technique of teaching. But it cannot choose ends or goals. And ends and goals are far more important than technique. Scientific technique can only be a curse when headed in the wrong direction. No better illustration of this truth

---

* Compare Gordon H. Clark, *The Philosophy of Science and Belief in God* (Jefferson, Maryland: The Trinity Foundation, 1987).—*Editor.*

could be desired than the constantly improving techniques of chemistry. Improved chemistry can work wonders in medicine. But if improved techniques are used to make biological warfare more horrible, we may well wish chemistry less success. Technique in education, similarly, will make the teaching of children more efficient; but if the educator teaches the wrong ideals, the more efficiently he does so, the worse the results. Scientific experiment may tell us how children learn, but no amount of scientific observation and experiment will tell us what they ought to learn. And this is the most important phase of education: not the description of the process, but the goal of the process. In philosophical language pedagogy is not a descriptive science. It is a normative science. It deals not so much with what is, but with what ought to be. And views of what ought to be do not come, as some educators envious of a scientific reputation claim, from observing how children learn. Views of what ought to be depend on the underlying philosophy. The anti-Christian educator wants to produce one kind of man; the Christian wants to produce a very different kind.

This argument may still be regarded as rather academic, in the bad sense of the word, particularly with respect to primary education. In college, it will be admitted, the religious issues come to light, and a young man is forced to take sides by the teaching of professors who have already discarded neutrality. But the arithmetic and spelling of the elementary grades are so innocuous that the thesis here defended is inapplicable. Further study, however, reveals that the thesis is equally applicable to primary education and scarcely less prominent.

The early American colleges were distinctly Christian institutions. But the public school system, unlike the colleges, was not so inspired. On the other hand, the public schools were not intended to be irreligious. In the readers of our grandparents' time God and Jesus Christ were mentioned. Today no such references can be found in the books of the public schools. The reason is not hard to find. The public schools were founded with the idea of not favoring one Christian denomination above another; of not favoring one religion above another; and the result is that they now favor no religion at all. They are completely secularized.

Originally the public schools, while not supposed to favor one Christian denomination above another, were not intended to attack Christianity. The idea was that they should be neutral. And because the majority of Protestants believed the promises of the schoolmen that they would not attack religion, the Protestants did not found primary schools as the Romanists did. Now it is clear that the Romanists adopted the wiser course of action because the promises of the schoolmen were soon to be broken.

Today Christianity is attacked all through the public school system. Reports from parents say that the evolutionary denial of the creation of the world by God is taught to the children of the second grade. How can a child of seven or eight stand up against an organized attack of the theistic world-view? How can parents protect their children? The public school makes no pretense of being neutral in religious matters, and when a parent here or there protests, he is promptly ridiculed and squelched. The notion of religious liberty, or even of the toleration of Christianity, that is, the original claim to neutrality, is not a part of the schoolmen's mental equipment.

Mention has already been made of the exclusion of Bible reading from the public schools. The result has been a generation of children who are handicapped in the English language and literature. It is an incontrovertible fact that the English Bible has had a greater influence on our language, our literature, our civilization, our morals, than any other book. The children who are deprived of the Bible are culturally deprived, as well as religiously deprived. Someone has well said that a knowledge of the Bible without a college education is of more value than a college education without a knowledge of the Bible. In view of this fact the prohibition of Bible reading is acutely significant of the hatred the public schools, and a large section of our society, have for Christianity. Books attacking Christianity are not illegal. Teachers can deny God, creation, and providence; but the law forbids them to recommend Christianity.

Since the cultural deprivation of this policy is so obvious, some of the educators want to teach the Bible as literature. This reintroduction of the Bible into the schools might also allay some of the criticism. It may turn out, however, that the Bible as literature will be worse than no Bible at all. Will the Bible be taught as divine literature? Or as human literature—mere literature, and not revelation? In one school where this was tried, the teacher required the pupils to write a paper. She was very flexible in her requirement: Each student could choose any part of the Bible for his subject. One little girl asked if she might write on Isaiah. The teacher asked, Do you mean first Isaiah or second Isaiah? Thus the teaching of the Bible as literature becomes an attack on its veracity. It will be used, it is being used, to undermine Christianity.

When public schools first became popular, the Protestants generally were deceived by the specious promises of the public school people. They thought that if they maintained Christian colleges, the primary schools could be entrusted to the state. But not all the Protestants were deceived by these false promises not to attack Christianity. The Lutheran Church and the Christian Reformed people early established primary schools for their children. They believed that the influence of the Christian home and the preaching of the Christian church should be strengthened by a Christian school system. But both the Lutherans and the Christian Reformed, with their European background, have remained somewhat closed societies as it were, and unfortunately have exercised little influence, in this respect at least, on the rest of American Protestantism. There was one man, however, among the English-speaking American churches who saw the implication of the public school system; he warned of what was to follow, but his warning went unheeded. It is interesting, sadly interesting, to read his warning today, now that ninety years have proved him to be right. For it was in lectures given prior to 1890 that A.A. Hodge made the predictions now to be quoted.

In his *Popular Lectures on Theological Themes*, page 283, he wrote:

> A comprehensive and centralized system of national education, separated from religion, as is now commonly proposed, will prove the most appalling enginery for the propagation of anti-Christian and atheistic unbelief, and of anti-social nihilistic ethics, individual, social, and political, which this sin-rent world has ever seen.

Two pages before, he had written:

> It is capable of exact demonstration that if every party in the State has the right of excluding from the public schools whatever he does not believe to be true, then he that believes most must give way to him that believes least, and then he that believes least must give way to him that believes absolutely nothing, no matter in how small a minority the atheistics or agnostics may be. It is self-evident that on this scheme, if it is consistently and persistently carried out in all parts of the country, the United States system of national popular education will be the most efficient and wide instrument for the propagation of Atheism which the world has ever seen.

What A.A. Hodge did not see, at least what he did not explicitly say, is that although the irreligious have seized the right to exclude Christianity, the Christians are denied the right to exclude attacks on Christianity. There is no neutrality.

Obviously the schools are not Christian. Just as obviously they are not neutral. The Scriptures say that the fear of the Lord is the chief part of knowledge; but the schools, by omitting all reference to God, give the pupils the notion that knowledge can be had apart from God. They teach in effect that God has no control of history, that there is no plan of events that God is working out, that God does not foreordain whatsoever comes to pass. Aside from definite anti-Christian instruction to be discussed later, the public schools are not, never were, can never be, neutral. Neutrality is impossible. Let one ask what neutrality can possibly mean when God is involved. How does God judge the school system which says to him, "O God, we neither deny nor assert thy existence; and O God, we neither obey nor disobey thy commands; we are strictly neutral." Let no one fail to see the point: The school system that ignores God teaches its pupils to ignore God; and this is not neutrality. It is the worst form of antagonism, for it judges God to be unimportant and irrelevant in human affairs. This is atheism.

The evidences so far adduced to show the schools' opposition to Christianity have been largely individual instances that have come to the present writer's attention. They cannot easily be checked by the reader. The following evidences will come from educational authors, and anyone can get the books and evaluate them for himself.

The first exhibit may disappoint those who expect to be treated to some ridiculous blast against Christianity by a radical publicity seeker. Quite the reverse: The scholarly attainments, the writings, and the personality of Professor B.A.G. Fuller of the University of Southern California command respect. He did not ridicule Christianity, and nothing in the following argument is intended to ridicule him. He may not even have intended to attack Christianity at all—certainly it was not his chief purpose; but sober and, it is hoped, convincing reasons will be adduced to show that Professor Fuller fell into error, and that this error is detrimental to Christianity in the minds of his readers. The quotations now to be commented on come from his *History of Greek Philosophy, Thales to Democritus* (pp. 25, 26):

> From the beginning Christianity has bade man seek God within himself, and has taught that the external, physical world and the ranges of experience with which it furnishes us are if anything obstacles to that search.

Since, now, it is natural to have an interest in the world about us, either from the viewpoint of scientific physics or of practical invention, it follows that a normal student, when told that Christianity considers the world as an obstacle or nuisance, will discount Christianity. But if Christianity does not so teach, then the paragraph, however unintentionally, is an unjustifiable attack on that religion. To show that Christianity does not teach that the physical world is an obstacle to religious development, one may point out that the Bible asserts that the heavens declare the glory of God, and that the invisible things of God, namely his power and deity, are clearly seen in the physical universe, and that one of the earliest commands of God to man was to subdue nature and turn it to his purposes. It may well be that the revelation of God in nature is not sufficient to give a sinful man a knowledge of God's provision for salvation through the expiatory sacrifice of Christ; it may well be that Christianity does not view the physical universe exactly as paganism does; but certainly Christianity does not view the world that God created as an obstacle to the worship that God requires.

Fuller continues:

> The process of salvation is essentially an inner process. It is the rescue of the inner life from dependence upon the outward world and a restoration of it to an immediate communion with God in which the physical and external are forgotten.

It is true, of course, that salvation is essentially an inner process. Repentance, the changing of one's mind from a love of sin to a love of God, is internal; the work of the Holy Spirit in causing him who was dead in sin to rise to newness of life, in removing the depravity of the natural man and enabling him to receive the things of the Spirit which before he could not receive, in enlightening our minds in the knowledge of Christ and causing us to grow in grace—all this is internal. But this does not imply that man, or even his inner life, is made independent of the external world, and certainly it does not mean that the physical universe is forgotten. The stages of sanctification with struggle and victory over temptations, the promulgation of the Gospel, the public worship of God, all occur by the proper use of physical means. It must be kept in mind also that God pronounced his creation good, and after man had been created, with a body, God pronounced it all very good. Then, most significantly of all, one of the distinctions between Christianity and the pagan philosophy of Greece is precisely that educated Greek religion argued for the immortality of the soul, while Christianity also preached the resurrection of the body. What Fuller says therefore may be true of some forms of paganism, but it is not true of Christianity. Christian salvation does not exclude the external and physical.

Doubtless it is true that Christianity opposes the world, the flesh, and the devil. And this may be his basis for thinking that Christianity regards the physical universe as an obstacle. But while the devil is literal enough, the world does not mean the physical universe, nor is the flesh the sort of flesh that Shylock wanted. The Scriptures teach that Adam was created originally righteous, that, nevertheless, acting as representative of the race he fell into sin, and so guilt and pollution came upon all his natural descendants. Hence human nature as it now is, is sinful, and in the Scriptures this sinful racial inheritance is sometimes designated as *the flesh*. Similarly the world, in the extended moral sense, refers to the whole social set-up with its anti-Christian principles. In this sense the world and the flesh are obstacles to religious development, but there is nothing in the Scripture to justify the contention that stones and stars, cats and cabbages, are evils from which the inner life must be rescued.

Doubtless it is also true that some people who have claimed the name of Christian have spoken as if certain objects in the world, like the body, and certain institutions, like marriage, are evil in themselves. It is therefore necessary to decide what criterion shall be used in judging whether this or that view is Christian or not. In the paragraphs above the Scriptures of the Old and New Testaments have been taken as the only criterion. But perhaps Fuller does not equate Christianity with what the Scriptures teach. At least there are those, even if it is not true of Fuller, who take Christianity merely as an historical movement, and anything is called Christian if it is in any loose way connected with this historical movement. The trouble with taking history as a criterion becomes obvious when all that is loosely connected with Christian history is compiled. It is then seen that Christianity teaches that Christ is the trinitarian Son of God, that he is a created angel, that he is a mere man; that the sacraments are the indispensable means of salvation, that the sacraments are the valuable but not indispensable signs of an inward work of grace, that the sacraments are not to be observed at all; that Christ died on the cross to pay a ransom to the devil, that he died to satisfy the justice of God, that he died merely as an example of humility.

The trouble is that history cannot be a criterion of what is Christian, because a criterion is needed to determine what is Christian history. There have been and still are many individual Christians who do not see all the implications in the Scriptures and who therefore hold views inconsistent with the Scriptures; but the only objective criterion as to whether a view is Christian or not is the Bible—it is not whether someone who is or merely calls himself a Christian holds such a view. To determine what is Christianity by history or experience is to make the name self-contradictory and meaningless.

Then when Fuller continues by understanding "the objective side of Christianity, the historic Incarnation and Redemption" as "but the lever for applying pressure from without to loosen the soul from the hold of the body," he adds further to his ascetic error. For if asceticism were truly Christian, the Incarnation would be ridiculous. God certainly would not become incarnate, if to be incarnate were precisely the evil from which all should flee. But more serious than simply giving a wrong explanation of the Incarnation is the paragraph's implicit denial that redemption is obtained by a vicarious, expiatory sacrifice that satisfies the justice of God. One who reads these paragraphs would get no idea of what the New Testament teaches with respect to its central and greatest doctrine. And to obscure, indeed to ignore the main message of Christianity, is an attack far more subtle and effective than ridiculous imaginations concerning the opiate of the people.

Now finally on the next page Fuller writes:

> The world for which the blood of redemption was spilled is the moral world. . . . No drop of that blood overflows into the outer and physical world. In the benefits of salvation no being,

animate or inanimate, save the human, shares. The physical world remains unchanged. But after all, from the Christian point of view, why should nature be affected by the process of redemption?

Now obviously the Scriptures are addressed to man, not to animals or inanimate nature, and consequently the plan of man's salvation lies writ large throughout the Bible. But Fuller's criticism is equivalent to asserting that Jesus Christ, whatever he may mean for man, plays no cosmic role. Is this then what the Scriptures teach? On the contrary they teach, in the first chapter of John's Gospel, that Christ is the Logos, the Wisdom of God and the rationality of the universe. In Colossians 1:16 it is revealed that all things were created by Him and for Him, including all animate and inanimate forms. Were this all that the Scriptures said, it would be sufficient to raise serious doubts as to the accuracy of Fuller's interpretation of Christ's death. For if Jesus is the Creator, would not so stupendous an event as the death of the world's Creator have some effect on the entire creation? Now as a matter of fact, we are not abandoned to mere conjecture; the Scriptures add to the above information and state positively that even the inanimate world shall be changed and that the lower animals and even plants shall share in the benefits of redemption. They benefit, to be sure, as plants and animals, not as human beings; but they are not, as Professor Fuller says, excluded from God's all embracing plan.

And the cow and the bear shall feed; their young ones shall lie down together: and the lion shall eat straw like the ox. And the sucking child shall play on the hole of the asp, and the weaned child shall put his hand on the cockatrice's den. They shall not hurt nor destroy in all my holy mountain: for the earth shall be full of the knowledge of the Lord, as the waters cover the sea (Isaiah 11:7-9).

Furthermore, Dr. Fuller's question, "From the Christian point of view, why should nature be affected by the process of redemption," has an answer which the rhetorical style of the question implies is impossible. In Genesis 3:14-19 the curse of sin is extended to the very ground; the effects of sin are not limited to the human race. Is it not therefore perfectly appropriate that redemption from sin should affect all the realms in which the curse applies? Nor is it true that this idea lies buried so obscurely in the Bible as to have been forgotten by the contemporary Christian community. If one cares to attend an orthodox Christian church about Christmas time, one is sure to hear the carol, *Joy to the World.* And in this carol, Christians sing,

> *No more let sins and sorrows grow,*
> *Nor thorns infest the ground;*
> *He comes to make the blessings flow*
> *Far as the curse is found.*

Professor Fuller is a competent scholar; he gives careful consideration to what exactly Thales and Democritus taught, even though he may not agree with them; why has he forsaken the ideal of historical accuracy when he describes Christianity —why, unless accuracy would put Christianity in too good a light?

In this volume by Professor Fuller one finds a specific case of the approved method of attacking Christianity. It is not the aberration of an embittered bigot, but the calm, seemingly unbiased statement of a disinterested scholar. Nonetheless the specific attack on Christianity by Fuller is an aberration—it is a misinterpretation. And the most effective attacks against Christianity are no doubt all misinterpretations, not wild misinterpretations, but plausible misinterpretations. These are most effective on students who are mildly favorable to Christianity, even on students who are definitely Christians. A slashing attack would not influence them. The more vicious attacks are effective on students who are in some degree already unfavorable to Christianity. They stimulate and augment animosity. A few pages further on an example of a vicious attack will be reported. It comes from William Heard Kilpatrick who was nearer the grade school level than Professor Fuller. And this fact will take care of the objection that one must expect reasoned objections to Christianity in college, though there is no evidence of anti-Christian animosity in the grade schools.

If this specific instance were unique, there would of course be little damage done. The multiplication of distortions is what finally makes Christianity seem repellent to the student world. When in philosophy, in history, in zoology, and in literature, the student is repeatedly taught distortions, the foreseen effect naturally takes place, and the Christian religion is no longer regarded as a respectable position.

Adding to the effect of such misrepresentations is another powerful factor. Had the student in his early years been taught the doctrines of the Bible, these deviations could be recognized and so lose some or all of their force. But unfortunately the elementary system of education through which nearly all children pass provides no instruction in the things of God and his revelation. Through grammar and high school the growing child is given the idea that God and education have nothing to do with each other. A family may have its religion for Sundays and church business, but education is a totally separate matter. Now, the Scriptures teach that the fear of the Lord is the chief part of knowledge. The schools, by their silence, teach that there is no room for God in intellectual matters. Thus because the public schools ignore God it is not difficult to persuade the college student that Christianity is unworthy of consideration.

From this analysis of the situation the Christian may learn two things about a counter strategy. The first thing is not to be silent. If anyone is to advance the cause of Christ, he must talk out. Silence is not proclamation. No one will accept the truth, no one will hear the truth, unless someone speaks the truth. The first measure to be taken therefore is to break silence and talk about Jesus Christ, the Son of God, the nature of his redemptive work, and its application to individual believers.

Or, perhaps, this is not the first step in counter strategy. No, assuredly it is not the first step. The first step is to learn what the Scriptures teach, for if one does not know exactly what Christianity is, how is it possible to preach the Gospel? Modern educational theories have so stressed methods of teaching, that even Christians have come to forget that the important thing is not *how* one is to teach, but *what* one is to teach. It is unfortunate that those opposed to Christianity misrepresent it; it is much more unfortunate that many who want to be true to the Saviour distort His Gospel. The first step then is to learn the whole counsel of God, and the second step is to publicize it.

The whole counsel of God involves a world-view; its principles have applications in all fields of study. For this reason the second exhibit to show the methods of opposing Christianity will be taken from a textbook on political science. Whereas Fuller's disparagement of Christianity was largely a matter of misrepresentation, the present example depends on a perversity of expression calculated to cast slurs on the Holy Scriptures.

Often an anti-Christian author so chooses his words that it is difficult to quote a single sentence to convict him of inaccuracy, and it becomes necessary to examine carefully an extended passage to discover exactly what is happening.

An instance of this type of attack is found in an *Introduction to Political Science* by James Wilford Garner, Professor of

Political Science at the University of Illinois. This textbook, in the section under consideration, states some things very well; in fact it is the mixture of excellence and carelessness which causes the difficulty. Were it largely inaccurate or absurd it would have little effect. But Professor Garner's book, like that of Fuller, is scholarly, and one does not expect crude blunders.

In chapter IV the subject is the origin of the state, and on page 87 these words are to be found:

> The oldest of these theories . . . is that which attributes the establishment of the state, mediately or immediately, to God or some superhuman power. The theory assumes that the will of God was made known by revelation mediately or immediately to certain persons who were His earthly vice-regents and by them communicated to the people by whom obedience was a religious as well as a civil duty. . . . Biblical support for it is found in such passages as Paul's admonition to the Romans: "Let every soul be in subjection to the higher powers; for there is no power but of God; and the powers that be are ordained of God."

First, one notes that this theory of the origin, or better the justification, of state authority is supported by the Bible. Therefore general condemnation of the theory involves rejection of the Scriptures. To be sure, Garner said: "Biblical support is found." Now a man might find support wrongly, so that a rejection of his theory would not involve a rejection of the Bible. But no such distinction is made by Garner. Had he criticized the theory of James I and showed that the divine right of kings is not the same as the Biblical doctrine of the divine authority of the state, no one could object. But as a matter of fact his discussion does not discriminate and his rejection apparently applies as much to the Bible as to James I.

On page 90, in a paragraph headed, *Theocratic Doctrines no longer accepted*, the reason for rejecting the divine authority of government is stated as follows:

> The state is no more the direct and immediate creation of a supernatural power than any of the multifarious associations into which mankind has entered. The authority which the state exercises, whatever its origin, must be exercised through human agencies and must be humanly interpreted, that is, in the last analysis, it is only what the state chooses to make it.

This reason for rejecting the Bible, however, does not even apply to the Biblical view as Garner defined that view. As quoted above Garner explicitly stated that the divine origin of government permits of a mediate working by God. Now he objects that since man is the means, God cannot be the source of authority. In other words, he argues that if God is the source of authority there can be no human means, no human rulers, no human government at all. The only condition on which God can be the source of human government is that there be no human government. It is this type of perverse argument that betrays a man's subconscious predilections. Had the author been at all sympathetic toward the notion that God is the Creator and ruler of the world, he would not have stumbled into such an elementary logical blunder.

Following the last quotation, Garner continues in this manner:

> We may accordingly dismiss the doctrine of divine right with the statement that it never was anything more than an invention of man, designed to bolster up the claims of certain rulers to hold their crowns independently of the will of the people. . . .

Now if the doctrine of divine right were never anything more than this, then it follows that Paul in enunciating the doctrine was interested in bolstering up the powers and claims of Caligula and Nero. Sober historians do not usually credit Paul with such political ambitions.

The paragraph heading which was placed at the side of the sentence last quoted, together with the sentence which immediately follows it, is further evidence of the author's anti-Christian orientation. The paragraph heading reads. "Element of truth in the theory." Thus one is led to believe that the author finds at least some good in the notion that God is the source of governmental authority. The text so far quoted merely dismisses the Scriptural view. Then the author writes: "If the theory meant simply that the Creator implanted in the breast of man the instinct for order . . . we could accept it. Or if it meant that magistrates should rule in accordance with the precepts and teachings of the Christian religion . . . few would dissent."

Note that the grammatical construction, condition contrary to fact, implies that while a fertile mind might have these elements of truth suggested to it by the divine theory, the theory properly understood does not contain them. Hence the paragraph entitled, *Element of truth*, etc., turns out to be a denial of any element of truth to the Scriptural view. This queer circumstance coupled with the previous elementary logical blunder shows clearly how difficult it is for a camel to go through the eye of a needle and how difficult it is for a non-Christian to tell the truth about Christianity.

A third exhibit will conclude the examination of the attacks on Christianity on the college level. It illustrates a different method of attack, and because it is chosen from a different part of the curriculum, it shows once again that a world-view is involved and that Christianity touches all spheres of human interest. The exhibit is John Dewey's well-known volume, *Human Nature and Conduct*, and its method, instead of being a misrepresentation of Christianity, consists of ignoring Christianity and of substituting something entirely incompatible with it. The page references are taken from the 1922 edition.

To show that John Dewey is not a Christian, little proof is needed beyond a reference to some incidental attacks on Christianity and some concrete proposals inconsistent with Christian ideals.

The first of these is exemplified on pages 49, 50, and 295, where Dewey brands as superstitious the belief in a future life with divine rewards and punishments. This leads him to repudiate the view that punishment of crime vindicates justice. On page 17 he writes:

> The abstract theory of justice which demands the "vindication" of the law irrespective of instruction and reform of the wrong-doer is as much a refusal to recognize responsibility as is the sentimental gush which makes a suffering victim out of a criminal.

Now since a dead man cannot be instructed and reformed, it follows that Dewey is here opposing capital punishment; and since capital punishment is given divine sanction in the Bible (Genesis 9:6 and Romans 13:4), it is clear that Dewey is advocating a non-Christian society.

The second is exemplified in the desire to abolish old institutions (p.73). One of these is the home, the family, with its parental discipline (p.98). Dewey complains that adults enforce habits on children because they distrust the child's intelligence. Apparently he thinks that a child is quite able to cope with the world without parental instruction. "The habits of the growing person are jealously kept within the limits of adult customs. The delightful originality of the child is tamed" (p.98). It is not unreasonable to see in this theory of progressive education, as it is called, the cause of a great deal of today's juvenile delinquency and of the general lowering of the academic standards of schools and colleges. Dewey describes the result of parental training as follows:

> These "infantilisms" account for the mass of irrationalities that prevail among men of otherwise rational tastes. These personal "hang-overs" are the cause of what the student of culture calls survivals. But unfortunately these survivals are much more numerous and pervasive than the anthropologist and historian are wont to admit. To list them would perhaps oust one from "respectable" society (pp.98-99).

In advocating that children be left to learn by their own intelligence without the evil of parental discipline, in attacking morality and respectability, Dewey is clearly attacking Christianity.

Still more important than the bare fact that someone does not like the divinely ordained institution of the family, is the method by which such an attack is made plausible to the reader. Christian faith is not injured so much by clear denials of it, as by the methods of persuasion used in bringing others to deny it. Dewey's methods of argumentation are worth studying.

The book is well named; it treats throughout of human nature and conduct. In the introduction there is the complaint, often repeated, that morals have been severed from human nature. "Until the integrity of morals with human nature and of both with the environment is recognized, we shall be deprived of the aid of past experience to cope with the most acute and deep problems of life" (pp.12-13). Apparently to support this proposition Dewey gives a series of oddities in common moral thinking. But why should one be so concerned to prove this proposition? Has anyone, regardless of his personal oddities, argued that morality should be divorced from human nature and conduct? Is not Dewey wasting words on what is perfectly obvious? No, Dewey is not saying what is obvious, at least he does not mean to say the obvious. The reader is at first struck with the obvious, that is, the superficial truth of the statement and is carried along by what seems to be good common sense. But at length it appears that Dewey has meant something else altogether. In the meantime the reader has adopted Dewey's position and fails to see that the meaning of words has changed. On page 52 Dewey is arguing against transcendental moral principles, principles that are not empirical generalizations but eternal verities. With respect to an appeal to such principles for moral guidance he says, "Objectivity is saved but at the expense of connection with human affairs."

Here one sees what he means by a separation of morals from human nature. Here the meaning of the integrity of morals with conduct becomes clear. To be connected with human nature, morals must have no connection with a supernatural world. If morality is regarded as a matter of God's law, then it cannot be connected with human conduct. Now, whether one accepts the Christian philosophy or not, it is evident that the two propositions, "Morals should concern human nature," and "Moral principles cannot be divinely ordained," are not logically equivalent. Let us grant that Dewey has proved the first proposition. It did not need proof. But what of the implication: Since morals must concern human conduct, it is impossible that God should require a certain type of conduct? This implication, on which his whole argument rests, Dewey does not even attempt to defend; he is content to begin with a truth superficially obvious and pass surreptitiously to his own, quite different, opinion.

Another illustration of this method of argumentation is his

attack on the institution of private property. It is fairly well summed up in the sentence, "Only a calloused imagination fancies that the institution of private property as it exists A.D. 1921 is the sole or indispensable means of its [the acquisitive instinct's] realization" (p.117).

From the fact that some accidental characteristic of the situation in 1921 could possibly have been improved, it is not right to cast doubt on the wisdom and morality of all forms of private property. Notice too how the word *sole* in the quotation beclouds the issue. No doubt acquisitive desires can be partially satisfied in other ways; but this does not prove that private property may be dispensed with. The acquisitive instinct can probably be pretty well satisfied by the acquisition of power. A dictator can command the most luxurious autos; he can confiscate the art treasures of the conquered nations; all his subjects are his servants. Of course, he has no private property. Private property is anathema. It all belongs to the state. But, *l'Etat, c'est moi*. In the paragraph Dewey connects private property with the acquisitive instinct. If "instincts" are good psychology—Dewey should know—no doubt there is some connection between them. But Dewey never mentions private property as the citizens' defense against totalitarian-minded governments. Remember Ahab.

This method of argument pervades the book. Dewey makes a statement obviously true in a superficial or literal sense, and then he passes to a new meaning unsupported by argument, analysis, or fact.

Turning now to the main thesis of the book, Dewey's view of human nature and conduct, one finds that like the ancient Sophists he holds that morality is conventional. And a thorough acquaintance with Plato's arguments in the *Protagoras* and the *Theaetetus* shows how changeless is the philosophy of change. For Dewey, morality is like language (p.79). Men did not intend language; rather, language grew unconsciously out of unintelligent babblings. Neither in grammar nor in morality is there any principle that should remain unchanged. "Life is a moving affair in which old moral truth ceases to apply" (p.239). True, history has provided "cumulative verifications which give many principles a well-earned prestige." And for this reason they are not to be "thrown away," but "revised," "adapted," and "altered." In any case moral principles are to be changed as their truth becomes obsolete. Consider in passing the effect of this view on the principle "Thou shalt love the Lord thy God with all thy heart, and with all thy soul, and with all thy mind."

To make matters worse, there is no criterion by which to judge of change, nor is there a goal which fixes the direction of progress. In arguing against utilitarianism, Dewey not only stresses the impossibility of completing the calculus of pleasures, but stresses even more the force of habit and instinct on conduct.

> The baby does not move to the mother's breast because of calculation of the advantages of warmth and food over against the pains of effort. Nor does the miser seek gold, nor the architect strive to make plans, nor the physician to heal, because of reckonings of comparative advantage and disadvantage. Habit, occupation, furnishes the necessity of forward action in the one case as instinct does in the other (pp.199-200).

And further on he repudiates all notions of a final end of action by approximation to which one may judge the amount of progress (p.284). He has no use for an ideal, stable condition toward which man may strive. In particular the Christian conception of heaven has less claim to ideal finality than the primitive simplicity of Rousseau and Tolstoi, the indifference of the Stoics, or Buddhistic Nirvana (pp.285-286). Dewey dislikes them all; but one may reasonably doubt that any one of them is less preferable to Dewey's view of an endless struggle in which problems only get more complicated. In the absence of a final goal the world is "open," and chance, luck, and accident cannot be denied. "A free man would rather take his chances in an open world than be guaranteed in a closed world" (p.311). And Dewey continues by indicating that a man who would choose a guarantee in preference to chance is a coward. But how is it possible on Dewey's position to say that cowardice is a vice rather than a virtue? Dewey constantly appeals to consequences as justifications of previous choices. Certainly the guarantee of a final end would guarantee the consequences. Does not this justify the choice? Dewey may call it cowardice and fatalism; but what is wrong with fatalism if it produces the results? A metaphysical ideal might provide a basis for rejecting fatalism, but Dewey without a stable standard cannot do so.

In fact Dewey, regardless of his categorical imperative "So act as to increase the meaning of present experience" (p.283), empties life of all purpose and meaning. Consider the following quotations in preparation for a pertinent question.

"There is no such thing as the single all-important end" (p.229); because, as he says at the end of the chapter, there is no fixed truth. "If quiescence were the end and it could be perpetuated, this way of removing disagreeable uneasiness would be as satisfactory a way out as the way of objective effort" (p.252). Here Dewey states that the quiescence of Nirvana, would, if permanent, be as satisfactory as the constant struggle toward no fixed goal. Then why not commit suicide? For him, with his denial of an immortal soul, death is permanent quiescence. The Christian with his belief in divine rewards and punishments has a reason—call it metaphysical, transcendental, or any other frightful adjective—has a reason for regarding suicide as immoral. Dewey has none. He says indeed that "Man continues to live because he is a living creature, not because reason convinces him of the certainty or probability of future satisfactions and achievements. He is instinct with activities that carry him on" (p.289). This no doubt explains why most people as a matter of fact do not commit suicide. But unless this instinct is a moral endowment from the Creator, it is no reason why men *ought* not commit suicide. Dewey urges us to reflect on experience. But does not reflection on the world's ills, its wars and brutalities, its endless struggle toward nowhere, bring us to the belief that suicide is best? Some have come to that conclusion and have killed themselves. Are they not the wisest and best of men? If there were a heaven to be attained, perhaps even if there were a goal to be approximated, life would be worth living; but Dewey's theory of morality in flux without norms and criteria makes morality impossible and life useless.

Most basically of all, morality is impossible because truth is impossible. Dewey eschews epistemology. And because he evades the problem of knowledge, he can the more easily slip into a behavioristic psychology. There is no distinction between overt behavior and consciousness (p.82). An individual mind is a complex of bodily habits.

> What then is meant by individual mind, by mind *as* individual? In effect the reply has already been given. Conflict of habits releases impulsive activities which in their manifestation require a modification of habit, of custom, and convention (p.87). The more flexible they [habits] are, the more refined is perception in its discrimination and the more delicate the presentation evoked by imagination. The sailor is intellectually at home on the sea, the hunter in the forest, the painter in his studio, the man of science in his laboratory. These commonplaces are universally recognized in the concrete; [now notice

the conclusion Dewey draws from this excellent premise] but their significance is obscured and their truth denied in the current general theory of mind. For they mean nothing more or less than that habits formed in process of exercising biological aptitudes are the sole agents of observation, recollection, foresight, and judgment: a mind or consciousness or soul in general which performs these operations is a myth (pp.175-176). Concrete habits do all the perceiving, recognizing . . . and reasoning that is done (p.177).

Although the importance of evading epistemology and of denying the existence of consciousness can scarcely be exaggerated, a long and technical discussion of them must be regretfully omitted.* It can only be said that Dewey follows in the skeptical footsteps of Heraclitus, Kratylus, and the Greek Sophists. All is flux. Nothing remains true. Morality is convention, and life is devoid of purpose.

One may soberly conclude that higher education in America is pagan and atheistic. It was not always so. The colleges that were founded before the American Revolution were almost without exception Christian colleges. Their aim may not have been to train ministers of the Gospel: but at least it was to provide an education in the liberal arts so that there might be an educated ministry. In some form or other their charters proclaimed them to be Christian institutions. And the world-view they gave their students was the theistic world-view. They believed in God; today they do not. So great is their deterioration, so thorough is the repudiation of their original purpose, that the boast of a humanist must be taken seriously. Mr. Corliss Lamont, in the Summer 1942 issue of *The Humanist*, wrote:

---

* For an excellent analysis, study Brand Blanshard's *The Nature of Thought*, Volume I, chapters ix and x.

In our own country of America it is obvious that the real spirit of the people is becoming more and more humanistic. There is the definite decline of supernatural religion and of church-going; there is the growing secularization of all phases of living and the constant spread of science and invention; and there is the American ideal of democracy, which means equal opportunity for all individuals and groups to share in the material and cultural goods of this life. In other words, while the American people do not as yet clearly realize the direction in which they are moving and while a large proportion of them still render lip-service to outworn religious forms, their every-day pattern of existence and their highest aims implicitly embody the philosophy of humanism.

The evidence of animosity against Christianity adduced here in the last few pages has come from books on the college level. Perhaps some people suspect that this has no bearing on the grade schools. Well, Dewey has had an immense influence on the public school system; hence the evidence is not too remote from the lower grades. To come still nearer, promise was made of a vicious attack on Christianity by one very intimately connected with the public schools. William Heard Kilpatrick taught Education to thousands, at least thirty-five or forty thousand, prospective school teachers. The following evidence can be checked in his book, *Philosophy of Education*. He opposes the view that it is the government's duty to protect private property and to respect unalienable rights (pp.53-54; 403). Most emphatically he opposes religious liberty. Not only would he prohibit religious groups, like the Lutherans, from maintaining private schools and colleges (p.354); he believes it is "undemocratic" to allow parents to teach the doctrines of their religion to their own children. Could there be any more vicious form of atheistic totalitarianism?

Some reference to grade school textbooks will serve as a

conclusion to this chapter. If one looks around, one can find more flagrant examples than the following. It is not spectacular. That is why it has been chosen. It will be quoted in full and then analyzed.

Scott, Foresman and Company, publishers of an excellent line of grade school textbooks, has one called *Our World and How We Use It,* by Campbell, Sears, Quillen, Hanna. On page 97, in a chapter explaining the domestication and use of animals, there is a section entitled, *Ideas about God.*

> You have seen how many of our ideas about property, about working together, and about war have come from these herdsmen of long ago. The herdsmen had many other ideas, too.
>
> The herdsman knew about the stars, because he had learned to read the sky as we read calendars. The sun was his clock by day, and the moon and stars told him the time at night. The night skies are very clear and the stars are bright in the dry climate of the grasslands and in the desert country.
>
> The herdsman watched the seasons come and go. He knew about times of plenty and about times of famine, too. He saw his animals born, grow, and die. He saw the head of the tribe punish his own children and his animals if they did not obey him, and reward them if they did right. Herdsmen had time to think about many, many things as they tended their animals.
>
> And so the herdsman came to know that there was a great God who took care of the world and everything in it, just as he himself took care of his own flocks and family. He taught his children to worship this God and to obey Him.
>
> The herdsman also knew that he had to protect his own animals and his family and his servants and workers. Many times he must have thought that the world would be a better place if there were no wild beasts or unfriendly people. And he came to believe that there must be something bad, something evil, which worked against God, just as wolves and bad men and

famine worked against him. This evil thing he called Satan.
Many of the thoughts of the herdsmen were made into
songs. You can read some of them in the Bible, in the Psalms of
David, the shepherd who became a king.

Confessedly the aim of the section is to teach the pupils
about God. Therefore it is a matter of religion; and religion,
whether preached in a pulpit or taught in a primary grade,
cannot be a neutral matter. To discover whether this textbook
favors Christianity or opposes it, let us list the five chief points it
teaches. It teaches first that the herdsmen discovered God or got
ideas about God by thinking as they tended their animals;
second, that they discovered God cared for them; third, that
they taught their children to worship and obey God; fourth, that
they learned, by reflection always, that there is a devil; and fifth,
that the Psalms of David are a result of this process.

Since this is the teaching of a textbook for the fourth grade,
it may be deemed unfair to offer profound, philosophical
criticism. And yet even pupils in the fourth grade can be told a
few simple, though profound, philosophic principles. The
section as written produces the impression that learning of God
is a purely empirical process. No reference is made to what a
philosopher would call the *a priori* equipment of learning. Now,
Kant's terminology is not for children, but even children can
understand when they are told that all men are born with the
idea of God. They may not know the terms *a priori* and *innate*,
but they can understand as well as they can understand
anything else that men are so made as to think of God
spontaneously: They are born that way. However, no particular
stress will be laid on the argument that the book teaches a
non-Christian empiricism.

But stress, great stress, is to be laid on the omission of all
reference to revelation. A true Christian, if asked how he has

learned of God, will answer immediately, "through the Bible, God's word." When a person replies, "by experience and reflection," it is instantly clear that that person is not a Christian.

In the second place, the textbook teaches that the herdsmen knew God cared for them because they cared for their flocks. What sort of argument is this? The herdsmen take care of their flocks in order to shear them, and eat them. Does such reflection lead to an ultimate trust in God?

Then third, the herdsmen taught their children to worship and obey God. This raises two questions. First, if there is no revelation, where do the herdsmen find the commands God requires us to obey? The Scripture speaks of the law of God as written on the hearts of men; it teaches that man was made in God's image and has an innate knowledge that right is different from wrong and that God punishes wrong. But the Scripture also teaches that man suppresses this knowledge by his wickedness, that he does not wish to retain God in his knowledge, and that God has given him over to a reprobate mind. Obviously the fourth grade textbook and Christianity do not agree. And the second question is still more to the point: How can the herdsmen teach their children to worship God? The Scripture not only says that no one, apart from the regenerating power of the Holy Spirit, seeks after God and that there is none that doeth good, no, not one; the Scripture also teaches that no one comes to the Father except by Jesus Christ. And this is as true of Abraham of old as it is of men today. Jesus said, "Abraham rejoiced to see my day, and he saw it, and was glad." The textbook gives no hint of this necessary prerequisite of worship. It teaches rather that one can obey and worship God without any reference to Jesus Christ.

The fourth point does not require any additional criticism; but the fifth point is the climax. Here it is stated that the Psalms of David are the products of purely human reflection. In direct antagonism to the Christian view, the textbook reduces the Bible to the level of the philosophically unjustifiable thoughts of a nomad.

David wrote, "The Lord said unto my Lord, Sit thou at my right hand, until I make thine enemies thy footstool." Is this a human fancy or a divine promise? David wrote:

> The kings of the earth set themselves . . . against the Lord and against his Anointed. . . . He that sitteth in the heavens shall laugh: the Lord shall have them in derision. . . . Yet have I set my King upon my holy hill of Zion. . . . The Lord hath said unto me, "Thou art my Son; this day have I begotten thee. . . . Kiss the Son, lest he be angry, and ye perish from the way, when his wrath is kindled but a little."

What is this? Nonsense? Or is it the voice of the Mighty God and Terrible?

The textbook from which the quotation was taken is pedagogically and mechanically excellent; it displays all the marks of technical competence. The inclusion of the section quoted therefore cannot be attributed to ignorance. It was deliberately planned. For these reasons the only possible conclusion is that the book and the educators behind it are definitely aiming to destroy the Christian religion.

Chapter 5
Ethics

The subject of ethics, the norms of morality, is not here introduced for the purpose of showing that neutrality is impossible. The previous chapter has done this sufficiently. Of course if neutrality is impossible in general, it will be impossible in ethics, too; and it will be made clear by the contrast between Christian and humanistic ethics. But the immediate purpose of this chapter is to explain Christian morality, to identify its norms, to uncover their foundation, and to suggest the implications for education. Education is an ethical undertaking. Schools cannot avoid making some sort of ethical impact on the students. This is so, not only in respect to such basic and all-embracing matters as pessimism and suicide, but also in many particulars, in very important particulars and in lesser, routine matters as well.

A current example of a very important particular is most apposite. An activist group at this moment is trying to introduce sex education into kindergarten. The present age is obsessed with sex. The Episcopal professor, Joseph Fletcher, advocates violating all of the Ten Commandments. He speaks favorably of swapping wives; he defends all forms of sex; hetero, homo, and auto. Various organizations publicize birth control and abortion. Some mothers give their daughters contraceptive pills when they leave home for college. So, for some reason or its opposite, sex education seems to be required, not only in high school, but in the elementary grades also.

What policies will control this instruction? One view is that sex should be treated as mere biology. No remarks on morality are to be allowed. Since morality may lead to religion and since public schools must have no religion, nothing more should be taught than the processes of coition, conception and contraception, abortion, and perhaps birth. With regard to this educational policy one must ask whether or not it has really avoided morality. Since the most important aspect of sex is its moral status, a purely biological treatment not only suffers from omission of what is most needed to be known; but, worse, it results in the impression that sex has no moral aspect at all. It puts sex in man on a level with sex in animals. Of course, this is what naturalism has to do; and in doing so it places all sexual aberrations on the same biological level: All are equally natural to the evolutionary process, and the fittest will inevitably survive. This view of human nature is sometimes called "a-moral"; on the Christian position it is immoral.

The second educational policy is perhaps the one that appeals to the greatest number of parents. They are aware of the widespread contempt of purity and virginity and think that it might be a good idea to have their children learn a little about sex in school. Maybe it will save their children from the worst excesses. Religion in the schools must at all costs be avoided; but a little morality may be taught. The plan proposed is to tell the children that premarital and homosexual sex may cause emotional conflicts in later life. It is easy to see what the young teen-ager will reply to such instruction. He will say, Perhaps premarital promiscuity may cause a little trouble in married life, but perhaps it won't. Who can tell? People are a lot different one from another. Furthermore, the more common promiscuity becomes, the more accepted it will be and the less emotional upset there will be. At any rate, the girl I marry will have had intercourse with several of my friends, so we shall be on a fifty-fifty basis, and neither of us will be so narrow-minded as to become emotionally disturbed. Therefore the present certain pleasure outweighs the unlikely future regret. In reply to this student-argument the teacher cannot consistently add that illegitimate children, venereal disease, and AIDS are possible penalties because these are the very penalties that modern education can prevent. Since, too, the teachers themselves are more and more the products of open visitation and contemporary sex propoganda, they probably will not be much concerned with what the pupils do. They may even have studied ethics under Professor Fletcher.

That this description is not an improbable surmise, an unreal nightmare conjured up to scare people, but a very sober appraisal of the present direction, can be seen in the results of sex education in Sweden. Socialism and secularism dominate Sweden. Hans I. Zetterberg, in an exhaustive study on Swedish sex education, concludes that "Sweden should be rightly thought of as The Contraceptive Society." This was not true a few decades ago. In 1938 it was still illegal to discuss contraceptive devices. When the liberal* politicians took over in 1932 a program to introduce sex education into the schools immediately began. Sex education began to be taught in 1940 and was made compulsory in 1956. The liberals did not want anyone to escape their immoral influence. Religious scruples count for nothing. At first the socialists, no doubt for publicity purposes, argued that sex education would build character. It did: bad character. One flaw in the program is the statement in

---

* *Liberal* as a contemporary term is the exact opposite of its nineteenth century meaning. Then it meant a restricted government, minority and individual rights, and free enterprise. Its principle was: The government that governs least governs best. Today liberalism means huge bureaucratic governments that regulate or want to regulate everything, including education and sex.

one of the teachers' handbooks that "It is neither desirable nor permissible [Christianity must be suppressed] for the school to teach a way of living as morally and socially right which does not agree with what the pupils know life actually is." Even this average loose morality was too idealistic and Christian. The socialistic leaders insisted that moralistic instruction was inappropriate for Sweden's "pluralistic and contraceptive society." Lars Gustafson in *The Public Dialogue* in Sweden opposed morality as "preserving prejudices. . . . Sex education is taught in an unsatisfactory way, and is more directed at warning the children about extra-marital relations than at really forestalling the various unwelcome results of such relations." Lars Ullerstam, M.D., in *The Erotic Minorities* asserts that "sexual deviations ought to be included [in the class room instruction] and these should not be described as diseases or abnormalities but as fully legitimate methods of satisfying the sexual urge"; and he advocates the establishment of brothels and government "bureaus to act as agencies for making sexual contacts."

To be noted is the circumstance, common to liberal theology and liberal politics, that Christian morality is to be excluded from public education because society is pluralistic; but pluralism is no bar to an attack on Christianity or to the inculcation of immorality. No wonder liberal Sweden is the most licentious nation in Europe.

But the United States has become as bad. The degree to which children are depraved by the public school system is unbelievable to many parents whose lives are mainly restricted to Christian circles. The utter viciousness of the public schools is well documented in a book that should be widely read. Claire Chambers has written a virtual horror story in *The SIECUS Circle*.* The school children are not taught to read these days;

---

*Claire Chambers, *The SIECUS Circle* (Belmont, Massachusetts: Western Islands, 1977).

they cannot do arithmetic; but they get plenty of instruction on the joys of copulation.

There is, finally, a third educational policy. It is to teach pupils that God gave the Ten Commandments and that one of them forbids adultery, lasciviousness, and fornication. But to tell public school children that God condemns sin is illegal. The Supreme Court reminds one of Louis XIV. The Jesuits had persuaded him to close the Jansenist abbey of Port Royal, where spirituality was so developed that even some miracles were reported to have happened there. On its closed doors some unknown wit tacked up a poster, which read:

Dit par le Roy: Défense à Dieu
De faire miracle en ce lieu!*

In contrast with the ineffective moral instruction of the second policy above—it is not really ineffective moral instruction; it is effective immoral instruction—the Christian view needs emphasis. Some people who think they know what the Christian view is, really do not. Others, though aware of several particulars, are hazy on the over-all theory. In any case the emphasis of contrast is needed.

The major difference between secular and Christian ethics is that the former (with the exception of Kant) judges the goodness or badness of an act by a doubtful calculation of its possible consequences, whereas the latter judges the rightness or wrongness of an act by precepts divinely revealed to the Hebrew prophets and Christian apostles.

Christian ethical standards have their source in the religion of the ancient Jews. Of all the peoples of the pre-Christian era, the Jews indisputably had the highest moral code. Even a

---

*Said by the King: Forbidden to God
  To do miracles in this place!　　　—*Editor*

Buddhist would admit this, and some, a few, contemporary humanists might be embarrassed to defend the Sodomites or the worshippers of Moloch and Baal. As individuals and as a nation the Jews were not faultless. Often they fell into idolatry and adopted the vicious practices of their heathen neighbors. But by and large over a period of two thousand years they not only possessed the purest moral code, but their actual conduct also was a green oasis of righteousness in a great and terrible wilderness, wherein were fiery serpents and scorpions.

Something more may also be said about the actual conduct of individual and groups: To wit, that western civilization until quite recently has been more moral than the peoples of Africa and Asia. Of course there has been corruption here. On November 24 and 25, 1960, *The New York Times*, which on principle minimizes the shortcomings of the liberals, carried some information as to the frauds in the election of John F. Kennedy. *Newsweek*, on December 5, 1960, told of a federal grand jury that discovered that Mayor Daley's machine, in a precinct of only twenty-two residents, was able to turn in seventy-four votes for Kennedy. The news media of December 12 and 13, 1968, carried stories of the infiltration of the liberal machines in New Jersey by the Mafia. The Mafia even infiltrated the IRS there. These are but two examples eight years apart. Nevertheless, even with the Tweed Ring of last century, corruption has not been so bad in America as it has been in Asia.

Without in the least modifying the doctrine of inherited depravity, we may cheerfully and thankfully admit that William James, repudiating Christianity and theism as he did, was a fairly respectable person. So it has been with many secularists. Their commendable character, however, is more the result of the Christian theism of their fathers than of their own non-Christian systems. The public preaching of the Gospel, which has elevated Christian moral principles to a position of supremacy, affects non-Christian individuals and restrains their evil human nature. Where the Gospel is not preached, brutality, corruption, crime, degeneracy, and cannibalism go on unchecked. With the Gospel now being silenced in America, our nation is sinking to the moral level of the heathen.

Yet herein lies a puzzle. Western morality has come from the Jews. When one stops to consider, does it not seem strange that while the secular culture of the western world traces its ancestry to ancient Greece, western morality, until World War II and the apostasy of the large churches, has been a more or less faithful development from the laws of a despised alien race? The Jews were and are despised. They were expelled from England until Oliver Cromwell brought them back. Long before Hitler the Germans did not like them; and the Communists follow the old Russian custom of oppressing and suppressing them. In antiquity, too, Claudius expelled the Jews from Rome; and Antiochus Epiphanes could not be satisfied with conquering Jerusalem: He must show his contempt by sprinkling pig soup in the temple. Now, we are accustomed to saying that the Jews influenced our civilization through Christianity. But does this not seem strange when we reflect that the word Christ itself means the Messiah of the Jews? Is it not peculiar that the Gentiles joined a church that was in those very early years entirely Jewish in its membership? How did it happen that a Jew crucified as a criminal is acknowledged as God by a hundred million Gentiles?

The history of the Jews—and all the more so because of the contemporary resurrection of the nation of Israel—may be too great an historico-psychological puzzle for scientifically-minded moderns who reject supernatural providence. But no one can doubt that an understanding of the Christian system of ethics requires a study of the Hebrew Scriptures in order to find its first principles, if not their developments. In making this search one is in harmony with the statements of Jesus himself and with the writings of the apostles. The Jews of today, or any other non-Christian group, may believe that Jesus and the apostles distorted the teaching of the Old Testament, but it remains a truth of history that they claimed to be in complete accord with Moses and the Prophets. Christian ethics, therefore, and Christian theology, cannot be understood apart from the Old Testament.

The Old Testament states the basic principles of Christianity, both cosmological principles and ethical, and these form a radical contrast with all forms of paganism. As this contrast is further spelled out, it will enforce the contention that the derivative principles of any system are determined by its presuppositions. The reason Aristotle differs from the Stoics on the nature of virtue is that they differ on the nature both of man and of the world. Unless one recognizes this, one fails to understand their motivations. Similarly, to comprehend the essential meaning and raison d'être of the derivative principle "Love thy neighbor as thyself," one must pierce beneath its surface to its systematically basic presuppositions. If it is true with Aristotle, it is equally true of the Bible that a *part* of a system can be understood only as a part of a *system*.

The Christian system starts with God—not just any sort of God, but with a very definite God, the God of the Bible. The preceding chapters contrasted a bare theism with Christian theism. Many systems use the term *God*, but this fact should not lead us to assume that all systems mean the same thing by that term. Just as Aristotle and the Stoics both use the term *virtue,* so, too, the term *God* in two systems may have little or nothing in common.

For the Hebrews and for the Christians, God is an Almighty Personal Being. In Plato and in Epicureanism God or the gods were personal but not almighty. With the Stoics, at least before the advent of Christianity, God may have been almighty but he or it was not a person. Furthermore, in the Hebrew-Christian system God is absolutely independent, for He is regarded as the Creator and First Cause of the world. And by referring to an Almighty Personal Creator, one makes a clean-cut distinction between God and the world. God is ontologically and eternally prior to the world, and while the world depends on Him, He in no wise depends on the world. No school of Greek philosophy prior to the introduction of Christianity seems even to have considered such a notion. Not a single school considered God as absolute Creator, and while there are in several schools elements of apparent transcendency, they all virtually make God and the world correlative terms and in one way or another fail to consider an absolute transcendency such as the despised Jews had in the Old Testament.

This concept of God, in contrast to all others, is indispensable for the establishment of ethical norms. In proportion as impersonal elements are included in the notion of God, and in so far as God is conceived as Nature or the Cosmos as a whole, it becomes impossible for men to have personal relations with the Deity. But in the Old Testament and even more so in the New Testament God had definite dealings with individuals. In the Old Testament he established a theocracy with a chosen nation for a specific purpose; in the New Testament the expansion of the church further emphasizes the same truth. Throughout, a man's relation to God is all important. In pagan systems, however, attention is drawn primarily to man's relation to other men, or to Nature as a whole, or as in the case of Plato, to a supersensible world of ideas. Pagan ethics always conceived morality as essentially an affair among men. On the contrary in the Bible man is first of all related to God, and then secondarily and mediately he is related to other men.

To put this same matter more concretely, reference may be made to the concept of responsibility. The choice between atheism and theism, offered somewhat abstractly in chapter two, is here seen again to force decisions in derivative subjects. The Hebrew-Christian religion takes the concept of responsibility quite seriously, while the same can hardly be said either of ancient paganism or of modern non-Christian systems. Responsibility means to give a response, that is, to be answerable for something; but to be answerable implies that there must be someone to be answerable to. In other words, responsibility implies a superior personal power. To the Christian it does not seem to make sense that one should give an answer to impersonal Nature as a whole; nor are other men so superior that one is called upon to give a final answer to his brother; and to give an answer to oneself is a little gratuitous. Without Almighty God to call all men before his judgment bar, there to require an account of the deeds done in the body, responsibility is meaningless. Responsibility is based on the Sovereignty of God; and only in a system where the world, the human race, and everything else are theistically explained, can responsibility be a serious element in human life.

It is the failure to understand this personal aspect of responsibility to an Almighty Person which has led Dewey and Tufts in their revised textbook on ethics to make a curious mistake. These two professors recognize that Hebrew morality and Jehovah are somewhat related, but the precise relation escapes them. Hence they picture Jehovah as a despicable person who would kill a man for innocently touching a wooden chest. Now we are not concerned to point out that that wooden chest was the symbol of the Divine Presence and was therefore to be treated with the proper reverence. The important point is that Uzzah—the man who touched the ark and was killed—in touching the ark deliberately disobeyed God. If Dewey and

Tufts wish to be consistent, they would have to say also that a buck private in the army should not be punished for disobeying orders. Touching a wooden box may or may not be innocent; but disobedience to God is not innocent. And just as in the army it is the officer and not the private who decides what the proper punishment is, so in the Hebrew-Christian religion it is God and not Uzzah—nor even Dewey and Tufts.

In view of this construction of the concepts of responsibility and obedience to God, it is clear that the Bible allows of no morality apart from religion. This is what underlies the Christian objection against public schools trying to inculcate a minimum of morality by hesitantly suggesting some possible unpleasant results of immoral conduct. Their argument is bad and their principles are wrong.

All serious thinkers have attempted to provide some sort of ethical position. Humanists must defend their type of life without an appeal to divine sanctions. Naturally they arrive at non-Christian particulars. Dewey is a good example of a humanist who expends considerable energy in formulating a theory of ethics, and whose system is so far removed from Christian ideals that he himself admitted that if he had published the details he would have been banned from public society. The reason for so great a divergence is that the humanists reject God and his revelation. They try to establish moral principles on some sort of observation of the world and human nature.

This sort of empirical procedure is logically impossible. Values in the sense of things men ought to choose cannot be discovered in experience. All that can be discovered are values in the sense of what men factually want. In the writings of some authors ethics has become a sort of sociology. They think they are discussing ethics when in reality they are only describing what various societies believe is ethical. In Robert Louis

Stevenson's *Treasure Island* Captain Billy Bones valued rum. He valued rum more than a long life. He would rather die young with rum than live to old age without. But such a sociological description avails nothing in proving that Captain Bones' evaluation was correct. John Dewey expended great energy in trying to pass from *de facto* value to *de jure* value, from what men actually desire to what is really valuable. His efforts ended in failure.*

Perhaps the best attempt ever made to establish moral norms on a non-theistic, non-revelational basis was that of the older writer, Henry Sidgwick, in his monumental volume, *The Methods of Ethics*. In turn Sidgwick disposes of egoistic hedonism and two forms of English intuitionism. Then he gives a penetrating but rather favorable critique of utilitarianism. Bentham's theory, however, needs an intuitional basis. This Sidgwick provides with the intuitions of justice, prudence and benevolence. Then he considers whether personal happiness coincides with universal happiness. Here he admits two things: First, there is no empirical evidence that the good of any one person is consistent with the good of all; second, if there were a God who imposed sanctions so as to make these two goods harmonize, then ethics would be rational. He should also have said that God would have to reveal the fact to mankind. But Sidgwick is unwilling to accept God and revelation. He is therefore forced to admit, reluctantly, that he has fallen into universal skepticism.

Ethics depends on revelation, and more emphasis should be placed on the necessity of revelation. A God who told man nothing would not be a satisfactory basis for ethics. The utilitarian method of judging right from wrong is the method of

---

* Compare my monograph *Dewey* (Nutley, New Jersey: Presbyterian and Reformed Publishing Company, 1960) and *Religion, Reason and Revelation* (Jefferson, Maryland: The Trinity Foundation, 1986).

calculating consequences. Sidgwick tries to minimize the difficulties; but it should be obvious that no one can calculate the amounts of pleasure and pain a proposed line of action will produce for the whole human race. One cannot calculate such a sum even for oneself. Later moralists sometimes repudiate utilitarianism, but they all seem to depend on some kind of calculation. Since this is impossible, the advantage of the divinely revealed Ten Commandments is obvious. And contrariwise even a theism without revelation would be ethically useless.

The necessity of revelation points to a very fundamental principle of Christian ethics. The Ten Commandments are commandments given by God. God is the law-giver. The laws depend on his will. Morality in the Old Testament is never conceived as loyalty to a set of Platonic Ideas. In Platonism the Demiurge—the Maker of the world—imposes order on chaotic space so as to change it from chaos into a cosmos. The order so imposed is originally contained in an eternal blueprint, the World of Ideas, which the Demiurge faithfully follows. Thus for Plato the principles of rationality, knowledge, and order, including the principles of morality, exist independently of and objectively to the God who makes the world.

Not so in the Old Testament. God is as much the creator, perhaps *determiner* would be the better word, of moral laws as he is the creator of the inanimate world. God determined that water would freeze at one temperature and gasoline at a lower temperature. Likewise God determined that stealing was to be wrong and that the Jews should offer certain sacrifices. Christian theism regards God as the *Law-giver*.

As this exposition of the Christian view develops, its utter incompatibility with humanism, and the resulting impossibility of neutrality, can hardly be missed. Consider the effect of an immoral act. Aristotle, for example, certainly recommends a life of virtue. He does not encourage wrong-doing. Nevertheless in his eyes a moral mistake is like a child's mistake in practicing the piano. One mistake does not produce a bad habit; and further attention to the correct fingering will erase the effect of one mistake. Virtue for Aristotle is a good habit. It is achieved by practice. In this view there are several glaring contradictions of Christianity. First, morality and immorality are divorced from any particular relation to God. In the Christian view Adam's one "mistake" was an offense against God. It was not just a temporary interruption in the formation of a good habit. Second, Adam's original sin resulted in universal, inherited depravity; whereas for Aristotle every child starts out from scratch, naturally inclined neither to good nor evil. In the third place, as a logical implication of the former, according to Christianity the inherent depravity of human nature, the inclination to evil and enmity against God, cannot be removed by an extra half hour of practice. What is needed is a change of nature, regeneration, and a change of mind, repentance. The incompatibility reminds one of a remark by William James: Referring to the Prayer Book's confession, "There is no health in us," James asserted that he was in very good health. Between these two views no compromise or accommodation is possible.

Some further elaboration of a point already mentioned will do no harm. It has to do with norms and the role of norms in education. What is the origin of norms? How is the distinction between right and wrong identified? It has already been said that God in the role of creator and law-giver establishes normative distinctions. But the contrast with secularism that this entails is greater than perhaps some people imagine. All non-Christian moralists from Plato to Hastings Rashdall, and contemporary humanists still more vociferously,* always as-

* Descartes expressed an opposite opinion concerning the creation of the world,

sume that the intellectual or "ontological" relationship between a person and a norm is the same for all persons, God being a person included with men. Leibniz is an especially clear example, meriting Spinoza's complaint that he had subjected God to the supremacy of moral principles. Plato is an even clearer example, partly because he lived before the Christian era; and having no knowledge of Moses as some Jews and early Christians thought he had, he could not have tried to combine into his system discordant elements from Hebrew-Christian sources.

In Plato's system there are three independent principles, all eternal but not all equal in rank. There is Space, out of which this world is later formed (not created). Second, there is a God who forms the world out of the previously chaotic space. And highest of all, even above God, is the World of Ideas, the source of all existence, good, and moral law. God is good because he uses the World of Ideas as the plan or model when he forms our world here below.*

In contrast with this Platonic world-view which makes law supreme, stands the Christian system which makes the law-giver supreme. The Christian system may still find a place for the Ideas (as Philo did), but they are God's Ideas, his Logos, his thought, his plan of the universe. This principle is popularly expressed in the phrase, the good is good because God said so, whereas in the various forms of Platonism, the Good exists independently of God's volition.

The consequence to ethics is this: Non-Christian systems must discover their ethical norms by arguments based in one way or another on observation of the universe. Even Plato used

---

though he may not have seen its application to ethics; but then he was not chiefly a moralist.

* One may of course contend that Plato's god is the World of Ideas, not the Demiurge. But the Demiurge is nonetheless the Maker of Heaven and Earth.

such arguments to prove the existence of the Ideas. But Christianity depends on a divine revelation. God, the Law-giver, promulgates his laws, and we learn what they are by this promulgation. This promulgation is of course the Scripture. The Bible makes known to men the divine precepts that should govern our lives.

This leads up to the final point. Perhaps it is better to phrase the thought in terms of an objection to the Christian system. Sometimes people object that the God of the Hebrews is immoral and that the ethical implications of the Scriptures violate their consciences.

No one, however, who understands the Hebrew-Christian system is much surprised or worried by such an objection; it is precisely the objection expected. The whole argument has aimed to show that a definite world-view must be chosen, and that neutrality is impossible—as impossible in ethics as in politics or geography. And if neutrality is impossible in ethics, the non-Christian thinker is logically bound to repudiate Christian morality. Naturally the Scriptures contradict man's moral consciousness, because man by rejecting the Sovereign God has corrupted his nature, darkened his mind, and has chosen other norms. This does not mean that the Scriptures should be changed; what needs changing is the mind of man.

Some writers do not openly repudiate Christian morality. Less consistent, or at least less frank than the Nazis and the Communists, they try to lift Christian ethical principles out of their proper setting and dress them up in foreign attire. For this reason many of the books written on Christian Ethics, or more particularly on the Ethics of Jesus, are completely misleading. They examine a few of the sayings of Jesus, discover that He spoke about love of God and love of neighbor, and then they place this love in a non-Christian context. They assume, for example, that the love Jesus meant is possible apart from the new birth, that the meaning of love can be known apart from revelation, and that God is not the Almighty Personal Creator to whom we are responsible. These authors may write apparently scholarly books and achieve a reputation for learning, but in reality they are as mistaken as a college student who (believe it or not) returned in his examination this choice sentence: "The Sermon on the Mount, in the Old Testament, was one in which Moses, one of the apostles, gave the moral rules of God to the chosen people."

But as in Platonism or Stoicism, so in Christianity, ethics cannot be understood without the context of the system. The presuppositions of any subject are always its most important part. If one insists on disconnecting Jesus' ethical teaching from his specifically theological teaching, an impartial student will see clearly that there is nothing particularly original to be learned from Jesus. With hardly an exception, his moral sayings can be paralleled in Plato, Confucius, or the Hebrew prophets, scribes, and rabbis. It is the basic theology which makes Jesus and Christianity unique in ethical teaching; it is the theology and the theology alone that provides adequate philosophic justification of Christian morality; and it is the theology which saves Christianity from the fate of being merely good advice, and makes it a vital religion.

A concrete example of distorting the Christian system of ethics may be seen in two quotations from contemporary textbooks. Instead of taking derivative Christian principles and placing them in a non-Christian system, they take the ethics of a non-Christian system and try to crown it with a respectable Christian halo.

"Perhaps the best way to introduce Kant is to conceive him as the last and most logical of the long line of Hebrew prophets and Christian Apostles."* The second quotation is:

---

* T.V. Smith, *Readings in Ethics*, by Clark and Smith, p.223.

Either then there is some way of defining a good end—an end
which justifies the means—or else there must be a moral
excellence that belongs to certain types of acts irrespective of
what they may lead to, if indeed they lead to aught in
common. . . . The second interpretation is in the spirit of the
Decalogue. . . . This world, we might call it the Old Testament
world, is then exactly the kind of world in which morality as
Kant defines morality could and would exist.*

That some have had doubts as to the truth of the view given
in the quotations is attested by the following footnote of the
second writer. "This image of the Old Testament World is not of
course supposed to be that of the ancient Hebrews. Rather does
it represent this world as reflected in the thought of a modern
Christian community."†

Now whatever the force of this last admission may be, the
two quotations strongly suggest a fundamental similarity
between the ethics of Kant and of the Old Testament. Because
of the footnote, however, one needs to distinguish between the
Testaments themselves and what that vague entity, a modern
Christian community, might happen to think of those ancient
documents. But both authors imply, and the second distinctly
asserts, that common opinion makes Kant's strict morality
essentially that of the Hebrew-Christian religion.

This opinion seems to be a definitely mistaken one. And
why those who express such an opinion, without some qualifi-
cation like that in the second author, are mistaken, admits of an
easy psychological explanation. The modern Christian community is simply not Christian. The views of the intelligentsia,
artistically if sometimes flippantly expressed in dilettante
magazines, err through a profound unfamiliarity with the

---

* E.A. Singer, *Modern Thinkers*, pp.132, 137.
† E.A. Singer, *Modern Thinkers*, p.137.

contents of the Old and New Testaments. The modern educated community is largely pagan, so largely in fact that the condition usually escapes notice. The educational system has fostered religious ignorance, and the great majority of college graduates go through life either with distorted views of the contents of Christianity or none at all—alternatives which in reality amount to the same thing. When asked in class the most authentic sources for the examination of early Christian thought, the instructor named the twenty-seven books of the New Testament; the student then asked again if the Epistles of Paul had been included in the list. Aside from scholars who are both trained in research and have made this particular research, the educated people of the United States are not in general capable of deciding whether Kant is fundamentally similar to the Old Testament or not. Nor does their inability arise from any meagre acquaintance with Kant. If they were presented with the pamphlets of Luther and Eck, the *Institutes* of Calvin or the Tridentine symbols, these writings would appear not so much untrue as unintelligible. In matters of religion these people are as advanced as high school pupils who think *hors d'oeuvres* means "out of work." For this reason it is appropriate to show that any similarity between Kant's ethics and the Hebrew-Christian system is accidental and superficial.

There are two main views respecting the intent of the Old Testament which must be considered. One is that of the Jewish people both of Christ's day and, so far as I am informed, of today as well. The second is the Christian view. There is little difficulty in showing that the Pharisees of the first century were not in harmony with the categorical imperative. For them, no one will deny, morality with the means of winning God's favor, of improving oneself until acceptable by God, in short, of achieving salvation. Omniscient Jehovah knows and balances each fault against each good deed and if by observing the multitudinous regulations of the Pharisees, a man's good deeds exceed his evil ones, God accepts him as worthy of heaven. Far from any suggestion that man should do his duty regardless of consequences, purely from the motive of vindicating an abstract formal duty, the Pharisees act deliberately for reward. Whether the reward be crudely or more intellectually conceived does not alter the matter. Any reward as a motive of action is inconsistent with Kant's theory.

On the other hand, articles are sometimes written to show how primitive the Hebrews, or more strictly, the Old Testament is in making fear of punishment so prominent in moral exhortation. They contrast Kant and the Old Testament. Kant, whose position is sounder, higher, more ethical, would never avoid evil through fear of punishment. With perhaps the exception of some obvious exaggerations, this attack on the Old Testament is far more accurate historically than the view under discussion. There is no need of quoting the penalties attached to infractions of the Mosaic code. Occasionally, through the lack of historical perspective, as in the case of eye for eye and tooth for tooth, these laws are understood more as vicious savagery than as an alleviation of the customary eye for an insult and a life for an eye; nevertheless the penalties, both civil and religious, are enunciated very explicitly. Likewise there are numerous promises to those who will honor father and mother, who will pay the tithe, or who have the faith of Abraham. Nor, in this respect at least, can there be drawn any antithesis between the Law and the Prophets. The Prophets protest against violating the law by means of evasive technicalities, they inveigh against a self-complacency in obeying parts of the law and not other more important parts, but they never annul the rewards and punishments, nor preach duty for duty's sake. Amos in particular is singled out as having attained to high ethical standards of social justice. But his very first verses give warning of punishment in a tone indiscernible from the thunder of Mount Sinai. These facts suffice to show that both the writers of the Old Testament and the Pharisees of Christ's day do not agree with any system which removes reward and punishment as motives toward morality.

But, it is maintained, Jesus attacked the Pharisaic interpretation of the Old Testament. He objects to their praying on the street corners to be seen of men, adding pointedly—they have their reward. Does his attack therefore apply to the point in question? Did he add some new spiritual principle abrogating the reward and punishment morality? No one can object to referring to the Sermon on the Mount as an important piece of evidence. Some members of the modern Christian community have placed this sermon, especially its specifically moral injunctions, in a position more systematically basic than sound scholarship would show it deserved. By making Jesus principally if not solely an ethical preacher, they have reversed the relation that obtains in the New Testament between ethics and theology. Yet on an ethical question, the Sermon on the Mount demands appeal. Its opening words are "Blessed are the poor in spirit, for theirs is the kingdom of heaven." Blessing and reward begin the sermon; rains, floods, winds and destruction end it. Can then anyone seriously maintain that Jesus preached a categorical imperative in the Kantian sense? "For if ye love them which love you, what reward have ye? Take heed that ye do not your righteousness before men, otherwise ye have no reward of your Father. Let not thy left hand know what thy right hand doeth, and thy Father shall recompense thee." Not less than three times in the sixth chapter of Matthew is reward mentioned. In other discourses punishment is as clearly stated as reward. "Depart from me ye cursed into everlasting fire prepared for the devil and his angels. And these shall go away into everlasting punishment but the righteous into life eternal."

It is not proper to minimize the differences between the Pharisees and Jesus. They held thoroughly inconsistent views respecting the sense of the Old Testament. They differed radically on the effective power of human morality with God, but neither obscured, it is quite permissible to say both emphasized reward and punishment. If Jesus objected to the Pharisees, it was not because they wanted a reward but because of the miserable reward they wanted. Perhaps then it was the apostles who changed Jesus' teaching in a Kantian direction.

Peter on the day of Pentecost testified and exhorted with many words, "Save yourselves from this untoward generation." At the Beautiful Gate he declared, "Repent so that there may come seasons of refreshing." Paul in II Thessalonians 1 asserted, "It is a righteous thing with God to recompense tribulation to them that trouble you." Indeed, Christianity must be a strange thing to draw upon itself the attacks of those who consider heaven and hell a barbarous philosophy and at the same time to be understood as teaching duty for duty's sake.

This confusion results from assuming that modern communities are Christian. Scholarly opinion is still in process of recuperating from the effects of nineteenth century criticism. Historical investigations are showing that certain popular conceptions of the God of the early Christians derive more from Kant than from the early Christians. The God of the New Testament strikes Ananias and Sapphira dead for fraud. He is indeed a God who so loved the world that He gave His only begotten Son, but He is also a God who reveals His wrath from heaven against all ungodliness of men who suppress the truth in unrighteousness. At present there are two classes of scholars who have seen something of the Christian genius. First are those who definitely and consciously oppose it. Among others there is George Santayana in *Winds of Doctrine*, p. 45, and *Genteel Tradition at Bay*, p.42, but for all of that he judges modernists to be in a state of "fundamental apostasy from Christianity," "worship[ing] nothing and acknowledg[ing] authority in nothing save in their own spirit." He accuses the modernist who thinks he is Christian of "an inexplicable ignorance of history, of theology and of the world," and of substituting a theory which "steals empirical reality away from the last judgment, from hell and from heaven." Santayana may have some queer views on the nature of Christianity, but the views of our modern Christian community are queerer still.

The second class of scholars who grasp the essence of Christianity is that small group which definitely and consciously accepts it. More and more is it being seen that the absolute anti-Christian radicals and the ultra-conservative evangelicals are historically accurate, while the third class, the "modernists," are befogged in a cloud of subjective mysticism. Theirs is a mere modern sentiment; the communities, to which the influence of Kant has finally seeped, insistently argue that the term Christian has noble connotations and therefore, refined and cultured as they know themselves to be, they must naturally be Christian. Therefore, in order to discover what Christian thought is, it is no longer necessary to study the New Testament or make erudite investigations into ancient centuries; one needs only to express one's own fine ideals and Christianity is thereby defined. Mysticism saves one so much trouble, you know.

This attitude, however, comes from Kant through Ritschl. These are the men, who, in separating scientific truth from value judgments, have led to the discarding of historical in favor of psychological investigation in religious matters. These men attempted to enclose intellect and religion in separate pigeonholes so that neither should disturb the other. Yet such a separation is a complete reversal of the Christian world-view. Now, while this modern development may be much nearer the truth and the Bible largely nonsense, as is usually assumed without much research, this would be just one more reason for not confounding Kant's morality with that of the Old Testament.

There still remains the question whether Kant and his followers, now shown to be at variance with Christianity, have provided a philosophically more acceptable ethic. It is doubtful. Any realistic ethic must provide room for one principle among others, which Kant would be sure to deny, *viz.* each individual ought always to seek his own personal good. Such a principle is usually designated egoistic, and egoism usually carries unpleasant connotations. Yet when unnecessary implications are avoided and misunderstandings removed, only some form of egoism can withstand criticism. A universalism, like Bentham's for instance, finds embarrassment in considering the possible incompatibility of an individual's good with the good of the community. Kant, representing a different system, is forced to resort to elements discordant with the rest of his philosophy when he considers the possible conflict between an individual's good and the same individual's duty. He attempts to harmonize duty and good by providing a *Deus ex machina* to reward duty, but he makes hope of that reward immoral.

On the other hand, neither Christ nor the Apostles thought it immoral to seek one's own good. They all made abundant use of hope and fear in their Gospel. If therefore anyone reproach Christianity as being egoistic because of rewards offered, the objector should say whether fear and self-interest are or are not worthy motives for preferring orange juice to carbolic acid for breakfast. The Bible appeals directly to fear and self-interest; it teaches that eternal punishment awaits him who rejects Christ; and it also teaches that although the Christian may have temporary tribulation, he ultimately loses nothing but gains everything in accepting Christ. Now this is what egoism means, and Kant would have none of it. Unfortunately, however,

egoism is sometimes regarded as countenancing sharp practices and shady morality. Yet it requires but little reflection to
conclude that sharp practices do not pay in the long run.
Honesty and all other forms of virtue are the best policy. Egoism
when correctly understood cannot in the least sanction viola-
tion of God's law. In this relation a paragraph may well be lifted
from the good Bishop Butler:

> Conscience and self-love, if we understand our true happiness,
> always lead us the same way. Duty and interest are perfectly
> coincident; for the most part in this world, but entirely and in
> every instance in the future and the whole.

If we agree that egoism does not counsel shady actions,
and that virtue is the best policy precisely because God rewards
it, we are ready to consider the position assigned in this scheme
to the good of others, for egoism in general and Christianity in
particular have been attacked as selfish.

This is not quite the same problem as that usually raised
about the compatibility of the good of all people. An egoist,
Christian or not, will find quite a little difficulty in proving that
the good of one individual harmonizes with the good of all other
individuals. As a matter of fact the Christian might well
conclude that had Judas done what was best for him, it would be
too bad for us. Apparently, then, the good of some people is
incompatible with the good of others. But whether we accept
this conclusion or not, that the good of two people may under
given conditions conflict, it does not follow that egoism teaches
selfishness. And yet Christianity has been assailed as selfish.
That one must save his own soul first, and only afterwards turn
his attention to others, and that his helping others reacts again
to benefit himself, Hastings Rashdall, for example, frankly
considers "nauseous." But is not the attempt to help others

before attending to one's own condition a case of the blind leading the blind? And why is there anything disgusting in regarding one's own development as a motive in Christian activity? We sing about stars in our crown, we speak of souls for our hire. If, then, I may be an instrument of effectual calling in God's hands, and if such instrumentality brings a blessing, I can see no good reason for denying that that blessing may properly be a part of the Christian motive.

Accordingly, if portions of the modern Christian community regard Kant as the last and most logical of the prophets and apostles, a polite acquaintance with the Bible would remedy their misapprehension. And when opponents claim that Christianity is a selfish, soul-saving, egoistic religion, the Christian should not be apologetic in the colloquial sense of the word but in the technical sense, and, with the aid of oranges and carbolic acid, follow the examples of Christ and the apostles in holding out to men the hope of heaven and the fear of hell as legitimate motives for availing themselves of Christ's gracious redemption.

Chapter 6

The Christian Philosophy
Of Education

The first chapter of this book aimed to show the need for a systematic and comprehensive philosophy—not just a narrow attention to immediate details—as a basis for educational theory, or for any other subject in which one may be interested. Unless a person revels in the paradoxes and contradictions of dialectical theology, he will admit that education in its relations to learning subjects (pupils) and to subjects to be learned (arithmetic) should be systematic and not disjointed. Chapter two never got beyond the basic theism of a Christian system. Then came contrasts with secular views and, in sharpening these contrasts, some further development of Christian theism. Now it is time to add to the sketch of Christianity and to indicate its implications for a philosophy of education.

The first and basic point in a Christian philosophy of education, or a Christian philosophy of anything, is Biblical authority. Just as Platonism is defined by what Plato wrote, and not by the decadent skeptical Academy of later years, so the ultimate definition of Christianity is not the decadent confusion of the liberal churches, not the pronouncements of the Pope, not the inconsistent opinions of a so-called Christian community, as is so frequently asserted in ecumenical circles, but what is written in the Bible. A philosophy of education therefore is more or less Christian as it more or less faithfully derives its contents from the Bible.

Of course many people and most educators reject the Bible as the truth of God. They note its errors and list its contradictions. They used to say that Moses could not have written the Pentateuch because writing had not yet been invented in his age. They were wrong. They used to say that Luke coined the word *politarch* (Acts 17:6) to disguise his ignorance of Greek political terms. They were wrong. They used to say that John's Gospel was written in the third century. They were wrong. The study of archaeology has been a continuous process of showing that the liberal critics were wrong. And when they reject its theism and theology, why may they not again be wrong as usual?

The modernists in their efforts to keep up to date, in their efforts to show that the old truths are all false and the new lies are all true, cannot afford the luxury of consistency. They must change with the temper of the times. This has become particularly noticeable in political matters. The liberal churchmen of 1918 wanted to hang the Kaiser for alleged atrocities in Belgium; but later they were thorough-going pacifists, urging college students to take an oath not to defend our country even if attacked. For a time in the thirties the *Christian Century* was favorably inclined toward Hitler, presumably because Hitler aided the ecumenical movement. From 1942-1945 the modernists had to show a little patriotism again; but what position they may take in the next decade cannot be predicted. At the same time they despise straight-laced conservatives who do not change their views. They are like the ancient sophist who complained that Socrates always said the same thing. Socrates replied pointedly that such an objection could not be leveled at the sophist, for he never said the same thing twice.

Aside from history and archaeology, there are other objections to acknowledging the Bible as authoritative. Kant stressed the autonomy of the will in the field of ethics; he ruled out a divine lawgiver and the sanctions of reward and punishment. Similarly humanistic philosophers today insist on the autonomy of man. James Bissett Pratt in *Can We Keep The Faith* (page 71), makes a clear assertion of autonomy:

> As rational beings we refuse to abdicate the throne of our autonomy. . . . And the final explanation of our refusal is to be found in the fact that we *cannot* abdicate. We cannot avoid the necessity of making a final decision; for even if we decide to abdicate, *it is we who decide*. Moreover, once we had abdicated (were that possible), the question would always be present . . . whether we should remain in our humble, do-nothing position, or should reascend the throne; and it would always be *we* who decided that question.

Reason cannot abdicate, he continues, in effect, because it must choose from among different alleged revelations. And to try to persuade a person of the truth of a revelation implies that there is a common basis for persuasion, and that common ground is reason. Anyone who argues or persuades at all recognizes reason as the final court.

This is a clear statement of a common objection, and if the Bible is to be regarded as authoritative, some reply must be made. The first observation is that a decision's being our own does not imply that we are the final authority. If we decide to obey the ninth commandment, Thou shalt not bear false witness, it is we who make the decision, naturally; but we do not make the commandment, nor do we make the commandment authoritative. The situation is similar to a person who wishes to measure a distance. He may look at the distance and guess its length. Likewise he may look at every instance of deceit and guess when he should and when he should not bear false witness. In neither case is it a very accurate method, for it is an appeal to unaided reason. The second method of measuring a distance is not such guesswork. It is the method of using an accurate measuring device, a yardstick or a micrometer. In this case it is still we who make the decision, but we appeal to the yardstick as a norm. And this second method has the advantage of being much more accurate. Strange to say, scientists do not object to abdicating the throne of their autonomy and to being bound by external authority when something is to be measured. Then when moral action is to be measured, or when educational norms are sought, why should they not gladly accept aid from authority?

Since all analogies have their limits, a second observation questions the meaning of abdication. To abdicate a throne, it is invariably essential first to be on the throne. One who has never been king cannot possibly abdicate. Those who argue like Pratt simply assume that man is on the throne, but that is exactly the point at issue. If God is on the throne, if it is he who decrees norms, and if we are not autonomous, then Pratt's remarks are completely irrelevant.

A third observation is all that can be permitted on this phase of the subject. Pratt argued that there are several alleged revelations, that we must choose one if we are to have any, and that to persuade others of the truth of this revelation is to appeal to the common ground of reason.

Before considering the proposition that persuasion is an appeal to common ground and therefore assumes autonomy, it is a matter of curiosity to see how the argument views the various alleged revelations. Sometimes the argument against Biblical authority is baldly based on the fact that there are several claimants to the status of revelation. The Koran, the

Book of Mormon, the Vedas, the Hermetic literature, the Avesta, as well as the Bible, all claim to be revelation. And because they cannot all be true, because some of them are internally inconsistent, it is concluded that none of them came from God. It is as if a judge were faced with twelve claimants to a large estate and, after he had discovered that eleven were not heirs decided that the twelfth also must therefore be a fraud. Further, it is strange that a philosopher should reject authority because the claimants are twelve, and then place his faith in experience when there are five billion centers of experience. We must appeal to experience, so the non-Christian tells us. But to whose experience? The experience of G.E. Moore caused him to conclude that the inadequacy of our causal knowledge is such that we can never have any reason to suppose that a given action is our duty. T.H. Green's experience was considerably different. Perhaps the anti-theistic philosophers rest their case on some unified, common experience. But to obtain unity in five billion experiences is quite a task. Kant wrote as if space, time, and the categories were the same in all human minds and that these *a priori* forms could guarantee a sort of unitary human experience. But when he argues against all types of preformation systems that would unify experience by grounding the possibility of knowledge in the Creator's ordering of human minds, he ruins every hope of discovering unity and of making knowledge possible. Only theism can do this. And if theism alone suffices, a few fraudulent claims cannot serve as reasons for abandoning the search for God's word.

But then we must choose from among the claimants; and if we would persuade others, there must be a common ground; and if there is a common ground, our judgment is autonomous. This objection, charging the Christian position with self-contradiction, is plausible, but it results from a misunderstanding of supernaturalism. To convict supernaturalism of inconsistency, it is necessary to represent it accurately. But the plausibility of the objection results from combining the supernaturalistic view of revelation with a purely naturalistic view of persuasion. The result is easily shown to be inconsistent. If however, persuasion and revelation both are understood supernaturally, no inconsistency will be found. For, be it observed, there is no such thing as a common ground between Christianity and a non-Christian system. From a world naturalistically conceived, one cannot argue to the God of the Christians. From a world-view that denies all revelation, one cannot produce a Biblical revelation. Persuasion therefore is not an appeal to a common ground or non-Christian experience. Persuasion must be regarded as a supernatural work of the Holy Spirit. The faithful Christian presents the Christian faith to an unbeliever, he explains it and shows it in all its fulness. Then the Christian prays that the Holy Spirit will regenerate his auditor, renew his mind, open his eyes, and enable him to see the truth of what was said. This is not an appeal to a common ground; it is an appeal to God.

This much must suffice for an assertion and defense of the position that a Christian philosophy of education must get its contents from the Bible. One of the immediate implications, and one particularly applicable to the subject of education, is the immutable distinction between truth and falsity. Christianity is not relativistic, pragmatic, dialectic, Hegelian, or anything else that views truth as mutable and temporary.

That Christianity allows no flux in truth is clear from the immutability and omniscience of God, who is truth itself. If God is truth and truth changes, a particular revelation from God would be useless a few years or even a few minutes after he gave it. God would have changed; and no one, even if he knew what God wanted us to do yesterday, could guess what God's truth might be today.

Various forms of relativism are rampant in this latter half of the twentieth century. Both among professional philosophers and among the ordinary populace, fixed truth has small honor. Nietzsche and his disciple Freud reduce man to a mass of irrational urges that give rise to "rationalizations" and changing opinions. John Dewey argued that Aristotelian logic is antiquated and that the present non-Aristotelian logic will change in time, too. The existentialists, each for himself, make their own "truth."

The public schools teach that moral codes differ from place to place and change in time. The cannibal morality of the Congo is different from the bull-fight morality of Spanish Catholics. But if "two plus two is four" and "Lincoln was President during the Civil War" are true in America, while "two plus two equals five" and "Lincoln was Pericles' successor in Greece" are true in Africa, while again "two plus two equals six" and "Lincoln was the first astronaut to step on the moon" are true in Asia, then there simply are no subjects such as arithmetic and history. And if moral principles differ from place to place, there is no morality. And if truth changes, there is no truth. And if there is no truth, the truth that truth changes is not true.

Christians therefore must evaluate the subjects in a curriculum in a radically different way from that of secular relativists. Also in a radically different way from that of religious relativists, for Kierkegaard, Brunner, and the dialectical theologians embrace self-contradictions with more gusto than the secularists. Not only does Christianity have a different view of the subjects to be learned, but even more importantly, if that be possible, it views the learning subjects differently. Instead of Nietzsche's amd Freud's view of man as an evolutionary animal governed by irrational urges, the Biblical view is that man was created in the image of God. Of course, men are often irrational, they often rationalize like natural-born hypocrites, yet in spite of sin and its hereditary effects, man is generically the image of God. And this elevates rationality beyond every secular estimation.

The main and most explicit Biblical data on the subject are the following passages: "Let us make man in our image, after our likeness" (Genesis 1:26-27); "In the likeness of God made he him" (Genesis 5:1); "In the image of God made he man" (Genesis 9:6); "Man . . . is the image and glory of God" (I Corinthians 11:7); "Renewed in knowledge after the image of him that created him" (Colossians 3:10); "Men which are made after the similitude of God" (James 3:9).

In addition to these explicit references to the image of God in man, there are many passages, perhaps even some not yet recognized as such, that have some bearing on the subject. Hebrews 2:6-8, with its appeal to Psalm 8, and whatever analogy may be found elsewhere between Christ as the image of God (cf. Heb. 1:3) and the image in man would be such passages, useful in developing the doctrine. Acts 17:26-29 also has implications; for example, with the support of Romans 1:23 and other passages, it gives the reason for the divine prohibition of idolatry. When, too, empirical philosophers deny innate ideas, inherited corruption, *a priori* forms of the mind, and stress environment to the exclusion of heredity, Romans 2:15 and Psalm 51:5 sharpen the contrast. An analytic mind will discover a great number of verses from which pertinent implications can be drawn.

Paradoxically there are some verses that make no reference, either explicitly or implicitly, to the image of God, but which by their complete silence contribute to the doctrine nonetheless. Chiefly this material is in the first chapter of Genesis, concerning the creation of animals. These were not created in the image of God; man was. Hence the characteristic of humanity, as distinct from mere animality, is somehow to be found in the divine image. From all the Scriptural material, the doctrine must be derived.

God created man after his image and likeness. This image cannot be man's body for two reasons. First, God is spirit or mind and has no body. Hence a body would not be an image of him. Second, animals have bodies, yet they are not created in God's image. If anyone should suggest that man walks upright, so that his bodily position could be the image, the reply is not merely that birds also walk on two legs, but that Genesis distinguishes man from animals by the image and not by any physiological structure. In fact, man himself is the image, as I Corinthians 11:7 indicates, in spite of the antithesis between man and woman found there. So also the other references quoted at the beginning. The image therefore is not an extra gadget attached to man after he had been created—not a *donum superadditum*—nor a suit of clothes that he could take off.

Man is not two images. To distinguish between image and likeness is fanciful exegesis. Nor can this single image be divided into parts, like our two arms or two legs. For example, "dominion over the fish of the sea . . . and over the earth" is not an extra ingredient mixed in with others. It is an extra, or, better, it is one of the functions of the single image. The point is important for the effect of sin on the image. One must not suppose that sin amputated one part and left a remnant untouched. Similarly, the Bible should not be interpreted as making morality and intelligence the two parts of the image; and an ontological division between the natural and permanent image versus the moral and accidental image, or any other supposedly scholarly but actually empty distinction, is confusion. Doubtless the image, *i.e.*, the man, performs different functions, of which dominion over the birds of heaven and over every creeping thing is one. These functions, however, add up to more than two.

The reason theologians have asserted a duality of the image, rather than the unity of the image and the plurality of its activities, the reason also that Paul indicates some sort of duality by mentioning righteousness in Ephesians 4:24 and knowledge in Colossians 3:10 is the occurrence of sin. Since Adam remained Adam after the fall, it looks as if some "part" of the image survived; but since also Adam lost his original innocence and Cain committed murder, was not some "part" of the image lost? Man did not lose dominion over the animals; he also retained some other items; but in comparison with his changed relation to God, animals are of minor importance and the other items require little discussion. Sin, on the other hand, and its effects are of such great importance and require such frequent mention that a duality in the image, one half of which is lost, appears as a natural interpretation. Such an ontological separation of two parts has seemed to many theologians the best method of maintaining both of two truths: that man after the fall is still man, and that sin is far from trivial or superficial.

At this point in the exposition it is necessary to spell out the second truth by an appeal to Scripture. Concerning the extent and intensity of sin, Romans 3:10-18 collects a series of Old Testament statements, chiefly from the Psalms. "There is none righteous, no not one. . . . there is none that seeketh after God. . . . there is none that doeth good. . . . there is no fear of God before their eyes." Really now! Isn't there anyone who does something good? "No, one one." Surely not Stalin; surely not the Pharisees; but also not even the obscure common people who are neither so brutal as the one nor so hypocritical as the others. The Old Testament passages include everybody, and Romans 8:7 indicates the state of human nature in general by saying, "the carnal mind is enmity against God: for it is not subject to the law of God, neither indeed can be." Men are "dead in sin" as the New Testment says several times. Jeremiah 17:9 says, "The heart is deceitful above all things and desperately wicked." One might even allow that Sigmund Freud had a more nearly correct estimate of human evil, rationalization, and hypocrisy than the semi-pelagian Romanists have; though of course he did not view this evil as an offense against God.

Before the flood "God saw that . . . every imagination of the thoughts of his [man's] heart was only evil continually." After the flood he said, "I will not again curse the ground any more for man's sake, for the imagination of man's heart is evil from his youth." Possibly this means that there is no use to send a second flood because floods cannot cure the human race; but if this is not the correct explanation of the clause, it nonetheless asserts that man's heart is evil from his youth. In fact, "I was shapen in iniquity and in sin did my mother conceive me."

Hence it is impossible for the natural or unregenerate man to please God. He is incapable of doing any spiritual good. Even the ploughing of the wicked is sin; not that turning over the soil is sin, but that the morality of an act cannot be judged apart from its motivation, and the motivation of the wicked is always wicked. Man then is totally depraved. Totally, not in the sense that every man commits every sin, nor even that every man, or any man, is as wicked as possible, but in the sense that all his acts are evil and that no "part," function, act, or state escapes the corruption of sin. Yet if this is so, can man still be the image of God?

Yes, the image is still there. Paradoxical though it may seem, man could not be the sinner he is, if he were not still God's image. Sinning presupposes rationality and voluntary decision. Animals cannot sin. Sin therefore requires God's image because man is responsible for his sins. If there were no responsibility, there could be nothing properly called sin. Sin is an offense against God, and God calls us to account. If we were not answerable to God, repentance would be useless and even nonsense. Reprobation and hell would also be impossible.

But if we say all this, have we not tied ourselves in theological knots? If we acknowledge that we are dead in sin, must we not affirm either that the image has been lost altogether (and then we would no longer be able to sin), or that the image has parts and that most of its parts, or at least the most important parts have been lost (thus destroying the unity of the person), or finally should we retract the doctrine of total depravity and minimize sin?

The solution of this paradox is very easy and very clear. We note for one thing that Christ is the image of God (Hebrews 1:3), and that he is the Logos and Wisdom of God. We note too that Adam was given dominion over nature. These two points, seemingly unrelated, suggest that the image of God is Logic or rationality. Adam was superior to the animals because he was a rational and not merely a sensory creation. The image of God therefore is reason.

The image must be reason because God is truth, and fellowship with him—a most important purpose in creation—requires thinking and understanding. Without reason man would doubtless glorify God as do the stars, stones, and animals, but he could not enjoy him forever. Even if in God's providence animals survive death and adorn the future world, they cannot have what the scripture calls eternal life because eternal life is to know the only true God, and knowledge is an exercise of the mind or reason. Without reason there can be no morality or righteousness: These too require thought. Lacking these, animals are neither righteous nor sinful.

The identification of the image as reason explains or is

supported by a puzzling remark in John 1:9, "It was the true light that lighteth every man that cometh into the world." How can Christ, in whom is the life that is the light of men, be the light of every man, when the Scriptures teach that some men are lost in eternal darkness? This puzzle arises from interpreting light in exclusively redemptive terms. If one thinks also in terms of creation, the Logos or Rationality of God, who just above was said to have created all things without a single exception, can be seen as having created man with the light of logic as his distinctive human characteristic.

For such reasons as these, the fall and its effects, which have so puzzled some theologians as they studied the doctrine of the image, are most easily understood by identifying the image with man's mind.

Since moral judgments are a species of judgment, subsumed under general intellectual activity, one result of the fall is the occurrence of incorrect evaluations by means of erroneous thinking. Adam thought, incorrectly, that it would be better to join Eve in her sin than to obey God and be separated from her. So he ate the forbidden fruit. The external act followed upon the thought. "Out of the heart proceed evil thoughts." Note that in the Bible the term *heart* usually designates the intellect, and only once in ten times the emotions: It is the heart that thinks. Sin thus interferes with our thinking. It does not, however, prevent us from thinking. Sin does not eradicate or annihilate the image. It causes a malfunction, but man still remains man.

The Bible stresses the malfunctioning of the mind in obviously moral affairs because of their importance. But sin extends its depraving influence into affairs not usually regarded as matters of morality. Arithmetic, for example. One need not suppose that Adam and Eve understood calculus; but they surely counted to ten. Whatever arithmetic they did, they did correctly. But sin causes a failure in thinking, with the result that we now make mistakes in simple addition. Such mistakes are pedantically called the "noetic" effects of sin. But moral errors are equally noetic. When men became vain in their imaginations and their foolish hearts were darkened; when they professed to be wise, but became fools; when God gave them over to a reprobate mind—their sin was first of all a noetic, intellectual, mental malfunction.

Regeneration and the process of sanctification reverse the sinful direction of the malfunctioning: The person is renewed in knowledge after the image of him that created him. First the more obvious, the grosser sins are suppressed because the new man begins to think and evaluate in conformity with God's precepts. Second and third, the new man advances to restrain the more subtle, the more secret, the more pervasive sins that have made his heart deceitful above measure. Errors in arithmetic may seem trivial in comparison, but these, too, are effects of sin, and salvation will improve a man's thinking in all matters.

The identification of the image as reason or intellect thus preserves the unity of man's person and saves theologians from splitting the image into schizophrenic parts. It also accords with all that the Scripture says about sin and salvation.

Secular opposition to the image of God in man can be based only on a general non-theistic philosophy. Evolution views man as a natural development from the neutron and proton, through atoms, to plants, to the lower animals, until perhaps a number of human beings emerged in Africa, Asia, and the East Indies. Evolution can hardly assert the unity of the human race, for several individuals of sub-human species may have more or less simultaneously produced the same variation.

This non-theistic, naturalistic view is difficult to accept

because it implies that the mind too, as well as the body, is an evolutionary product rather than a divine image. Instead of using eternal principles of logic, the mind operates with the practical results of biological adaptation. Concepts and propositions neither reach the truth nor even aim at it. Our equipment has evolved through a struggle to survive. Reason is simply the human method of handling things. It is a simplifying and therefore falsifying device. There is no evidence that our categories correspond to reality. Even if they did, a most unlikely accident, no one could know it; for to know that the laws of logic are adequate to the existent real, it is requisite to observe the real prior to using the laws. But if this ever happened with sub-human organisms, it never happens with the present species man. If now the intellect is naturally produced, different types of intellect could equally well be produced by slightly different evolutionary processes. Maybe such minds have been produced, but are now extinct like the dinosaurs and dodos. This means, however, that the concepts or intuitions of space and time, the law of contradiction, the rules of inference are not fixed and universal criteria of truth, but that other races thought in other terms. Perhaps future races will also think in different terms. John Dewey insisted that logic has already changed and will continue to change. If now this be the case, our traditional logic is but a passing evolutionary moment, our theories, dependent on this logic, are temporary reactions, parochial social habits, and Freudian rationalizations; and therefore the evolutionary theory, produced by these biological urges, cannot be true.

The difference between naturalism and theism—between the latest scientific opinions on evolution and creation; between the Freudian animal and the image of God; between belief in God and atheism—is based on their two different epistemologies. Naturalism professes to learn by observation and analysis of experience; the theistic view depends on Biblical revelation. No amount of observation and analysis can prove the theistic position. Of course, no amount of observation and analysis can prove evolution or any other theory. The secular philosophies all result in total skepticism. In contrast, theism bases its knowledge on divinely revealed propositions. They may not give us all truth; they may even give us very little truth; but there is no truth at all otherwise. So much for the secular alternative.

Therefore the Christian evaluation of subjects in the curriculum and of pupils or students in school is rational and intellectualistic, in opposition to the emotionalism and anti-intellectualism of the present age. For those who know a little French it is worthwhile quoting Pascal's sublime words.

Car enfin qu'est-ce que l'homme dans la nature? Un néant à l'égard de l'infini, un tout à l'égard du néant, un milieu entre rien et tout. Il est infiniment éloigné des deux extrêmes, et son être n'est pas moins distant du néant d'où il est tiré que de l'infini où il est englouti. . . . L'homme n'est qu'un roseau, le plus faible de la nature, mais c'est un roseau pensant. Il ne faut pas que l'univers entier s'arme pour l'écraser. Une vapeur, une goutte d'eau suffit pour le tuer. Mais quand l'univers l'écraserait, l'homme serait encore plus noble que ce qui le tue, parce qu'il sait qu'il meurt et l'avantage que l'univers a sur lui; l'univers n'en sait rien. Ainsi toute notre dignité consiste dans la pensée.*

---

*For, in fact, what is man in nature? A nothing in comparison with the infinite, an all in comparison with the nothing, a mean between nothing and everything. He is infinitely removed from two extremes, and his being is no less distant from the nothing from which he is drawn than from the infinite where he is engulfed. . . . Man is but a reed, the most feeble thing in nature; but he is a thinking reed. It is not necessary that the universe arm itself to crush him. A vapor, a drop of water suffices to kill him. But if the universe were to crush him, man would still be more noble than that which killed him, because he knows that he dies and the advantage that the universe has over him; the universe knows nothing of this. Thus all our dignity consists in thought.—*Editor*

This majestic passage from Pascal places man's dignity in thought; and though the quotation does not say so explicitly, presumably the purpose of thinking is the knowledge of truth. Chess is undoubtedly the best game ever invented, but it is not a proper course in the curriculum because, although it trains the mind and requires intense concentration, it is not a thinking of truth. The object of education is truth; the transmission of truth to the younger pupils and the discovery of new truth by more advanced students. The aim of education, at least the aim of the purest and best education, is intellectual understanding. Home economics and secretarial science (science! no less) have no place in liberal arts because they are matters of vocational training and not rational explanation.

No doubt there must be vocational training for the retarded. Some people cannot think very much. More than others more gifted they suffer the effects of Adam's sin to a greater degree. This is not to say that they are personally disgraced by vocational training. Christianity views humble labor as entirely honorable. Only, vocational training should not be called education.

The curriculum and the administration of Christian education must be controlled by the Christian view of man. Like the plant, man is a living being, he needs food, he reproduces; but the nature or peculiarity of man is not found in so wide a genus. Like the animals he has sensations and visual images; but if this were all, he would be merely another animal. Education supposedly deals with man as man; so-called physical education deals with man as a brute. What man is and what education is are questions to be answered by appraising the different levels of human activity. Keen sensation does not mark an educated man, for savages often have keener sensation than the well-educated. Carpentry and plumbing are distinctly human activities beyond all animal possibility, and factually beyond the savage; and yet these two useful and honorable trades are not an education. Music and art rank higher than carpentry and plumbing; colloquially we speak of a musical education, but strictly music and art require training. All these are different levels of activity—all honorable but not all equal. Some men are born capable of one but not of another. The Lord did not berate the man to whom he gave one talent for not being able to earn five; he condemned him for not using the one he had. However there is no denying the fact that it is better to have five. God does not require the unskilled laborer to write the critique of all future metaphysics nor to finish Schubert's symphony; but I.Q. 150 contains greater possibilities than I.Q. 85.

All phases of life should glorify God, and if a man is a carpenter or a plumber, he should and can glorify God by his trade as well as a student or professor. To serve God acceptably, one does not need to be a monk, neither does he need to be a scholar. God has given some men five talents, some two, and some one. He has given scholastic aptitude to some and to others mechanical ability. What is required is that each should use faithfully what he has received.

In view of this it cannot be said that education is in all respects democratic. In politics, representative democratic government, amenable to the will of the people, is decidedly preferable to irresponsible totalitarianism and arrogant bureaucracy. All men are created equal—in the sense that political justice should be impartially administered. But economic and mental equality never have existed and never will. The economic handicaps can be equalized to a degree by private aid through scholarships. But there is no cure for mental inequalities. Education, like art, can never be democratic; both are inherently aristocratic. Some students simply cannot learn. Try as they may, they cannot grasp the significance of the material. And instead of benefiting by a college education, their spirit and self-respect may be ruined. As plumbers they could serve a useful purpose, and if they recognize that God is glorified in honest plumbing, they can walk among men with Christian dignity.

A word about art too. Surely a great artist is superior to a great coal miner. Rembrandt's *Night Watch* is indescribably impressive. Rembrandt *knew how* to paint. But I am not aware that he *knew* art. Beethoven *knew how* to write music; but I doubt that he understood music. Artistic ability is one thing—a precious gift from God. The intellectual understanding of art, of its function in society, of its relation to religion and morality, is another thing—a still more precious gift from God. The latter is a subject of education. The former is skill.

Christianity, however, is intellectualistic. God is truth, and truth is immutable. The humanists, of course, oppose any theistic conception of truth. Immersed in the flux of pragmatism, guided by Nietzsche, James, and Dewey, they hold that truth changes, moral values change, and the only fixed truth is that there is no fixed truth. What works is "true." Skill and success make "truth." Because there is no final truth in humanism, the humanist cannot consistently give adequate recognition to the intellect. If he praises intellectual endowments, he means only the vocational skill to get what you want.

Yet secular humanism is not the only, nor even the most vociferous opponent of intellectualism. If Nietzsche, James, and Dewey have their disciples, including the existentialists, Kierkegaard, with Schleiermacher's emphasis on emotion, is an even worse enemy of truth. So it happens that large numbers of religious people despise the intellect and exalt the emotions. Brunner says that God speaks falsehoods, that man should believe contradictions, and that God and the intellect are mutually exclusive.

Religious activity of necessity assumes many forms. Noah was discharging a religious duty in building the ark; Moses was religiously engaged when receiving the Ten Commandments; and David served God both by killing Goliath and by writing the Psalms. Surveying these dissimilar activities, one naturally asks, Is any one of them more intrinsically religious than another? Does one of them above the others offer a closer approach to God? Since Christ commended Mary rather than Martha, it is clear that some activities are higher than others; but how may this distinction be explained in technical terms?

To answer this question some grouping of activities is necessary. In the past the various mental functions or conscious states have been classified according to different schemes. For example, Augustine spoke of memory, intellect, and will; a later Augustinian, Bonaventura, listed the faculties of the soul as vegetative, sensitive, and rational—the latter uniting both intellect and will. At the present time a more common division is emotion, volition, and intellect. Without in the least denying value to such schemes of dividing conscious activity, it is necessary, in order to avoid misunderstanding, explicitly to reject the so-called faculty psychology. A man is not a compound of three things, an intellect, a will, and an emotion. Each man is a single personality. Long ago Plato showed the sophistic, skeptical results of making man a wooden horse of Troy and destroying his unitary personality. Emotion, will, and intellect are not three things, each independent of the other, mysteriously and accidentally inhabiting one body. These three are simply three activities of a single consciousness that sometimes thinks, sometimes feels, and sometimes wills. For this reason one must recognize that religion in general and Christianity in particular makes its appeal to the whole man. Strictly speaking, there is no such thing as a discrete part of man; other than conceptually it is often difficult to separate these functions. When a normal human being experiences an emotion, he may easily will an action; when he exercises his volition, he ought to have some knowledge of the situation; though to be sure he may employ his intellect and his will without emotion. Since these three, then, are actions of one person, the unity of personality must be regarded as basic throughout the whole discussion—it is the individual person who acts in several ways. Therefore, although expression is facilitated by using will, emotion, and intellect as abstract terms, and while the term "faculty" is still a good English word, the exact question proposed may more clearly be stated as follows: Granting that religion does not appeal to a thing called emotion or intellect but to a real human being, by which of these three actions does a man best respond, most fully grasp God, most perfectly worship and most closely commune with Him?

The meaning of the term *emotion*, it must be recognized at the outset, is exceptionally vague. Philosophic or scientific accuracy is not to be expected in a dictionary, for a dictionary must record colloquial usage; but with respect to the word *emotion*, colloquial usage is not only the starting point for scientific definition—as is true always—it also fixes the only generally accepted meaning. Contemporary psychologists usually avoid giving a scientific definition of emotion or any accurate account of it;* instead they merely enumerate states of

---

* Tiffin, Knight, and Josey, *The Psychology of Normal People* (D. C. Heath and Co., 1940), are to be complimented on trying to frame a definition. They write, p. 187, "emotion [is] an experience involving a disturbed condition of the organism brought about by the prospect of some 'values' being gained or lost, and involving also an impulse to act." To comment: that emotion is a disturbance may be granted. That it is necessarily dependent on the prospect of gaining or losing values may be doubted. That it necessarily involves an impulse to act may be denied, for depression is an aversion to action. Other psychologists are wiser in admitting that they have no clear idea of what an emotion is. Compare the several works of Robert Plutchik, Wenger, Jones and Jones, and Ernest R. Hilgard.

consciousness which they are willing to call emotional. And this a dictionary can do perhaps as well as a psychologist. More systematically-minded thinkers, both ancient and modern, not confined to any one school but varying as do Plato, the Stoics, and Leibniz, attempt to define emotion as confused thinking, or as a physiological hindrance to rational activity. Writers on emotion who have not thought out the whole problem so deeply as Plato and Leibniz should not object to such a definition; but admittedly it is not a widely accepted view. Therefore one is almost forced to the dictionary.

Webster's New International Unabridged, 1935, reads as follows:

1. Obsolete. (a) Migration; transference. (b) an agitation, disturbance, or tumultuous movement, whether physical or social. 2. Any such departure from the usual calm state of the organism as includes strong feeling, an impulse to overt action, and internal changes in respiration, circulation, glandular action, etc.; any one of the states designated as fear, anger, disgust, grief, joy, surprise, yearning, etc. 3. Agitation of the feeling or sensibilities.

Accordingly, unless a student of this subject is prepared to follow some well integrated system like that of Leibniz in which the place of emotion is accurately located with respect to all other knowledge, the dictionary has to be accepted. Now the most noticeable quality common both to the obsolete meaning and to its modern derivative is that of agitation, a departure from a state of calm, accompanied by physical disturbances. Disturbances and agitation, therefore, are the chief criteria of an emotion.

In theology, when one claims that emotion is the basic religious activity, it is not usually meant to imply that man comes into contact with God by means of each or all in the list of emotions, but by one of them. In some less profound and more popular religious circles the one chosen is the emotion of love, though it is significant that the dictionary did not include love among its examples of emotion, and it is particularly to the point that for centuries the theologians have classified love not as an emotion, but as a volition. Apart from popular religion, the more philosophical advocates of emotionalism do not stress love but choose a peculiar religious emotion, the feeling of piety or dependence. The reasons for such a choice, at least the reasons for the adoption of emotionalism, are most clearly seen in the philosophical development starting from Kant.

Briefly, Kant had taught that behind the sense perceptions present to the mind there were *things-in-themselves* which caused the sensations. But just as we see railroad tracks apparently converging in the distance, so all our perceptions are received under a certain perspective. Common sense says that the tracks are really straight but they appear to converge. Kant says that the things of perception appear to be spatial and temporal, but strictly *things-in-themselves* are not really in space and time at all. Furthermore, the scientist by his laws describes nature as it appears to him. There are causes and effects, substances and accidents, action and reaction. But nature has these only in perspective; *nature-in-itself* must not be conceived as subject to such categories, which after all are only human forms of perspective. To proceed rapidly, the cosmological argument for the existence of God is therefore invalid, not because of any minor fallacy but because it has used the concept of causality beyond the range of sensible experience. God cannot be conceived as a cause or a substance for these categories apply only within sensible experience. Hence thinking, which receives its real content only through sensation, can never grasp God.

With Kant's position thus briefly summarized, the post-

Kantian development is not hard to anticipate. Jacobi epito-
mized the situation in his famous phrase to the effect that
without the *thing-in-itself* one cannot get into Kant's system, but
with it one cannot stay in. *Things-in-themselves* had originally
been posited as causes of sensation, and then causality had been
denied application beyond sensations. Since the categories and
the forms of space and time constitute Kant's main contribution
to philosophy, there is no reason for retaining the notion of
things-in-themselves. God, too, must keep company with the
things-in-themselves in their banishment from thought.

But, continues Jacobi, God is banished only from thought;
and after all thought is neither the whole nor the most important
part of man. Kant's theory which limits causation to phenomena and identifies every cause with a preceding temporal event
shows that thought is imprisoned in the infinite series of
conditioned events and is forever incapable of grasping true,
unconditioned actuality. Since the knowable is the phenomenal,
a God who could be known would not be God at all. He would
be merely an event in time. Thus the attempt to make religion
rational is deadly to religion. He who would bring into his
intellect the light of his heart extinguishes the light. Jacobi's
salvation, therefore, must lie in the fact that man has a "heart,"
that man has feeling and emotion as opposed to thought; and
while man cannot know God, he may by faith *feel* Him. Jacobi,
in championing a faith which has no evidence, gives free rein to
a romanticism which Hegel justly characterizes as rhapsodic.

Unfortunately, the interesting philosophic development
must give way for the specific application of these views to
theology. In this field Schleiermacher, 1768-1834, was easily
the outstanding exponent of the theology of feeling that grew
out of post-Kantian philosophy, and his influence extends even
beyond the nineteenth century. Although it may seem ungener-
ous to those who revere his name, yet from the restricted scope

of this discussion Schleiermacher can hardly be called an original philosopher. As a theologian he is important for shaping actual religious movements after the pattern already indicated. Hence, he repeats, God cannot be an object of intellect, nor of the will. Rather it is in the feeling of piety, not to be identified either with a form of knowledge or with a form of right action that man attains communion with God. Romanticism in philosophy, therefore, corresponds to mysticism or pietism in religious life. The forms in which this anti-intellectualistic philosophy has manifested itself have been various since the time of Schleiermacher, but one of the most conspicuous examples in the United States is the estheticism of which Dr. Harry Emerson Fosdick was an exponent.

The history of pietism and emotionalism reveals the chief considerations militating against this type of theology. In the first place it is a matter of experience that man has many emotions—a list was given above. Since, now, they are all equally parts of man's nature, why should one emotion, the feeling of piety, be singled out as able to bring us into communion with God rather than some other emotion or all of them together? Certainly if Schleiermacher feels that the feeling of piety is the most valuable for him, why cannot some one else feel that the feeling of pleasure feels best to him—or the feeling of anger? If an individual's emotions are the most important activities of life, as they must be if by them alone one reaches God, then no person has any basis to complain against any emotion which another person cares to make supreme. Emotion is supreme and is therefore its own and only judge. The intellect is enjoined from interfering. The emotionalist must therefore assert that there is no *reason* for selecting one emotion above another. The emotion which emotes most emotionally is on its own authority best and most valuable.

If at present we do not feel like tracing out these Dionysian consequences and feel like discussing Schleiermacher only, there is another implication of emotionalism that needs to be made explicit. Since it is the feeling of piety that brings man into contact with God, it follows by a simple logical conversion that God is to be defined as the object which gives rise to the feeling of piety. On this basis some contemporary thinkers have concluded that polytheism is the only possible religion. Many objects by their aesthetic appeal produce feelings of awe, reverence, or piety, and hence these objects are by definition gods. Emotionalism, therefore, involves polytheism.

But the chief objection to the theology of feeling is its assertion that God is unknowable. It should be perfectly clear that no man knows enough to assert the existence of an object of which he knows nothing. And not only so, but the assertion that an object exists of which nothing can be known reduces to skepticism. The right of each man to assert the kind of unknowable he chooses throws all objectivity into confusion; and the implicit contradiction contained in asserting that something cannot be known cuts the foundation out from under any and all knowledge.

Because skepticism is the logical outcome of the theology of feeling, its advocates take refuge in deep obscurity. James Orr, in the first chapter of *The Christian View of God and the World*, neatly characterizes the verbiage of those who object to the clarity of intellectualism and defend the theology of feeling:

> Here I cannot forbear the remark, that it is a strange idea of many who urge this objection [and defend emotionalism] in the interests of what they conceive to be a more spiritual form of Christianity, that "spirituality" in a religion is somehow synonymous with vagueness and indefiniteness; that the more perfectly they can vaporize or volatilize Christianity into a nebulous haze, in which nothing can be perceived distinctly, the nearer they

bring it to the ideal of a spiritual religion.*

If the argument so far developed is sufficient to dispose of emotion as the chief religious activity, one also finds in the history of philosophy and theology proponents of the will as the religious faculty par excellence. It is not through emotion, they hold, nor is it through knowledge, but rather it is in the act of volition or love that man grasps God. While these thinkers have rejected emotionalism, they are at one with it in its anti-intellectualism. For this reason their attack on the intellect is at least as prominent as their defense of the will. No criticism, no just analysis of the complete thought of any one man can here be attempted; some borrowings of typical phraseology must suffice to represent the basic position.

The intellect, they write, deforms and mutilates reality. Real things exist in their rich individuality, but the intellect abstracts from and divides this individuality, with the result that unreal abstractions take the place of the original object. Thus artificial unities become substitutes for immediately given experience. Petrified categories obscure the ever changing life of history; and even worse, God is brought into subjection to the limitations of human reason, and the religious person is fettered by dogmas and creeds. Pulsating faith in a person, says one author as he waxes eloquent, is laid to rest in a tomb over which is set the stony monument of Gnosticism, and a Gnosticism devoid even of the picturesque fancies that served to make early Gnosticism at least interesting.

Religion, another writer protests, seeks union with God, but it is a union of will. Thought and the object of thought are never the same, and hence thought can never truly grasp any object. Reality, he repeats, is something other and deeper than

_____

*Pages 21-22.

thought. Personalism, the philosophy he acknowledges as his own, is more voluntaristic than rationalistic. It lays more stress on the will than on the intellect and inclines to the view that life is deeper than logic. Mere reason, he asserts, cannot bridge the gulf between thought and reality.

One of the gentleman's basic arguments makes voluntarism the bulwark against skepticism. Rationality or intellect of itself apparently cannot justify itself. We must, he therefore continues, as rational beings assume the validity of reason, but this assumption is itself a matter of faith. To accept reason, quite as much as to reject it, is at the bottom an act of volition. Contrary to the standard arguments showing the contradiction inherent in skepticism, this thinker holds that skepticism is not theoretically impossible, and hence the only escape is not theoretical or speculative, but volitional.

This capitulation to skepticism becomes clearer as we trace the developments. For if reality is deeper than thought, it follows that thought is not real. Or, more clearly expressed, if thought and the object of thought are never the same, as he says, then we never know the object. At best we have only a representation of the object, but a representation that cannot be known to represent it. The same author continues to say that reality is deed as well as idea, but how it is constituted we do not know. There is about reality, he admits, a mystery that the human mind can never penetrate. The embarrassment increases when he says that to think is to create, but how creation is possible we do not know. The immaterial soul combines unity and plurality; this is a fact we assert, he writes, but which we do not understand.*

Here again it is clear that anti-intellectualism has affirmed the existence of an unknowable, and in spite of all verbal

---

*A.C. Knudson, *The Philosophy of Personalism*, pp. 33, 65, 67, 143, 147, 209, 225, and 244.

denials the result is skepticism. In the light of the devastating admissions that produce this conclusion, it is hardly necessary to proceed further. The original thesis comes under the suspicion of being not only false, but meaningless. Religion seeks union with God, it was said, a union of will. Now, what can such a union be? Would it be some mystical confusion in which the human being loses his individuality? Perhaps this is not what the voluntarists mean. One might hope that by a union of wills they mean human obedience to divine commands. This makes very good sense; but it does not seem to fit in with voluntarism. Obedience to divine commands depends on a revelation that is intellectually grasped; it requires a knowledge of God; and hence alleged obedience must be judged by the norms of truth; but this makes truth and intellect superior to will. Furthermore, one may ask whether obedience, however reasonable and necessary it may be, is the equivalent of communion with God. Certainly, if an illustration be of any value, obedience is not the most intimate form of human friendship.

Since so much of the voluntaristic argument was an attack against intellectualism, the criticism of the former from this point on can only with difficulty be distinguished from the advocacy of the latter. There can therefore be no abrupt division between these two parts of the subject as there was between emotionalism and voluntarism. For the basic consideration in the views of voluntarist and intellectualist alike is the nature of the intellect as seen by each of the two. The voluntaristic position is that intellectual activity consists in abstraction, and that abstraction mutilates reality by substituting artificial unities for immediately given experience. Now, presumably the advocates of voluntarism would include sense perception under the heading of immediately given experience. And yet the sense of sight abstracts color and shape alone from the rich individuality of a plum pudding and fails to grasp the smell and the taste.

Smell and taste similarly fail to grasp the color. It follows then that every sensation, the immediate experience in which the voluntarist glories, mutilates reality. But who at Christmas dinner, for that reason, cares to will rather than to taste a plum pudding?

In the second place the voluntarists seem to assume without sufficient basis that abstraction is the sole example of intellection. In the history of philosophy this point has received considerable attention, and here it can be noted only that a respectable school for centuries has held that intellection is the grasping of an object as a whole. Concepts, they teach, are built up out of discrete parts; but ideas, far from being progressive reconstitutions of an object by the putting together of fragments drawn from experience, are global or integral representations arising within us. Unless the voluntarist can effectively dispose of this view, his objections to intellectualism fall to the ground. And a reading of personalistic authors does not give evidence that this view has been adequately studied.

The intellect, therefore, on the part of its defenders, instead of mutilating reality, is that faculty, or better, that mode of action by which man comes into possession of or contact with reality; while volition is considered as the act of striving to gain possession. The energy used in going to an art museum forms a rough analogy to the will, whereas the enjoyment of contemplating the picture may represent intellection. Before the enjoyment or possession of the object, whether it be picture or God, there is desire, love, or volition; afterward there is enjoyment, possession, contemplation. The will is directed toward an end or aim that is future; possession present. Clearly the desire of an end is not the attainment of that end. Now the Scriptures make certain definite characterizations of the end of our endeavor. The Apostle John records the words of Christ in his High Priestly prayer: "This is life eternal, that they should know thee, the only true God." See also I John 5:20. There is also the remarkable statement of I Corinthians 13:12. Our knowledge, it says in effect, is now obscure and hesitant; when we shall be glorified, we shall see God face to face. And as we contemplate him, he will so quicken our intellectual activity that we shall know Him as he knew us. It may be possible to read too much into this verse; obviously it does not mean that we shall become God; but no one can deny that it raises human knowledge to an astounding height. However, the clearest and perhaps the most beautiful of all the Scriptural expressions that express these thoughts is found in the ancient writing of Job. On the truth of Job's words depends the whole of this argument, and on the truth of Job's words depends the Christian's hope of glory: "For I know that my Redeemer liveth, and that he shall stand at the latter day upon the earth; and though after my skin worms destroy this body, yet in my flesh shall I see God; whom I shall see for myself, and my eyes shall behold and not another."

This end is something we long for now; it is something we desire. When we come to enjoy this final state, we shall still desire it to continue, we shall still love to see God face to face. But the act of desiring and the act of seeing are two conceptually distinct acts; the former is the means and the latter, the beatific vision is the end. Therefore volition cannot be the ultimate end itself. Voluntarism or dynamism, in refusing to accept such a consideration, is involved in the absurdity of making desire itself the end of desiring. Nothing is permanent except change. Life must therefore be deeper than logic because life and reality are too chaotic and unstable for logic to represent. In intellectualism, on the other hand, life is no deeper than logic, but this implies not that life is shallow but rather that logic is deep. Or to rephrase the distinction: Voluntarism conceived reality as fundamentally irrational, as ultimately an unknowable mystery before which man must remain a skeptic; whereas intellectualism with a love of truth resolutely affirms that reality is essentially rational, logical, and knowable.

Some voluntarists have seen more clearly than others that their irrationalism provides no room for truth. This is at least indirectly admitted by their stress on value judgments. It was Ritschl who last century popularized this conception, and his vogue has become widespread. But in antiquity the Sophists also, when by reason of their inability to cope with the philosophic situation they despaired of attaining truth, taught that each man for himself could by an act of will set up an object of value. The effective means of attaining these subjectively erected values was the nearest equivalent of truth they admitted in their system. And these means in the course of a century degenerated noticeably from the standpoint of common morality. Today also, the duplicity of modernists in using for their religious work as large a proportion as possible of the traditional phrases of historic Christianity, simply because these phrases with their sacred connotations are valuable in gaining the none too intelligent adherence of unsuspecting common folk to their ecclesiastical and political programs is nothing but a surface reflection of the technical viciousness of the basic philosophy. There are such things as values, of course; but to be truly valuable, a value must first be true. Truth is primary, value secondary. And the supreme value in the life of man is to be sought in the activity of the intellect as it grasps truth. It is no mere accident of history that the term *sophist* became one of disrepute. And it will not be surprising if the term *modernist* also becomes identified with intellectual dishonesty, for however pious and humble skepticism may at first appear, the unknowable will always prove unspeakable.

Hence much of the defense of intellectualism is provided by the old arguments against an unknowable object and ultimate mysteries. Instead of transforming the Kantian thing-in-itself into an object of feeling or will, it will be necessary to reject the position that gave rise to such a development and to formulate an epistemology in which reality can be known. Hegel attempted just this; and while much of his logic is worthless, the argument of the *Phenomenology* that the unknowable is a self-contradictory concept is so final as to cause astonishment at the resurrection of this unmanageable idea.

In the past the systems that emphasized rationality have always assumed a world of static perfection. At least the enemies of the intellect call it static; its friends think of it as stability. Plato, in the *Sophist*, protested against the criticism that his ideal world was one of petrified categories or unreal abstractions, and urged that it be viewed as a living mind. But at any rate, even Plato would have denied change in the truth the divine mind knows. Change in perfection could only be change toward the worse. The connection, therefore, between intellectualism and stability is too stable now to be overthrown. An intellectualist today must accept the onus that history has placed upon him, but he accepts it gladly. In voluntarism immutable truth is replaced by a radical dynamism. One seeks for God and ultimately finds only a Heraclitean flux. Nor does the lesson of antiquity need to be pointed out again that flux results in skepticism. The exponents of voluntarism embrace dynamism because they are enamoured of progress; to them stability is sterility, but they fail to see the aimlessness of an evolution that has no goal. "What is the ape to man? A jest or a bitter shame. And just that shall man be to the Superman, a jest or a bitter shame." But after the Superman, what? And if we must all travel this way again, where is progress? Or, if we need not travel this road again, if we must travel always new roads that lead nowhere, where is progress? The skepticism to which voluntarism as a system is reduced is nicely balanced by the despair to which it reduces us. Its restlessness is matched by its futility. Progress is possible only when there is a fixed goal, and goals belong not to voluntarism but to intellectualism.

Finally there is one last danger to be avoided. Each of the theories so far discussed has made two assumptions: First, emotion, volition, and intellection are distinct; and second, one of them is superior to the other two. Perhaps someone might wish to question the first assumption, but the resulting discussion would be much too tedious to include in this chapter or in this book, even though its omission placed the foregoing in the position of an *ad hominem* argument.* It is the second assumption to which attention is directed. In an endeavor to do justice to all sides of man's nature, in an endeavor to maintain the fundamental unity of personality, a writer whose view is more eclectic than synthetic might try to place all three activities on exactly the same level. Instead of one's being superior to another, emotion, volition, and intellection would be said to be completely on a par. Such a man would repudiate Schleiermacher's theory of feeling: Emotion is not to be set above reason. But he would also reject intellectualism: Reason is not to be set above emotion.

This eclectic view removes the possibility of solving moral problems. Suppose, as is often the case, that a man's desires and emotions incline him toward some evil; and suppose also, as is sometimes the case, that he knows the contemplated act is wrong. What shall he do? If intellect is supreme, if truth is authoritative, he will know that he ought to resist his evil inclinations. But if emotion is completely on a par with intellect, then there is no need of subjecting his emotions to the intellect. In fact this eclectic attempt to save the unity of the person destroys that very unity, for the man is torn between two equally

*See Clark, *Religion, Reason and Revelation* (Jefferson, Maryland: The Trinity Foundation, 1986 [1961]).—*Editor.*

sovereign powers. Unless there is a supreme ruling in man, unless one faculty or function is superior to another, a man becomes a split personality—an appropriate result of a schizophrenic philosophy.

Now, at last, to clarify the implications of the whole argument with respect to positive religion, to Christianity specifically, the suspicion arises that anti-intellectualism in general is an attitude engendered, nor merely by the complexity of the epistemological problem, but also, and perhaps in greater measure, by the fact that truth in philosophy implies truth in religion, and truth in religion is unwanted. Petrified categories fetter a person by dogmas and creeds; pulsating faith in a person (about whom no true statement can be made) is entombed in an unartistic Gnosticism. This hatred of creed is openly admitted to be one motive among others. One can easily suspect it of being a most important motive because the modernist's pseudo-pious appeal to something inexpressible is a good disguise for his inability or unwillingness to answer straightforward creedal questions.

On the contrary, if truth can be expressed—and only a skeptic dare deny it—then a love of truth must lead to a love of its expression. Creeds are not fetters to hinder man, but are essential aids to his progress. As Orr said, spirituality is not vagueness; rather the spiritual man is the honest man, the most truthful, the most accurate in his expression. Certainly it is clear that historic Christianity with its acceptance of a written revelation is more in accord with intellectualism than with either of the rival theories. Its view of education and its view of worship must accord. A creed in church and a formula in chemistry, even if the latter is not unchanging truth, agree in that both the chemist and the theologian value accuracy. A love of accuracy witnesses to a respect for truth. Since God is truth, a contempt for truth is equally a contempt for God.

Chapter 7
Academic Matters

Among the various particulars that could be included under this chapter heading, only two are selected for discussion. These will be complicated enough without adding others. One reason for the complexity is that these two are problems of subsidiary detail—important, unavoidable, but subsidiary none the less. The previous chapters were philosophical. They treated of general principles. Such matters are profound; sometimes the terminology is obscure and unintelligible; but philosophy is essentially simple. Particulars, however, are complex and confusing because the application of general principles, no matter how clearly they are expressed, to the minutiae of academic administration is never so certain as one could wish.

This is as true for secular schools as for Christian education. For example, J. Ronald Hutler has published at least three editions of *Four Philosophies and Their Practice in Education and Religion*. He gives summaries of the basic philosophy of Naturalism, Realism, Idealism, and Pragmatism. Then he desires to show how each of these philosophies works out in the field of education. This is an excellent idea. Everyone interested in education wants to know how contrasting philosophies work themselves out in educational practice. Unfortunately the book is superficial. Worse, the author is plagued by his initial choice of an awkward classification; he cannot keep his philosophies separate. Nevertheless a perceptive reader with some background easily sees that instead of four distinct programs of education, the applications are largely similar. Naturalism and pragmatism, for instance, cannot particularize their general principles so as to produce educational programs as mutually exclusive as their epistemologies.

This circumstance may also be urged as an objection to a Christian philosophy of education. Is there a Christian arithmetic, not to say spelling, different from pragmatic or idealistic arithmetic? Surely the application of Scriptural teaching to academic programs does not seem so definite, so detailed, and so unambiguous as it is in deducing the doctrine of the Atonement or Justification by faith. Yet it is at least as definite as the secular attempts, and perhaps more so.

Now, in addition to whatever uncertainty there may be in applying Christian philosophy to academic administration, each of the two problems selected are themselves sufficiently complicated. The first problem is the perennial, inescapable, and ordinary difficulties of producing a good school. This includes curriculum, training of teachers, methods of teaching, and all the daily burdens of the principal or president. If this is not sufficiently complicated, it becomes more so in this chapter because an attempt will be made to say something about grade schools and colleges. Their problems are clearly different: yet in some basic ways they are the same.

While this first problem is essential and perennial, the second is contemporary and accidental. At least one may anxiously hope that it will prove to be such. Unlike the situation obtaining during the past two or three centuries, the contemporary school administrator must contend with drugs, crime, riots, arson, and sexual immorality. Hopefully this matter will become outdated, but any book on practical educational problems written at the present time can barely omit it. These then are the two problems. They overlap and affect each other; but the one is more internal, absolutely essential, and strictly educational; the other is more external, having to do with the school's relationship to politics, therefore accidental in its present aggravated form, and educational only in the sense that a school must have civil peace in order to function.

The first of the strictly internal problems is the curriculum. Neither grade school nor university can escape it. The soundest principle governing the curriculum is to stress those subjects that will prove useful to the student no matter how he may choose later to earn his living. It makes no sense to require bookkeeping or mechanical drawing of persons who will never make blueprints or become accountants. The principle is easiest to apply in the early grades.

Indispensable to everyone is the ability to read. Yet in a stupid effort to democratize society, liberals have tried to defend illiteracy on the ground that people who cannot read have other, equally valuable, non-verbal skills. Reading, writing, and arithmetic have been degraded as the primitive accoutrements of the benighted nineteenth century. Unfortunately, there are some retarded children, morons, who cannot learn to read. They will never live independent lives, and if they can be trained to do even a few things for themselves, we shall have to be thankful for that little bit. But surely this is not the ideal for average children (I do not say normal, much less superior) who, now in high school, can hardly read fourth grade material because their early grade schools operated on utterly stupid educational principles.

Since World War II some schools, especially the private schools, have abandoned the look-see method. They now pay attention to words and sounds. They have even improved their literary taste by moving above the level of such scintillating stories as *Jane runs, see Jane run, run Jane run.* But even in the eighties the public schools promote pupils all through high school who cannot read fourth grade material. Admittedly I hardly know what fourth grade material is; but my memory goes back to fifth grade when we read *The King of the Golden River.*

A parenthetical paragraph at least should be devoted to the principals. Schools have principals as well as pupils. The wife of one of my best friends was a school teacher. Social changes brought in a new principal. He might have been able to read, but he surely could not write good English. He had this teacher correct the grammar of his reports to headquarters as well as other documents he had to send out. Then in the same city a boy wielding a switchblade attacked a teacher. She wrested the knife from him and called the police. The principal interfered and ordered her to return the boy's toy. Of course he dismissed the police. Is it not clear then that public schools are inferior?

Further paragraphs on writing and arithmetic are unnecessary. But an example can be crowded in. Jane's brother Tom got through high school without learning any of the three R's. His father wanted the Navy to take him, but the Navy declined the honor. Eventually he was drafted into the Army, but somehow got into the Marines. This made his mother happy because, as she said, he did not have to serve in the Army with all the dummies.

The question is, Why should public schools give none too bright parents the impression their son graduated from "High School"? Another question is, Why should tax money be spent to baby-sit these boys for six, eight, or ten years? In Scotland (for example) such a lad would have left school at twelve or fourteen and taken a job running an elevator in a hotel, or something else he could do acceptably and contentedly. This decreases the tax burden, adds to the economy, and serves to maintain the integrity of an educational system.

The poor work in the grades lowers the level in high school. Over the years I have found few arrivals in college who know the difference between an axiom and a theorem in geometry. Not many more can carry on algebra beyond one x plus one x equals two x.

An example, just one, of the pitifully low standards of American high schools was the college entrance examination given by Dr. J.C. Keister to a hundred or so high school graduates plus a few transfers. The date was 1978. The test was simple arithmetic. Before giving the test to the prospective college students, Dr. Keister gave it to his son, a sophomore in high school, and to his daughter in eighth grade. The boy got 28 answers right out of 40, and the girl tried ten questions and got the right answer in five. The questions were made up by the Educational Testing Service. They were multiple choice questions, four answers, out of which the student was to check the right one.

The first question was, "At the beginning of a certain month, a man's bank balance was $315. If he deposited $75 and withdrew $15 during the month, what was his bank balance at the end of the month?" The students were offered the choice of $255, $365, $370, and $375. Fifteen percent of the entering college students could not solve the problem.

Another question specified that in a certain township the emergency fund was allocated two percent of the property taxes. A circle showed the distribution of the tax dollar into the different funds. The question was, "If the township collected a total of $2,500,000 in property taxes, then the amount paid to the emergency fund was (a) $25,000 (b) $50,000 (c) $75,000 (d) $100,000. Thirty-one percent of these college entrants checked the wrong answer.

Another question was: "To make a quart of orange drink, the directions on the can call for one can of the frozen juice to be mixed with three cans of water. How many cans of frozen juice are needed to make a gallon of orangeade?" The students had to choose from among 4, 8, 9, 12. Thirteen percent got it wrong.

A final example was: "After Dan spent one-third of his allowance for a movie, and three-eighths for a shirt, what part of his allowance did he still have?" The students did not have to figure out that the two fractions had to be expressed in twenty-fourths. The multiple choice did it for them. They could choose from among seven, eleven, thirteen, or seventeen twenty-fourths (printed out in numbers). Exactly forty percent of the students gave the wrong answer.

Since these students had applied for entrance to college, and had not graduated from high school simply to take a job without going to college, it may be reasonably supposed that they were somewhat the better part of their graduating class. Imagine what the others might have done. The conclusion is that government high school education is deplorable. Christian high schools always do better.

In the dim, dark days beyond recall, before the present age of social relevancy and rock music, the present writer was required to take two years of algebra, a year of plane geometry, and a semester each of solid geometry and trigonometry. Physics, chemistry, and either botany or zoology were required. And in that Northeast Manual Training High School in Philadelphia (for I suffered the misfortune of not attending a classical high school) I had four years of Latin, three years of Greek and three years of French.

High schools today do not provide the same opportunities. An Oregon and a Wisconsin high school—to mention only cases that have come to my attention—made it impossible for students to take a foreign language before the junior year. A Pennsylvania school offers a survey course in language: Three weeks of Latin, three weeks of Greek, three of French, three of German, three of Spanish. The aim of this remarkable procedure, which could have been invented only by an addlepated Educationist, was to discover whether the student had an aptitude for Greek instead of French, or whether he would do better in German than in Latin. Read again the first sentence of chapter one.

The attitudes of some educators are amazing. The principal of a large high school, a school of more than three thousand pupils, after hearing a lecture on the value of foreign languages, explained to a small group that he had risen to the top without knowing French and therefore it was obvious that his students did not need French. Accordingly he allows no student to offer more than two units of French toward graduation.

Irrational as this high school principal was, one may still ask what relation there is between French and a Christian program of education. Well, first, in general, a student who knows a foreign language can take advantage of opportunities from which another student ignorant of the language is debarred. One such opportunity, and this time the Christian aspect is more prominent if the language is Greek, would be the study of the Bible in its original language. Only a person who reads Greek can exegete the New Testament. Only a person who knows Latin, French, and German can do much in church history. How many times, on the radio or in large churches, do we hear ministers making unfortunate blunders because they do not know their languages! Recently a radio preacher quoted Jude 14 as "The Lord cometh with ten thousands of his saints," and made a point in dispensational theology. But this is not what Jude said. The gentleman was quoting a mistranslation.

Now the Scripture says, "Thou shalt love the Lord thy God

with all thy heart, and with all thy soul, and with all thy mind."
Many people who do not know Greek think that heart and mind
are antithetical, representing the emotions and the intellect.
Because of this blunder they frequently distort the Gospel,
make faith an emotion, and disparage sound doctrine. Yet even
without knowing what the Bible means by heart, they can see in
this verse that it is necessary to serve God with the mind. The
word used here means *intelligence, understanding, logical ratio-
cination.* Therefore a person who is too lazy to study violates
this first of all commandments.

If it be asserted that not everyone is called by God to be a
minister of the Gospel, no one can disagree; but this is not an
argument against learning foreign languages, for it is required
of all men that they serve God with their minds. A scientist must
indeed be a mathematician, but what scientist can rise to the top
without also reading French and German? Naturally a physicist
will not study how Provencal developed from Latin, nor will a
theologian know all the Germanic dialects in use before Luther
translated the Bible. But each scholar must have a working
knowledge of his tools. Christian principles therefore prescribe
a strong liberal arts curriculum.

The trend of public education is increasingly vocational. In
addition to the diminution of offerings in foreign language, not
to repeat the point that Johnny can't read, arguments against
drop-outs stress preparation for jobs. Comparisons are made
between the life-time income of a high school graduate and a
drop-out, or between the high school and the college graduate.

Admittedly, vocational training has its place. And if a
Christian is to be a plumber, he should be an excellent plumber.
But even in vocational training the public schools are not often
up to par. Illustrative of this is the experience of a Philadelphia
lawyer (in both senses of the term) who must from time to time

employ stenographers. He testifies that girls who receive their training in the public high schools are uniformly incompetent, whereas the ordinary business "colleges" can generally be depended on to produce a satisfactory secretary. The public high schools fail to insist on correct spelling. Any college professor can produce a long list of horrors he finds on papers and examinations.

Further discussion of *vocational training* is unnecessary because, first, training is not education—plumbers, physicians, dentists, stenographers *per se* do not qualify as educated people —and this book concerns education; then, second, since Christians find it difficult to support financially sound education in grade schools, high schools, and colleges, they have no resources to establish trade schools also. There is no theological reason why they should not establish vocational schools. When they had the money, they established hospitals. In Canada they have a labor union (though I am not sure that its principles are strictly Christian); and many other things might be done. The difficulty is not theological but financial. It is a matter solely of how much is most practical and most necessary.

Before the discussion of the curriculum is ended, something should be said about its purpose. Two sub-points can be made here. First, the advantages of a liberal arts curriculum can be more explicitly stated, and applied to secular as well as to Christian schools. Then, second, it should be shown that a Christian private school can clarify and implement the purpose of education better than any public school can or should.

The superiority of liberal arts over vocational curricula lies in the fact that the latter tend to turn men into machines. The stenographer trains her fingers. She can type faster and more accurately than machines, with an equal absence of thinking. So long as the vocationally trained person is actively engaged in his or her little rut, everything runs smoothly. But after hours the stenographer must decide whether to take benzedrine and go to a party or sleeping pills and go to bed. Or she could for a while turn on the television. Whatever noises and nonsense blare forth, at least they fill the vacuum between the ears.

The liberal arts curriculum has the opposite aim. Instead of turning a man into a machine, it aims to prevent him from becoming one. The liberal arts tend to make the student independent of pills and television. The fingers are not trained, but the mind is developed. The student does not learn to do, he learns to understand. If successful, he becomes a rational man, instead of an over-age dependent child in need of amusement. Like Spinoza, he may have to grind lenses for a living—he can train his fingers in a short time—but he will spend his evening thinking and writing books that will influence mankind for centuries.

In the past, secular colleges have provided professionally excellent liberal arts education. They may be much less successful in the future. The City College of New York has maintained high standards for years; but lately a perverted notion of democracy that asserts the right of everybody to a college education has forced the C.C.N.Y. to admit students without entrance requirements. At the very best this ruins the freshman year. When half the class has an I.Q. of 125 or above and half 85 or below, instruction suffers. The wry part of this situation is that the liberal politics, in which the faculty of the C.C.N.Y. indoctrinated their students, is the proximate cause of this academic collapse. When the left-wing deserts scholarship and calls for social involvement, and when the college is regarded as an organization for producing social change, academic standards become a hindrance. Agitation needs numbers, not scholarship. For all their boasted claims to superior intelligence, the liberals are solidly anti-intellectual.

In addition to the C.C.N.Y., a number of state universities

are compelled by liberal legislators to admit any graduate of a state high school, even though he cannot read fourth grade material. Because this ruins the first year, the capable students, the only ones who deserve a college education, and the taxpayers are forced to pay four years' tuition for three years' instruction. But it will not be only the first year that is ruined. This first indignity will affect both faculty and school, and deterioration will be progressive.

Private schools can avoid these governmental compulsions, at least so long as a little American liberty remains. Granted, the democratic ideal of forcing the whole populace to the lowest rung, of eradicating the "middle class" with its "Victorian morals," and of establishing a bureaucratic elite to control the herd, exercises great political power. But so long as the conservative right-wing is not completely overwhelmed, perhaps some private schools with decent academic standards will survive.

Even aside from the deterioration of the curriculum forced by political liberalism, private Christian schools can be more single-minded in achieving liberal arts goals than any present public school can be. The chief reason for this is that the Christian school can be and should be directed in all its operations by a Christian philosophy of education; whereas a tax-supported school cannot completely and ought not at all be so directed by a Christian or any other philosophy of education.

Scripture teaches that man is essentially a rational being. Sin has indeed caused great deterioration in a man's use of reason, but man still remains in essence a rational creature. Consistently with this, Scripture also places great emphasis on truth. The single Gospel of John, which near its beginning describes Christ as full of grace and truth, contains a score or more references to truth. This truth, since it is the complex of propositions that constitute the mind of God, is fixed, final, and eternal. On such a view a liberal arts curriculum can be solidly based.

Secular, tax-supported institutions are not operated on this view of man and truth. Freudian psychology, even if modified by later psychologists, teaches that man is essentially emotional or irrational. Argument is merely hypocritical "rationalization." The existentialists, the dialectical theologians, and mystics like Bergson insist that life is deeper than logic and that contradictions are acceptable. Along with this the various kinds of relativists decry and ridicule the notion that truth is fixed, final, and eternal. Truth is simply the complex of inconsistent propositions that form the minds of those who can maintain a reputation for superiority. On this basis the ideals of liberal arts cannot be defended.

Since the relativists and humanists have conflicting opinions, they stress academic freedom in their own defense. Taxes and public schools should not be used to inculcate one set of truths rather than the opposite set of truths. Academic freedom is understood as the liberty of each professor to teach his own opinions. So construed, a college cannot have a single aim or guiding philosophy. It cannot even inculcate academic freedom, for this is only one relativistic opinion among others.

The Christian school also claims academic freedom, but it construes this as the freedom of a group of people to cooperate in the propagation of Christianity. The claim is that the government should in no way hinder Christian philanthropists from establishing educational institutions for the development of a Christian understanding of the world.

Further, the establishment of private schools is essential to the academic freedom of many teachers and professors. The secularists deride Christian schools for placing their faculties in strait-jackets. The truth of the matter is that the secularists, in spite of their advocacy of academic freedom, put some of their faculty in crooked-jackets. The reason is that little academic freedom is granted to Christian professors. Examine the faculties of American universities, from Harvard, Yale, Princeton and down: How many of these have even a few professors actively propagating Christianity? Here and there a small number may recommend some dilute form of subsidiary Christian themes. But how many stress the sovereignty of God, the depravity of man, and justification by faith alone?

Quite the contrary, the secular schools, instead of granting academic freedom to Christians, use their organized power to hinder and oppose Christianity. Documentation of this accusation can be found, not merely with respect to universities, where secularism is too blatant to need documentation, but in the elementary schools, where, above all, tax money should not be used to force children's minds into a prescribed political and religious mold. The Bulletin of The State Department of Education, *Suggestive Outline for Studies in the Elementary Grades* by L.A. Woods, State Superintendent of Public Instruction (No. 337, Vol X, No. 10, Austin, Texas, 1934), tells the teachers that the first aim of Geography is "to develop a liberal attitude on social questions." Note well that the first aim of Geography is not to teach the location of the Hudson River, or even of the Alamo, but the first aim is to develop a liberal attitude on social questions.

This is a significant statement, and it should be pondered. The first aim of the State Department is to develop an *attitude*. Its primary aim is not to provide the child with some information. It wants to control the child's social, and therefore moral, attitudes. These attitudes are to be "liberal." Imagine how the National Education Assocation would scream if a school system aimed to produce conservative instead of liberal attitudes!

Notice also the confusion resulting from the twisting of the English language. *Liberal* arts is conservative. *Liberal* attitudes in education are anti-intellectual, anti-informational. *Liberal* politics is a reversion to the totalitarianism of Louis XIV and George III, against whom "liberals" like Washington, Adams and Jefferson fought in order to institute a *liberal, i.e.,* a closely restricted government.

Now, regardless of what type of politics and sociology a State Department may wish to inculcate, there will always be some parents, and often many parents, who dislike or even abhor that attitude. They do not want a state officer perverting the morals of their young children. But this is what the state educators do who deliberately aim to produce "attitudes."

This is precisely what they ought not do. If there is anything a tax-supported educational institution ought not do, it is propagandizing against the social, therefore the moral, therefore the religious, beliefs of the parents.

But the liberals in government, particularly in Departments of Education, make great efforts to abolish Christian private education. In 1976 in the state of Ohio the Department tried to put a Christian school out of business. Fortunately, the Ohio Supreme Court upheld the liberty of parents to send their children to a private Christian school. In 1978 the state of Kentucky imposed a jail sentence on Christian parents whose children went to a Christian school. In the 1980's the state of Nebraska sent Christian parents to jail for sending their children to a Christian school. We hope that these bigotted liberals will be soundly defeated. These liberal politicians have much to lose because the students of Christian schools are so far ahead of the public school children, in arithmetic and spelling, that they are an embarrassment to the State Departments of Education.

A private Christian school has the privilege and the right to inculcate Christian moral principles because it does not violate the authority of the family. Since parents who dislike Christianity are not compelled to send their children to Christian schools, their home training is not hindered by Christian schools. Thus the integrity of the home is maintained. Unfortunately "liberals" do not have a high regard for the sanctity of the family. To force left-wing sociology on children in the elementary grades is an inexcusable breach of elementary justice. This state department, therefore, with many others like it, is convicted by its own admission of being a propaganda agency. It is willing to destroy the morality and religion of the home, to turn the children against their parents, for its own ulterior political ends.

Embedded here is another question purely about the curriculum. Why should high schools, not to mention the elementary grades in Texas, teach sociology or economics at all? The educators who have introduced these things into the lower schools put before mere children a type of problem that the President's Cabinet members cannot agree upon. Economics is a terribly complicated subject; and sociology is positively disreputable. In physics there are fairly definite units of measurement: a centimeter, a gram, and even a volt. A volt is a derivative measurement. So is density. Derivative measurements are absolutely indispensable to any physics that goes beyond the length of a string. But there can be no derivative measurements unless there are definite basic measurements, and sociology has few if any carefully defined basic units. Sociologists cannot even count unemployed persons, for there is no universally agreed definition of the term. Great Britain, though more socialistic than the U.S.A., uses a more politically conservative definition, and the U.S.A. uses a more socialistic definition. The figures of the two nations are not comparable.

Since the definitions themselves are chosen in order to advance a given type of legislation, it seems incongruous to teach sociology in high school. It is bad enough in college.

Even medical statistics are undependable, for the definitions of diseases change. To put it briefly, statistics are undependable. It is not that "figures don't lie, but liars figure"; it is the figures themselves that lie. If the elementary grades in Texas would teach the location of the Alamo instead of social attitudes; if Indiana would drop economics and teach geometry; and if Pennsylvania would teach spelling, I feel sure that the Ladue School district in Missouri would also improve.

Let this long section suffice for a discussion of the first and most important of the ordinary academic problems. The second problem is the education of the teachers. This is also very important, but its discussion need not be so lengthy.

Nothing need be said about the preparation of college professors: a Ph.D. with a solid liberal arts background is the sufficient formal requirement. Grade school teachers also should have a college education. At present, however, they are mostly restricted to two years of college plus two years of cutting papers dolls and playing ring around the rosy. Some such methods course can be very useful for teachers of the lower grades; but sixty semester credits is a tragic waste of time. Even after graduation these victims of the National Education Association pressure system are forced to take more courses— not in any subject matter, but in Education. However, Education and education are antithetical. Methods of teaching arithmetic are taught by an Education professor who knows no mathematics; and methods of teaching Economics are taught by one even more ignorant. Really, there is no need to know the subject, so long as you know how to teach it.

Although some hints on method are beneficial to a young teacher, Educationists are not always able to distinguish a good method from a bad. This is one reason, and probably the most significant reason, why Johnny can't read.

Some new methods are useful. Flash cards, matching games, and the like are of real help. It strikes me that flash cards are not so new. In high school during World War I, I used flash cards to learn my Greek vocabulary. It was of some use, I believe.

But consider more recent methods. Albert J. Harris in *How to Increase Reading Ability* lists six methods of teaching reading: 1. The Alphabet method; 2. The Phonic and Phonetic methods; 3. The Word method; 4. The Sentence method; 5. The Experience method; and 6. The Intrinsic method. By so enumerating them, the author gives the impression that there are six independent methods, each of which with more or less efficiency can be used to teach a child to read. It is hardly likely that the first two, the older methods, were ever used separately. Together they are one method, and they can teach a child to read. The newer methods cannot be used separately; nor can they be used together to complete the task at hand; they can be used only in conjunction with the older methods. For example, if a child were required by the third method to learn every word as a whole, without identifying the component letters, the task would be similar to memorizing Chinese characters. Obviously this method would never teach a child to figure out a new word or to use a dictionary. Learning sentences as units is even worse. In how many books is a given sentence repeated? These six items therefore are not methods of teaching reading, as Dr. Harris says. They may be subsidiary devices of a method, and possibly could be useful in some situations and for a limited purpose. But they cannot teach a child to read. How then can Professor Harris hold that "the mechanical alphabet-spelling and phonetic methods *should have no place* in teaching reading to beginners"? Such stupidity can only be found in professors of

Education.

The conclusion is that schools of Education with their uneducated faculties should be abolished. The lobbies that win governmental coercion for them should be retired. Somewhere a place could be provided for a one semester course on pedagogical tricks to amuse children and catch their attention. But nothing should prevent a prospective teacher from taking a four year college course.

Now, the second set of academic problems is not so essentially educational: It is more external, having to do with the schools' relationship to political agitators, vandalism, and violence. At the present time the solution of this set of problems is essential in the sense that unless law and order can be maintained, the school simply cannot exist.

The enormity of the problem hardly needs documentation. Cornell University was forced to capitulate to a group of heavily armed thugs in the late 1960's. A second grade teacher was robbed at gunpoint in her classroom at School 41 in Indianapolis. Berkeley is a hall of shame. Only S.I. Hayakawa made a reasonable attempt to subdue the criminals. Well, let this suffice for a token documentation of the problem of violence.

The fact that armed robbery, murder, arson, and dope can take over the public schools is the result of a widespread anti-Americanism that liberal professors have fostered in the colleges. They are willing to accept tax money, indeed they clamor for more, but they hate the hand that feeds them.

Two instances will be mentioned. The first is the downgrading of science at M.I.T. and elsewhere. On January 1, 1970, Dr. C. Stark Draper was forced to resign from the Massachusetts Institute of Technology. Dr. Draper was one of the scientists who made notable contributions to the United States space program. It was for this very reason that liberal professors and left-wing students bludgeoned the M.I.T. administration to force him out. Similar hostility to the best interests of the American people resulted, on January 16, 1970, in Columbia University's decision to end research for the Defense Department and for industries engaged in defense projects.

This weakening of our nation delights the Communists and it must be a very naive person who does not surmise that this was the motivation of some of the left-wingers. Furthermore the downgrading of basic science and a preoccupation with petty utilitarian details is contrary to scholarly ideals.

Chapter 8
From Kindergarten to University

This last chapter, recommending the establishment of Christian schools from Kindergarten to University, depends, as a conclusion, on all the evidence presented so far. Briefly the evidence can be arranged in three categories. First, the preservation of law and order, without which schools and civilization cannot exist, is aided more by Christian schools than by public education. Christian schools have fewer riots, less dope, more authoritative administrations, and therefore greater safety within their walls. Second, private schools can and usually do maintain a more serious interest in liberal arts. There is less vocational emphasis; the fads of the secular populace can be ignored; and Greek will not be abandoned. Admittedly, not all Christian schools are intellectually ideal, of which more in a moment. The argument simply is that private schools can have a more thoroughgoing intellectual emphasis than government schools because the administrators of the latter are politically controlled and the faculties are largely relativistic and anti-intellectual. Then in the third place, Christian philosophy and Christian theology can be taught. Instead of viewing the human race through Darwinian and Freudian glasses, instead of reading history in a Marxist perspective, and instead of ignoring justification by faith and other revealed doctrines, the Christian school can give a Christian education. For these three reasons, with all the details that fall under each, it is highly desirable, indeed vital, to establish and support Christian schools.

The initial establishment and continuing operation of a Christian school do not occur in a social or political vacuum. Clearly it is impossible to maintain Christian schools in Communist countries. The first thing the North Koreans did when they invaded the South was to shoot all the Christians they could find. When the Army in Brazil stepped in to prevent a left-wing revolution, it found in the leftists' headquarters lists of names of the people whom the leftists intended to murder. It is clear then that political liberty is essential for Christian schools to exist.

This is one reason why Christians should always oppose the trend toward totalitarianism. The leftists and liberals, however much they talk of liberty, free speech, and individual rights, show by their actions that they are intent on destroying these things. When conservatives attempted to address a college audience, the agitators grabbed the microphone, raised pandemonium, harassed the speaker, and prevented the speech. The not quite so left liberals use less obvious methods. When Edmund Muskie, early in 1970, presented Ted Kennedy to an audience, the audience booed. Not very polite perhaps, but a non-violent method of disapproving of an adult boy-girl party, without wives present, and a death unreported for half a day, all very efficiently hushed up. However, the liberals edited the film and on television no booing was heard. Yet when Governor Wallace was booed, the liberals' television left the booing in.

The same antagonism to freedom of speech, the same attempt to utilize the colleges for propaganda purposes, the same intent to control instruction is seen in the radicals' demand to determine the content of the courses and to hire and fire the faculty. The great majority of college students come to college to learn. They may not espouse the ideals of scholarship, but they know enough to know that they don't know everything. Naturally they think that some courses and some professors are useless; and so they may be for those students' purposes. But they still acknowledge that other courses, even most courses, and most professors are worth at least one semester's time. But the leftists know everything; there is nothing left for them to learn; all they can do is to try to disrupt and destroy the institution. Therefore schools, whether secular or Christian, require a government that will protect academic freedom and suppress the criminal element.

So little can Christian schools operate in a social and political vacuum that they must support and strengthen governments that favor Protestantism and resist Romanism. A government favorable to Romanism will not long permit Christian schools. The Roman church has a long history of political intrigue and oppression. It is quite true that many Roman Catholics are kind, decent, intelligent, and charming people. Many of them do not follow the hierarchy to the extremes of clericalism. They do, however, vote for Congressional and state candidates who will siphon off tax money for the hierarchy's benefit. It must be remembered, too, that the Roman church has never changed its policy of trying to govern the world. The papacy has always held that the state should serve the Roman denomination, and it has claimed the right, exercised the power, and has never repudiated the privilege of persecuting other religions. One need only remember the massacre of St. Bartholomew's Eve, Queen Mary who earned the title of Bloody, the Roman atrocities in Holland, and the Spanish Inquisition. But, say the gullible, this is all ancient history. History it is; but it will be ancient only so long as Protestants are strong enough to protect themselves. In 1940 John A. Ryan and Francis J. Boland published a book, *Catholic Principles of Politics*. It carries the *Imprimatur* of Francis J. Spellman, then Archbishop of New York, later a cardinal, and the *Nihil Obstat* of the Censor. The book approves and develops the papal encyclical *Immortal Dei*, which holds that the duty of the state is to prefer Romanism above all other religions, that freedom of religion is contrary to the dictates of nature, and that to exclude the Roman church from the power of making laws is a fatal error.* These Romish professors would permit unbaptized persons to practice their own form of worship secretly in their homes,† but the state should prohibit the preaching of such a religion publicly where Romanists might hear it. That Romanists are willing and eager to put these policies into effect is seen in their actual conduct in parts of Canada, in their attempt to have the United States government prohibit Protestant missionaries from preaching in South America, in their treatment of Protestant missionaries in Ethiopia when they had the backing of Mussolini's armies, and in the clericalism regained by the fascist war in Spain.

This point is sufficiently important to justify a lengthy quotation from the papal encyclical just mentioned.

> Just as the end at which the [Roman] Church aims is by far the noblest of ends, so its power is the most exalted of all powers, and cannot be held to be either inferior to the civil power or in any way subject to it. . . . Now this authority, which pertains absolutely to the Church herself, and is part of her manifest rights, . . . she has never ceased to claim for herself and to exercise publicly. . . . There was once a time when the priesthood and the government were happily united by concord and a

---

* Pages 298-300.
† Pages 316ff.

friendly exchange of offices. And the State composed in that fashion produced in the opinion of all [especially in the opinion of the Huguenots] more excellent fruits, the memory of which still flourishes, and will flourish, attested by innumerable monuments which can neither be destroyed nor obscured by any art of the adversary. . . . But that dreadful and deplorable zeal for revolution which was aroused [by Luther and Calvin] in the sixteenth century, after throwing the Christian religion into confusion, pervaded all ranks of the community. From this spring, as it were, came those more recent propositions of unbridled liberty. . . . Of those principles this is chief: that as all men are understood to be alike in birth and nature, so they are in reality equal throughout the whole course of their lives: . . . that he is free to think what he likes on every subject. . . . When the conduct of affairs is in accordance with doctrines of this kind, to the Catholic name is assigned an equal position with, or even an inferior position to, that of alien societies in the State; no regard is paid to ecclesiastical laws. . . . Thus Gregory XVI, by Encyclical Letter beginning *Mirari vos*, of August 15, 1832, inveighed with weighty words against those doctrines which were already being preached, namely, that in divine worship no preference should be made; and that it was left to individuals to judge of religion according to their personal preferences, that each man's conscience was to himself his sole sufficient guide, and that it was lawful to promulgate whatsoever each man might think. . . . The uncontrolled power of thinking and publicly proclaiming one's thoughts has no place among the rights of citizens, and cannot in any way be reckoned among those things which are worthy of favor or defense.

These considerations show under what political conditions Christian schools can operate. Contemporary so-called liberalism is secular and anti-Christian. Romanism is totalitarian. Only rightist politics is propitious.*

---

* Again note the confusion of language brought about by leftist propaganda. Hitler and

A recurring objection to the line of argument here outlined is that the church and presumably the Christian school should not meddle in politics. It seems more reasonable, however, that the church should take an active interest in anything that threatens its existence. This more reasonable principle naturally covers cases of legislation that would prohibit private schools. About fifty years ago there was a saying that the United States was composed of forty-seven states and the soviet of Oregon. The remark was partially based on Oregon's attempt to legislate private schools out of existence. Fortunately the United States Supreme Court in those days was conservative and declared the legislation unconstitutional. But there still remain people who look on the family as an extension of the public school, rather than vice versa. Education is regarded as a state monopoly. Christians who disagree, like the Amish, are harassed and some emigrate to Mexico to find freedom.

The objection to the church's meddling in politics is sometimes presented in the form of the statement: Christianity is not tied to any political system. This statement is a half-truth of propaganda. In one sense it is true that Christianity is not "tied to," *i.e.*, dependent for its existence on, any particular political system. Even in Russia and China the church survives —barely. Though I am not very enthusiastic about the phrase, "the blood of the martyrs is the seed of the Church"—for the Romish massacre of Huguenots on St. Bartholomew's Eve did not make France Protestant—nevertheless Christ has promised that the gates of hell shall not prevail against his Church.

The present argument, however, does not center on the worst conditions under which the church can survive. The question is whether the church is "tied to," *i.e.*, required to

fascism are often called rightist. But the word *Nazi* means national *socialist*. Hitler was a leftist, so far left that there was only one other position more so. In Europe, Romanism and absolute monarchy might be called rightist. But conservatism or rightism in America is Jeffersonian democracy—that government is best which governs least.

recommend some political system above others. The answer, though qualified, is affirmative.

In the first place Christianity must affirm and support the divinely-given powers of the State and also its God-imposed limitations. The church cannot be neutral or silent on this point. The most immediate danger today is totalitarianism, ushered in by violence and anarchy. Just as the French Revolution by its excesses against absolute monarchy produced Napoleonic dictatorship, so today's radicals, if they can succeed in disrupting our social processes, will produce a so-called proletarian dictatorship. Christianity must indeed support individualism against totalitarianism—man is not just an expendable cog in a social organism—but Christianity must also oppose the pseudo-individualism of those who claim a right to criminal activity and destruction of other individuals' property.

The previous chapter made the point that one of the rights and obligations God gave in establishing the State was the power of the sword. This means capital punishment and war. Not that any nation should go to war just for the fun of it. But refusal ever to go to war, i.e., pacifism, is anti-Christian. God himself commanded the Israelites to engage in certain wars, and the power of the sword, referred to during the supremacy of the Roman Empire, cannot be combined with pacifism.

The power of the sword also includes capital punishment. The church is "tied to" this, for the Bible is not silent. Even Cain at the beginning recognized that his other brothers would kill him for murdering Abel. The account implies that God had already revealed the penalty. When the account reaches the time of Noah, we have the death penalty explicitly spelled out. Christians must therefore resist the liberal attempts to outlaw capital punishment. (Strange, isn't it, that liberals object to executing murderers, and approve of murdering innocent unborn infants? But it's consistent.)

There is more that Christianity is tied to. Ahab's confiscation of Naboth's vineyard is an example of totalitarianism both in politics and economics. Christians must defend the right of private property. Today the muddle-headed liberals like to contrast human rights with property rights. This is a device that helps them in their plans to confiscate what does not belong to them. They are muddle-headed because the right of private property is itself a most important human right. The right of private property is not a right that property has: It is the right of a person to have property. This right is infringed upon by the irresponsible fiscal policies that produce inflation and runaway taxation, as well as by the medieval trick of clipping coins. The conclusion at this point is that Christianity is definitely committed to certain political and economic principles.

Now, if capitalism and liberty can be preserved, the next question concerns the actual organization of Christian schools. The possibilities are church schools, conducted by one or more congregations, and private non-ecclesiastical corporations. The best known parochial system of schools is that of the Roman Catholic church; but the Lutherans also operate more than a thousand parochial schools.

For Christians who are considering the establishment of a new school, the parochial system has an obvious advantage. The congregation is already in existence and may be persuaded to support a school. To interest enough scattered individuals to form a private corporation able to raise the needed funds is more difficult. If one congregation does not have adequate resources, it is still easier to secure the cooperation of two or three church bodies than to find eight or ten wealthy individuals.

However, there arises the question whether general education is a legitimate function of the church. Granting that the church should teach the Bible and the catechism, ought the church to teach geography and arithmetic? Does Scripture give any indication whether liberal arts lie outside the scope of ecclesiastical activity?

This question may be enlarged to include theological education also and the operation of seminaries. At the same time one should realize that what the church is commissioned to do in the case of theological education may not apply to liberal arts. It is possible that a church should train its own ministerial candidates, even if it should not provide a general education for all students. But complications arise. In the nineteenth century college graduates could read Greek before they started seminary. Now they cannot. If so, is the church at liberty to teach Greek and Hebrew grammar? Then why not German and French, since they are also useful in the study of theology? Why not also economics and sociology? These two are both reflected in the Old Testament, and in the New as well.

Now, the Old Testament, where God revealed so many fundamental principles, places the responsibility for the children's welfare upon the parents, not the Church or the State. Children are not creatures of the State, nor were they born to the Church. Children are born to parents and are their parents' responsibility. A characteristic pronouncement of the Old Testament is:

> Therefore shall ye lay up these my words in your heart and in your soul, and bind them for a sign upon your hand, that they may be as frontlets between your eyes; and ye shall teach them to your children, speaking of them when thou sittest in thy house, and when thou walkest by the way, when thou liest down, and when thou risest up.*

And the New Testament says, "Ye fathers, provoke not your

---

*Deuteronomy 11:18-19.

children to wrath: but bring them up in the nurture and admonition of the Lord."*

If we are limited precisely to what Scripture says, and if we cannot add or subtract, these verses, strictly interpreted, and without further information, might be taken to imply that the church is prohibited from organizing even theological education; for these verses refer to theology rather than to liberal arts.

There is, however, other information. While the children's welfare is the parents' responsibility, the Bible does not prohibit the church from engaging in theological education, and maybe general education too. Hannah brought Samuel to the tabernacle at a very early age. The training he received there could hardly have been narrowly restricted to the duties of a priest. One of his studies must have been Hebrew grammar. Also whatever instruction he received to prepare him for his civil office as judge must have been given in the tabernacle.

Once again, Moses gave directions for the feast of tabernacles: "Gather the people together . . . that they may hear and learn. . . ."† This then is a provision for the church's giving theological instruction to children.

Another instance of instruction given outside the home, if not in the temple at least in a religious organization, was the education of prophets in "schools." Samuel, Elijah, and Elisha presided over such schools of prophets. Since no human instruction could give a prophet his message, for this came directly from God, these schools must have given a more general theological education. One may surmise that the presiding officers taught Church History and the Mosaic Law. One may also surmise that they discussed current events. A mention of the sons of the prophets (whether *sons* be taken

---

* Ephesians 6:4.
† Deuteronomy 31:12-13.

literally or figuratively) could indicate that there was elementary education as well as more advanced studies for the prophets themselves. Granted, the details are nebulous; but there was clearly some organized program.

In the later Jewish economy there were doctors of the law who gave instruction in the synagogues. Since this program, like the schools of the prophets, was fundamentally religious, the question of secular liberal arts does not arise. There was no secular instruction. But this does not prove that the church today should not organize liberal arts institutions, for the church of that day provided *all* the organized education there was. If anyone opposes the parochial school system in favor of parent-controlled schools, he must at best use an argument from silence. Note that the Old Testament passages requiring parental instruction of children refer to theological instruction rather than to reading, writing, and arithmetic. In any case it is clear that the church supervised theological education. If now anyone opposes placing seminaries under church control, he has the Scripture against him, and while the elementary grade schools can in actual practice operate as parent-controlled schools, it is rather hypocritical to use this concept for independent theological seminaries.

The New Testament also, while like the Old it does not discuss liberal arts as such, indicates that the church should provide theological education. In the great commission Christ commands the church to teach all nations. One of the qualifications of a bishop is that he be apt to teach. Of course this teaching is primarily theological; but how can the church be denied the right to reduce tribal language to writing and teach illiterate savages to read? It would seem therefore that the church may properly organize elementary instruction as well as theological seminaries.

These arguments are not to be taken as opposition to

parent-controlled schools. The people of the Christian Reformed church, acting as parents independently of their ecclesiastical organization, support an excellent system of primary and secondary education. They are indubitably right in asserting the Scriptural obligation of parents to provide for the welfare of their children. There are also practical advantages. In some cases it is easier to organize a group of parents than it is to persuade two congregations to cooperate. A congregation in a certain city had split in two a dozen years before; there was still an amount of bad feeling, and some honest disagreement on principle; the congregations would not think of cooperating; yet parents from both churches, with the tacit approval of both congregations, formed a school corporation, and both churches offered their facilities until a school building could be built. Within ten or fifteen years the enrollment rose from ten or fifteen to four hundred.

There is no scriptural objection to such parent-controlled schools. One might as well argue that only the church should run a butcher shop because there were religious principles governing the slaughter of animals for food. There is, however, scriptural objection to state-run schools.

In this age of apostasy and crime it is imperative to establish Christian education from kindergarten to university. In this age of ignorance and anti-intellectualism it is highly desirable to establish schools that can maintain high standards. When a visiting lecturer remarked that "Ecclesiastes says . . . ," the wife of a college professor later asked her husband, "Who is that man Ecclesiastes the speaker quoted?" Public school authorites use the slogan "quality education." The quality is the poorest. Christian schools almost automatically avoid disciplinary problems because that type of pupil does not want a Christian school. With so little internal trouble the Christian school can give its full time to instruction. This is neither empty talk, boasting, nor exaggeration.

Christian high schools and colleges have another *raison d'etre*. They rescue Christian students from discrimination and injustice. Throughout history totalitarian governments have denied minorities the right of education. Either certain groups are rigidly excluded from the schools, or, to save appearances where necessary, a very few of the hated minority are permitted to enroll. Thus it is that Christians are barred at least from higher education in Russia and China. In Russia, too, parents are prohibited from teaching religion to their own children. There are proposals to inflict this program on parents in the United States. Earlier William Heard Kilpatrick's teaching at Columbia was cited. In 1953 UNESCO published certain booklets entitled, *Toward World Understanding*. Their assumption is that the State and not the parents should control the education of children, and that the State should aim at eliminating all religious differences among children. To do this they propose the abolition of neighborhood schools, religious schools, private schools, and schools whose pupils are of one sex. To meet this and other threats, Christians should organize as many schools as possible, and seek to dismantle the tax-supported school system. The exercise of liberty is essential to its preservation.

In the meantime public schools, or more accurately, public school teachers with liberal views, degrade Christian students. In one high school a girl of fifteen regularly received A's on her English themes. After one of these themes revealed she was a Christian her grades dropped to C. In another case a college graduate applied for a scholarship to take graduate courses in Chinese language and culture. The examiner showed pleasure at the student's preparation; but when he learned that the student's wide knowledge came from having been raised in China by missionary parents, and that he wanted the extra training in order better to preach the Gospel in China, the examiner's face faded and he precipitously ended the interview. Thus the need for high schools, colleges, and for a university that can grant the doctorate is established. The latter would be an enormous task, for the funding of Christian colleges is difficult enough.

There is also an objection. Many Christians hesitate to support such institutions because so many Christian colleges have become secular. It is well known that most of the oldest and best educational institutions in America were founded for the promulgation of Christianity; and it is equally well known that they are now secular and anti-Christian. Therefore many Christians wonder whether they should risk their money in a venture that might defeat their most cherished ideals.

This objection is to be handled in three different ways by three groups of people. Very wealthy donors, who contemplate gifts of thousands of dollars, may well ponder how to preserve their money for Christian purposes. They must investigate and consider and try to guarantee the desired results. Men of such wealth realize that no book can give sound advice on individual cases. The responsibility must be left to them alone.

For donors of smaller sums the objection grows less with the sum. Most Christian colleges are so hard pressed for funds that small amounts donated to current expenses are used up within a year; and if the college at the time is maintaining Christian standards, the gift will accomplish its aim. The buildings must be heated this winter; some students need tuition help this September; the faculty salaries must be paid every month and should be increased, for it is not just that a devoted faculty should finance the college out of their own sacrifices. So long as the college is functioning at all well, these smaller gifts of a thousand or so, or of a hundred can be given with great confidence.

The third group to face the objection of apostasy is the administration. Its problem, the problem of the president and the trustees, is to prevent apostasy and to continue the original purpose of the institution. Some trustees think that faculties are usually the initiators of decline. This was not true in the case of Princeton Theological Seminary in 1929. The faculty was largely orthodox. It was the trustees who plotted to put the Seminary in charge of a Board that would include trustees who denied the Scripture and who may have also denied the Atonement and the Resurrection. When the trustees succeeded, the most orthodox professors resigned.

Not only do trustees succumb to financial pressure, worldly glory, fame, and popularity, they also are frequently incompetent in theology. They have not studied Calvin's *Institutes*, nor memorized the Westminster Confession, nor can they state the arguments for the immediate imputation of Adam's guilt. If they have been chosen for their office because of their financial ability, this ability itself has ordinarily prevented their attainment of theological competence. Trustees simply cannot be trusted.

Of course, professors cannot be trusted either. One conscientious president told me that professors applying for a position would assent to any creed required of them. Liberals have little regard for the truth. They sign statements of faith they do not believe and secretly work to change them. This is abundantly in evidence in the churches themselves. Hundreds of candidates for the ministry commit perjury when they take their ordination vows. This was especially true in the Presbyterian Church U.S.A. before the adoption of the Confession of 1967.

Honest conservatives find this situation hard to manage. They dislike suspecting perjury when a man takes a solemn vow; and colleges find it difficult to fire a professor when, after several years of service, some of his personal disbelief begins to appear. Nevertheless, the most trustworthy people are to be found among the faculty rather than among the trustees. Princeton Seminary was mentioned a moment ago. Fuller Seminary is another example. When the Seminary refused to adhere to the evangelical principle of *Sola Scriptura*, not only did Winona Lake School of Theology dissolve its connection with Fuller, but the best of the Fuller faculty resigned and went elsewhere.

To avoid such tragedies, a conscientious president, with the support of the faculty, may think of some useful and practicable expedients. These cannot be listed in order of importance, except that the first is indispensable. This first is a detailed basis of faith, preferably the Westminster Confession. The fundamentalist idea of a brief creed of six or seven articles is unsatisfactory, both because it gives relatively little guidance in the formulation of educational principles, and because trustees who think such fundamentalistic creeds are ideal go beyond them and enforce on the faculty standards that the faculty did not accept when they accepted employment. The radically oriented American Association of University Professors, compelled by public opinion to recognize religious schools, insists that the religious requirements imposed on the faculty be fully published and presented to a candidate for a teaching position. In this point the A.A.U.P. is to be commended.

Beyond this first expedient for preserving a college's original purpose, the remainder can be listed in a more or less haphazard order. Each is of some use in some situations. One of these procedures is the selection of the student body from among friendly constituents. No doubt this is normal. But there are cases where, because of proximity to home, low tuition fees, or other factors, a very sizable minority of unsympathetic students can influence and hinder the college's program. It is not wise to require a creedal subscription from students—they do not know enough to assent intelligently—nor it is necessary to exclude every unsympathetic or indifferent student; yet a solidly appreciative alumni body helps to preserve the original standards better than a religiously heterogeneous group could.

Another procedure is the constant reiteration of the institution's purpose. Of course, it must be publicized in the catalogue and publicity material, prominently publicized and constantly reiterated. Then at convocations and graduations the matter should be kept before the attention of the audience. In this way deterioration will be arrested; or if in some case not arrested, it will be made obvious and can be remedied. For example, the unconscientious liberal who signs his name to a document he does not believe may weary of being publicly pointed out as a supporter of this policy. He may become embarrassed before his friends, quietly look for another job, and resign. No doubt other procedures would suggest themselves as various situations arise. The old adage always applies: Eternal vigilance is the price of liberty.

One further point, however, second in importance only to the original adoption of a creed, must be listed, and it can serve as a conclusion to this volume. The professors can and should construct their courses in conformity with the faith. This is easier in some subjects, more difficult in others. The courses in English literature do not have to feature every depraved author, nor even the more respectable humanist authors. No doubt examples of humanism and even depravity can be used for contrast; but as much Christian flavor as possible should be included. The discussion, aesthetic, social, moral, will give ample scope for Christian instruction. History also can be utilized to serve the purpose of the college. Though the

Napoleonic wars are a legitimate area of study, the Christian Department of History can include and emphasize the eras reflected in Scripture: Babylonian, Egyptian, Greek, and Roman; and of course Church History, with strong emphasis on the Reformation. If the Napoleonic era is given, the professor, in addition to explaining Egypt and the Rosetta Stone, in addition to Moscow and Elba, Waterloo and St. Helena, can explain the religious results in France that for a century denied to the Reformed churches the right of holding a Synod meeting.

Besides History there are Physics and Mathematics. So far as their details are concerned, it is harder to infuse the courses with Christian material. But it is not hard to do so when the discussion turns to their significance. This is the Philosophy of Science, and is of great importance.

Then, as this reminds us, there is Philosophy. Of all subjects this profits most from Christian presuppositions. The method, however, or at least one part of the method, deserves a special note. Philosophy concerns the interrelationships of all subjects. It examines the broadest possible principles. Some courses in chemistry, on the contrary, are highly specialized. The more advanced courses are even more so. So minute are the investigations of researchers that they are unable to converse with other scholars even in the same general field. The jest about knowing more and more about less and less until one knows everything about nothing has almost come true. Of course, the chemist might reply that philosophy is so general that it knows less and less about more and more until it knows nothing about everything. There is truth in both quips. Yet as a scientist must press on to further detail, so must the philosopher advance to wider generalities. This philosophic endeavor, if all the faculty will engage in it, will prove extremely useful in constructing an integrated Christian curriculum. If truth is a system, as the omniscience of God guarantees, and if an institution of higher learning aims to transmit some truth, then a professor ought to have at least an elementary grasp of the system in order to locate the position of his subject in the whole. The material of the several courses should dovetail. Victor Hugo, for example, was not only a literary romanticist, he was also a French politician; the second law of thermodynamics is often said to have a direct bearing on the doctrine of creation; and social phenomena, rightly or wrongly, have sometimes been reduced to zoological terms. A liberal education may be said to consist largely of a knowledge of such relationships. To know these relationships, it is necessary of course to have some acquaintance with the particular subjects; but it is also true, and more important, that to know a subject well, a knowledge of the relationships is indispensable. Every competent professor, by definition, knows enough of these relationships to teach college students; but none knows enough. And if the function of a college or university is not only to transmit learning but to improve on the past and extend scholarship, what better method can be devised than periodically to hold faculty meetings for the discussion of these interrelations. Such a faculty discussion could well be conducted as a clinic with the students sitting in the gallery. There they could watch the contents of the curriculum expanding. A curriculum such as this will do two things: It will of course give the students what they came to get; and second, by making these ideas a part of the life of the college, it will be of great help in protecting the original purpose from erosion.

The kindergarten and grade school, by way of contrast, have in all their problems an easier time than the college and university. There is less financial strain—though with a more restricted clientele it is considerable; and there is not so much danger of doctrinal decline. Furthermore the Christian elementary school can easily outperform the public schools. The

Christian colleges, because of their low salary scale, find it difficult to get enough first rate professors. They also suffer from a deficiency of expensive scientific equipment. Therefore their offerings are restricted.

But no grade school, secular or Christian, needs to worry about a restricted curriculum. Many of them would improve considerably if their curriculum were still more restricted than it is. Then, too, the Christian school ordinarily gets and can always insist on pupils of interested parents. Christian pupils, to be sure, have not achieved complete and perfect sanctification. But the worst disciplinary problems never arise, and the total is less. Thus the intellectual or educational standards of Christian schools are almost automatically higher than those of the public schools. There is always some danger of a lapse, but such a fall from grace can rather easily be avoided, or can be more easily remedied than the unfortunate conditions in the public system. Therefore congregations and parents should forthwith assume the financial and administrative burdens and establish Christian grade schools everywhere.

So well endowed as affluent America is, including Christians, and so antagonistic to Christian faith and morals is contemporary society, can Christian parents refuse their children the blessings that are greater than material prosperity and licentious indulgence? Does not your child deserve a Christian education from kindergarten to university?

Appendix A
The Relationship of Public Education to Christianity*

The subject of this morning's address is of such breadth and depth that many and important phases must be omitted. Since the theme of this conference is *Perils Confronting the Christian Church*, one might expect the paper on public education to deal with accounts of young men and women whose faith and life had been ruined in college. Yet this phase of the matter is one which must be omitted. As a matter of fact, at the opening of Westminster Theological Seminary this autumn, the speaker, the Rev. John H. McComb, of New York, asserted he had never known a case of Christian faith ruined by college contacts. In the alleged cases, he said, the young man had no true faith to begin with; and further, wherever a boy or girl is properly instructed by parents and forewarned of the existence of enemies, the enemies do little damage.

---

*More than fifty years ago, on October 31, 1935, Dr. Gordon H. Clark delivered the following speech to the 42nd Annual Convention of the Ruling Elders' Association of Chester Presbytery in Kennett Square, Pennsylvania. In the following 50 years, the burgeoning Christian school movement has sought to thwart the menace to Christianity represented by public education, but we still have a long way to go. The "complete Christian culture" of which Clark spoke is not yet in sight. But more and more people are beginning to understand the necessity of replacing public education with Christian education. Clark understood that need fifty years ago.—Editor

Now while my experience has been the same as Dr. McComb's, it may well be that my experience is limited. There has been recently published a book entitled, *Crucifying Christ in our Colleges* by Dan Gilbert. Mr. Gilbert states and then gives his evidence that "for many, a college education has meant an applied course in immorality." He quotes the anti-Christian Aldous Huxley as saying, "American college boys and coeds copulate with the casual promiscuousness of dogs." And he further refers to statistics which show that a certain college town in Michigan has a greater population of venereal cases than New York City.

Although the book is distressingly extreme, the collection of incidents and cases compiled by Mr. Gilbert is probably true and accurate. The author then traces this immorality to temptations and seductions presented to the student by anti-Christian professors. He has amassed a large number of quotations from college textbooks on psychology, sociology, biology, in which the Christian religion and the Christian standards of morality are attacked and repudiated in favor of promiscuity in sex, revolution and bloodshed in politics, thievery and even murder in private affairs. Assume, if you will, that the author has collected the most outrageous statements, it is nonetheless true that this is what the students get in some textbooks and in some colleges. If other textbooks are more cautious, it still remains possible that the lectures in the classroom promulgate paganism. Lectures, moreover, have this two-fold advantage over textbooks—they are more effective than textbooks in molding the ideas of the students, and in the case of dangerous doctrine they vanish in air and leave no accurate evidence behind.

All this is a menace to Christianity; it is an urgent phase of the problem; nevertheless it is a phase we must omit from this morning's considerations. We omit this phase for a reason, and the reason is that these distressing facts are the result of underlying causes. The causes are not as spectacular as the results, but they are the root of the trouble and require recognition in a proper diagnosis.

No doubt these causes are numerous. Perhaps the basic cause is the inherent depravity of human nature. Born in iniquity, implicated in Adam's guilt, a man is naturally a sinner. However, the most basic cause of the evil educational situation is not restricted to the field of education. Anyone who has worked in a factory knows that "one taint of nature makes the whole world kin." And so it might seem proper to pass by the subject of human depravity as being a theological consideration and not peculiar to education. On the other hand, although it is not peculiar to education, an educator's belief or disbelief in hereditary depravity determines his attitude toward school problems. The non-Christian educator who believes that the child's nature is inherently and positively good, or at very worst neutral, aims to develop that nature as it is. Restrictions and inhibitions are regarded as evil, and self-expression is regarded as good. That the result of such an attitude is often a decidedly immoral life is not surprising; but even in the very limited field of intellectual attainment, the results are disastrous, for the child chooses to learn what he feels like learning. The child chooses the project, and the teacher is there only to amuse him. The Christian educator, on the other hand, believes that every child he teaches inherits an evil nature, praises self-control rather than self-expression; he believes the teacher, rather than the pupil, knows best what lessons should be studied; and he is convinced that the popular shibboleth, learning by doing, is unmasked when we see that evil learned in such a manner does irreparable harm. The theological doctrine of human depravity, it is true, is not limited in its application to education; but certainly it has a very definite bearing on the problem, and should be so recognized.

It may be well, however, to attempt to limit this discussion to purely educational theory. At least the attempt will prove whether such a limitation is possible or not. But what is educational theory, and what is education? Disagreement on this initial question produces divergence all along the line. It should be obvious from the mere statement, that a school system founded on the idea that education is a moral and spiritual preparation for all of life, will train children in a manner totally different from a school system which conceives education as a preparation for getting the most money in the shortest time. It would be difficult if not impossible to find in the United States a public school system whose operation is based on the supremacy of moral and spiritual values. It would be relatively easy, however, to find proponents of an education more or less completely materialistic in its philosophy and purely vocational in its contents. It sees only this world, and in this world it knows only economics.

Aside from any religious implications, this type of education tends to turn men into machines. As long as the victims of this type of instruction are actively engaged in following their own little rut, as long as they are occupied by their business, the machine works smoothly. But take away the business, get the machine out of the rut, give the man an evening of solitude or leisure, and his essential poverty of spirit is revealed. If he can find no acquaintances to prevent him from boring himself, he must turn on the radio. What noise the radio transmits is irrelevant; at least it fills the vacuum between the ears.

Other educators attempt to substitute a view of education more plausible to common sense. They assert either that there is no ultimate aim of education, or, if they are more cautious, declare they know of no such aim. Enamoured with scientific experiment and observation, they have discovered, so they say, that education has many disconnected and unrelated ends. Discarding what they consider impractical metaphysics, they hold that everyone agrees that spelling is useful, and arithmetic, and, let us say, football. To develop the student along these unrelated lines, then, is the purpose of education. Of any synthesis of human activities, of any primary purpose in life, they profess ignorance or disbelief.

Plausible as this theory is, the person who reflects stumbles on some embarrassing questions. In any list of unrelated aims of education, one may ask, has anything been omitted? Is the list complete? Certainly every consistent Christian would regard the list of a pagan educator woefully inadequate. Does the professional educator, in particular does the public school system of our country, wish to force on Christian people a type of schooling from which all spiritual values are banned? When the educator composed his list, what was the motive behind his omissions? Was it his concealed conviction that certain ends, especially the more comprehensive ends, are valueless? It may be that such lists occasionally include subjects omitted from the purely materialistic vocational theory; but on the whole, these two theories, the dogmatic materialism of the one and the dogmatic skepticism of the other, amount to much the same thing.

A third theory, however, seems definitely more promising. It is precisely the opposite of the first theory. If the aim of vocational education is to make man into a machine and to regiment him in a rut, the aim in this case is to prevent man from becoming a machine and to save him from a rut. The aim is to make him independent of radios, in short to make him a *man*, a complete man instead of a dependent child in need of amusement.

A pertinent suggestion for modern school systems is that they banish everything vocational, and banish it on the ground that it is not education. Technical schools are to be encouraged —the finer they are the better; but let not the common confusion remain that technical training and education are the same.

Education, properly understood, does not prepare a youth for this or that specific type of life; education is not for the purpose of producing chemists, brokers, or engineers; it is for the purpose of producing men. It does not prepare for any one type of life in particular, but for any and all kinds in general. Its lessons are applicable to all life, not to just some life.

Let it be perfectly well understood, however, that this education can be and should be as thorough as technical training. The theory does not imply that the school year is a holiday, that hard intellectual labor can be dispensed with, or that college is a young gentlemen's finishing school. A course at the Sorbonne will impress one with the thoroughness of French education, and while their system is not ideal, American systems would improve if they should copy some of the French thoroughness. Education should be as thorough as technical training, but not so narrow and restricted; for the aim is a complete man and a well balanced life.

Unfortunately, just as we are arriving at an apparently satisfactory view of what education aims to do, we are confronted with the most basic and most serious problem of all. Education may well aim at a well balanced life and a complete man; but what is a well balanced life, and what constitutes a complete man? No strictly educational theory can answer these questions; the attempt to exclude all but purely educational material fails, because each educator adopts a particular philosophic world view and bases his educational theory on his philosophy. Some educators hold that man and the world he lives in should be humanistically conceived. They do not believe in God; religion in their estimation is superstition; and the well balanced life becomes the gratification of as many senses as possible. Some of the worst results of this view give Mr. Gilbert material for his book mentioned above. Other educators, too few in number, hold to a theistic world view. They assert that God is, and is Sovereign; that disregard of God results in inevitable calamity, and that the chief end of man is to glorify God and to enjoy him forever. On the one side we have John Dewey and most of the professional educators; on the other side, the Christian.

It cannot be too strongly emphasized that the educational policies of a public school system derive their character from the philosophy of its higher officials. Let these directors, superintendents, and principals claim they base their views on experiment and observation; their claim is untrue. Experimentation in psychology and pedagogy may indeed improve the technique of teaching, but it cannot choose ends or goals. And ends or goals are far more important than technique. Scientific technique can only be a curse when it is headed in the wrong direction. No better illustration of this truth could be desired than the constantly improving technique in chemistry. Improved chemistry can work wonders in medicine; but if improved technique in chemistry is used to produce poison gas for war, we may well wish chemistry less success. Technique in education will make the teaching of children more efficient, but if the educator teaches wrong ideals, the more efficiently he does so, the worse. Scientific experiment may tell us how children learn, but no amount of observation of children will tell us what they ought to learn. And this is the most important phase of education; not the description of the learning process, but the goal of the process. In philosophic language pedagogy is not a descriptive science, it is a normative science. It deals not so much with what is, but with what ought to be. And views of what ought to be do not come, as some educators envious of a scientific reputation claim, from observing how children learn. Views of what ought to be depend on the underlying philosophy. The anti-Christian educator wants to produce one kind of man, the Christian has chosen a far different goal. They may both talk about a complete man; but that they mean different things is obvious when we quote perhaps the best verse in Scripture on the goal of education: "All Scripture is inspired of God and is profitable for teaching . . . for instruction in righteousness, that the man of God may be complete, furnished completely unto every good work."

If now as Christians we have some idea of our goal, it is time to pay attention to the methods for providing children with the education we favor. Methodology could be discussed indefinitely; its intricacies are infinite. This morning only certain very general principles of method can be mentioned. First of all education is and should be regarded as the responsibility of the family. It is primarily to parents, not primarily to the State, nor even to the Church, that God has entrusted the children and their upbringing. This principle needs emphasis in these days because so many educators neglect or deny it. There are powerful forces at work in the world and in these United States to destroy the family and to make children, yes and adults too, the creatures of the State. Loose morals and easy Nevada divorces go hand in hand with dictatorship to destroy the family and to exalt the State. Americans need not point the finger of scorn at immoral, atheistic Russia, nor at the efforts of Hitler and Mussolini to make of public education a means of political propaganda. Centralization of authority is well developed in this country too. Never before in this country has so much power been put into the hands of one man. If these tendencies toward loose morality, exemplified both in easy divorce and in the repudiation of debts and laws concerning potatoes, if these tendencies are not combatted and overcome, the family stands to lose. Dictators never have and never can annihilate the family, simply because it is an institution established by God, and ingrained in the human constitution, but dictators can ruin many families, cause widespread misery, and even civil war. In education the dictatorial policy is pursued with every centralization of authority. A

Federal Board of Education which could control local systems would turn the schools into instruments of party politics, and in short would be the most effective method possible for preventing any true education. All this, too, is in line with the so called Child Labor amendment, which, if it should ever become a part of the United States Constitution, at least in the form in which it was originally presented, would take the control of children from the parents and give it to Congress. If I am correctly informed,* its sponsors are communistic and they emphatically rejected limiting the scope of the amendment to industrial employment, but insisted on including the power to take control of children away from the parents. In these troubled times, the Christian must make himself vocal and reassert the responsibility of the family for the education of the child.

Parents, however, because of the exigencies of life, cannot personally give the children the instruction they need. Schools are necessary. But to what sort of school should Christian parents send their children? Does it seem reasonable that a Christian child should be given pagan instruction? There are Christians, even Christian ministers, who refer to Moses as being learned in all the wisdom of the Egyptians and from this fact conclude, by some sort of private logic, that there is no need for Christian schools. We agree that Moses' character was so formed by his mother's training that his Egyptian education did not ruin him, but if pagan education did not ruin Moses and does not ruin true Christian young men today, we should give glory to the power of God's grace instead of being satisfied with pagan education. Just because a young man survives pagan instruction is no reason for subjecting him to it. Children sometimes survive diphtheria or infantile paralysis, but we do not try to give it to them.

Now, in public schools, children receive a pagan education.

---

* *The Child Labor Amendment and What It Means,* by Sterling E. Edwards, Esq., St. Louis, Mo.

One hardly expects the public schools to teach that most compact and most consistent expression of Christianity, the Shorter Catechism. But the teaching of the Bible is also prohibited, and in some places even the reading of the Bible is outlawed. Obviously the public schools are not Christian. But many people reply, though they are not Christian, they are not anti-Christian, they are neutral. But, let one ask, what does neutrality mean when God is involved? How does God judge the school system which says to him, "O God, we neither deny nor assert thy existence; and O God, we neither obey nor disobey thy commands; we are strictly neutral." Let no one fail to see the point: the school system which ignores God teaches its pupils to ignore God, and this is not neutrality but the worst form of antagonism, for it judges God to be unimportant and irrelevant in human affairs.

Any Christian, it seems to me, should have sense enough to see that subjection to pagan influences works an injustice to the child. Any Christian should see that, but a Presbyterian should see it still more clearly. Unfortunately the Presbyterian Church in the U.S.A. is dominated by men who share the views of the heretical Auburn Affirmation. The Bible is repudiated and the chief events of Christ's ministry, his Virgin Birth, his vicarious Atonement, his bodily Resurrection, are called unessential to the Christian religion. The Westminster Confession with its glorious Calvinism is a dead letter. But a true Presbyterian, one who really believes the system of the Confession, one to whom total depravity, limited atonement, perseverance of the saints, mean something, such a one can see more clearly than any other type of Christian the injustice of subjecting a child to pagan instruction. With his profounder and more consistent understanding of Christianity, the Calvinist sees this more clearly because he more fully appreciates the Covenant of Grace.

In Genesis we read that God established a gracious

covenant between himself and Abraham; but it was not with Abraham alone that God established the covenant. The words are, "I will establish my covenant between me and thee and thy seed after thee. . . ." The covenant therefore definitely included the children. Hence the children of Abraham stood in a relation to God different from the relation of heathen children to God. In Paul's letter to the Galatians God teaches us that the New Testament dispensation is but the revival and fulfillment of the covenant with Abraham. This does not mean that actual salvation is a natural inheritance from father to son. Much less does it deny the need of regeneration. But it does mean that God ordinarily works through families; and for these reasons Presbyterians administer baptism to infants, just as the Hebrews circumcised their sons, to show their formal inclusion in the covenant. The parent at baptism promises to bring up the child in the nurture and admonition of the Lord, or in some other terms promises to educate the child along Christian lines. It is inefficiency to say the least to restrict this education to home training and Sunday School; logically the day school also should be utilized for Christian instruction.

Now once upon a time our country was two-thirds Calvinistic and the civilization in a large sense was Christian. This unfortunately is no longer true, and schools and colleges are accused with some degree of truth of giving the students courses in applied immorality.

What suggestion can be made to help the parent in the present situation? There is one very concrete suggestion—whether it is practicable or not the parents must decide for themselves. Suffice it to be said that the suggestion is in actual operation in a number of places. The suggestion simply is that Christian parents band together to form Christian schools. A single family cannot provide a Christian education for its children, but a large number of families can. Some financial sacrifice no doubt, would be needed, but Christianity in general and in particular its most consistent form, Calvinism, are not known for shunning sacrifice. Christian civilization and Christian culture are disappearing. Large groups of earnest orthodox Christians are totally unaware of the rich heritage that is theirs; they are as babes drinking milk, and they need strong meat for maturity. They believe the fundamentals, they preach the heart of the Gospel, and souls are saved through their instrumentality. We praise God for that. But they are not completely furnished unto every good work. A system of Christian schools will give us a knowledge of Christianity as it embraces the whole of life, and will produce a complete Christian culture for a complete man.

Appendix B
A Protestant World-View*

News reports of the last religious census contained some significant, if not encouraging, information. On the whole the increase in church membership did not keep pace with the increase of population, but the Lutherans showed the greatest proportional increase among all Protestant denominations and the Romanists showed the largest proportional increase of all religious organizations.

In view of Romanism's superstitions and idolatrous practices, repugnant to an enlightened age, in view of the dark history of Romanism with its persecutions and massacres, repugnant to human sympathy, and in view of allegiance to a foreign Pontiff who claims spiritual and temporal power, repugnant to historic Americanism, it might prove profitable to speculate on the causes of Romanism's increasing strength in these United States of America.

One will make no mistake in looking for a variety of causes. The mere force of numbers, the momentum of geometrical progression, so to speak, undoubtedly produces considerable effect. There is a power in a crowd that draws a larger crowd, and when throngs pour in and out of a great cathedral,

---

* A commencement address delivered at Westminster Theological Seminary, Philadelphia, May 6, 1941, published in *The Trinity Review,* April and May, 1979. Copyright 1979, The Trinity Foundation.

people are more inclined to follow the crowd than to generate the necessary stamina to attend a small congregation. There is political power with the crowds; there is money to be spent where it will do the most good; and in Romanism there is also a rather efficient organization for consciously giving direction to this power. Two items testify to the truth of this: First, according to a three-month survey of fifty-six leading daily papers, Romanism got 26.8% of the newspaper space devoted to religious news, and the next highest percentage, that of Methodism, was 9.7%. And second, the President of the United States, violating a fundamental principle of the nation, appointed an ambassador to the Pope.

For very obvious reasons, such denominations as the Orthodox Presbyterian Church will long be unable to gain Machiavellian wisdom by imitating the procedures suggested. But organization and the power of numbers, while they are elements of the situation and elements not to be despised, are not the only factors. They do not, for example, adequately account for the conversion to Romanism of a number of well-educated people.

Cardinal Newman is an illustration from last century. Heywood Broun, if we may join these two names, is an illustration from this century. Of course the organization takes pains to advertise such conspicuous examples, and there may be a psychological fallacy in using distinguished names as examples of Rome's gains in educated circles. But there is perfectly sound objective evidence of intellectual attainment sufficient to attract influential minds. If one were to examine the list of books, articles, and periodicals published by Roman Catholic writers, one would be amazed at the wealth of productivity. The subject matter, not confined to theology as such, ranges through philosophy, anthropology, biology, education, history, and political science. Nor is it the mere quantity of books that is significant. The strength of all this production lies in the fact that Romanism is attacking all these problems systematically. Whether the author writes on psychology or politics, the views expounded and advocated are the implications of the Thomistic system. And it may be said pointedly that on the whole the discussions are very ably conducted. The Roman Church, with its European background, with its consciousness of the long past, with its willingness to make haste slowly, maintains standards superior to those of typically American Protestantism, whether modernistic or fundamental.

Now, when system and quality are combined, they make a tremendous psychological impact on society. Protestantism, on the other hand, suffers from what may most politely be termed an uneven quality in production, and what is worse, from a complete absence of system. The result is that in the learned societies of our country, Roman speakers are heard with respect, while orthodox Protestants either are rarely invited or else perhaps do not exist. Let no layman in the pew, let no evangelist in the pulpit, make any mistakes. The various learned societies may not number a large proportion of the total population; but their views, their honors, and their contempt are soon shared by civilization in general. If they give the impression that Romanism and modernism are respectable, while Scriptural views are indefensible, great numbers of people will be inclined in either of the former two directions and influenced against the latter way of life. The work of the special evangelist and the work of the regular pastor are sensibly aided or hindered by the dominant intellectual outlook. People enter the pew either predisposed in favor of orthodox Christianity or predisposed against it. In times when the great majority of the population paid at least lip service to the Word of God, the faithful minister did not face extreme opposition; but in these days when books, radio, and periodicals generally condemn, deride, and distort the orthodox position, when they substitute another religion and bedeck it with attractive phraseology, the difficulties of the minister of the Triune God are multiplied. For example, it must soon be possible to notice the deteriorating effect of the articles on religion, prayer, and church attendance that have been reproduced during the past year in the *Reader's Digest*. These articles are religious, to be sure, they encourage church attendance; but they are a subtle attack on Christianity nonetheless.

If, then, the dominating outlook of a society may be called its philosophy, and if this popular philosophy is the result of a technical synthesis of all the fields of knowledge, a synthesis which postulates major principles to govern every particular investigation, one need not wonder that a Roman official asked the Knights of Columbus for funds to train ten young philosophers, for, he said, the coming battle is to be fought on the fields of philosophy. And the Papacy intends to be ready for the battle.

This determination and the resultant scholarly productivity have their source in a consciously adopted long-range policy.

Toward the end of last century the Roman church was experiencing the disorganizing influence of modernism. Had the hierarchy allowed this influence to spread unchecked, there might well have been the same lack of philosophic agreement in Rome as there is now in Protestantism. But at the beginning of this century, Pope Pius X in his Encyclical *Pascendi* and in some other pastoral letters condemned modernism, and its advocates were soon deprived of prominent positions. Accompanying the condemnation of modernism was the acceptance of Scholastic philosophy, with the result that today the Romish scholars present a fairly well unified front. They differ, of course, on various details, but they all are obviously Thomistic.

In Protestantism there is no ecclesiastical machinery to enforce a particular system of philosophy, and we fervently hope there never will be such machinery. Even within the limited circle of a single, small denomination, such machinery would be both unwise and unwelcome. Nonetheless, we ought to consider what basic philosophic principles would best serve the Reformed faith. If individually and spontaneously each of us is convinced by clarity of argument that one particular philosophic approach is best, we too, by continuing our discussions and pushing into every field of thought, may acquire greater unity and strength.

Would it be too bold on this occasion to suggest such a basic position? A suggestion of this type would be a very serious matter with far-reaching implications and should not be made thoughtlessly. On the other hand, some may think such a suggestion not so much bold as unnecessary. At any rate, could we agree that of all the systems of history, the general philosophic position of Augustine is more promising than any other?

The choice of Augustine as a point of departure is not made simply to be opposed to Thomism. Rather the choice is made, or more accurately, the choice suggests itself by a dim anticipation that the philosopher who came closest to the Scriptural doctrines of grace may also have come closest to their necessary philosophic context.

This may at first seem a bold suggestion; on second thought it may appear as useless. For one who chooses Augustine's guidance walks a harder road than one who follows Thomas. It is harder in the sense that Augustine is not nearly so explicit as Thomas. The latter obviously has a system; it is not so clear that Augustine has one. Thomas goes into great detail; Augustine leaves many questions unanswered. Hence the guidance may be less explicit, and we are in danger of losing our way; yet if Thomas is headed in the wrong direction, his more explicit instruction will not prove ultimately beneficial.

Progress, therefore, requires attention to the difficulties. A modern Augustinianism must supplement the teaching of its father by working out an enormous amount of detail. Broad views of the sovereignty of God as affecting all parts of the universe, and the consequence that science and theology form a single, organized, intelligible system, are both inspiring and necessary; but the only proof of which they are capable is their application to the details of physics, psychology, education, politics, and all else. An Augustinian must guard himself with vigilance to avoid the charge Hegel made against the romanticists. "But if we look more closely at this expanded system," he says, "we find that it has not been reached by one and the same principle taking shape in diverse ways; it is the shapeless repetition of one and the same idea, which is applied in an external fashion to different material, the wearisome reiteration of it keeping up the semblance of diversity. The idea, which by itself is no doubt the truth, really never gets any further than just where it began, as long as the development of it consists in nothing else than such a repetition of the same formula."

Plato in the *Philebus* expresses the same thought by the warning that a student should not jump from one to infinity or back again. The basic unity must be carefully divided and subdivided before reaching the multiplicity of individuality. To have any large effect on the educated world, therefore, the adherents of the Reformed faith must give detailed applications of their principles to particular problems.

Let us take several examples, not from the whole sphere of scholarly investigation, but merely from the more restricted sphere of epistemology. Let us ask whether Augustinianism can answer such questions as these. Is knowledge the result of forming a concept by the process of abstraction, or does no such process exist? Is the word *concept* merely a symbol for an embryonic concrete idea and should we say that only a lazy mind contents itself with the vague, poorly-defined objects called abstractions? Or, coming into closer grips with the concrete, one may ask whether in sensation we see an image, perhaps on the retina, or whether we see an external object. Detailed questions on other subjects, such as politics, education, and aesthetics are more conveniently imagined than mentioned.

On this commencement occasion it would be ungracious, though certainly less dangerous, to leave such questions unanswered. Any technical discussion of these problems involves extreme difficulty; nevertheless, to implement the promise of Augustinianism one is under obligation to say something, however little and however cautiously. Accordingly, let us plunge into the middle of things and attack the crucial and plaguy problem of sensation and psycho-physics.

In the history of modern psychology the investigation of the relation between the body and the soul has come to an impasse because the underlying assumptions require a mechanical production of a state of consciousness. The notion that a state of consciousness can produce mechanical action was early regarded as impossible; it has taken longer to see that the reverse process, of which sensation is the chief example, is equally impossible. For this reason epiphenomenalism, which held to the impossibility in one direction and denied it in the other, must be rejected as hopelessly inconsistent. The result of these considerations is that psychologists in general adopt a parallelism without subscribing to Spinozistic or other necessary philosophical bases for parallelism. To put the matter plainly, they have given up the problem in despair. Considerable sympathy is due them. The perplexities of the strictly philosophical problem and the complexities of the physiological data, not to mention the investigations and discoveries that must yet be made, make of despair an insurance against insanity.

Idealism has been acclaimed as furnishing a solution to these difficulties by reducing the so-called corporeal attributes to items of mental existence. It is with reluctance that this device must be judged inadequate. Perhaps idealism, rejecting the notion of an unknowable substratum in order to eliminate skepticism, has been of use in establishing the possibility of truth; but however that may be, the bare principle of idealism leaves practically untouched the difficulties in sensation. The reason is easy to state. Whether or not corporeal attributes are phases of mental existence, there is still the problem of relating the stimulus we call a sense object (whether idealistically conceived or not) with motor reactions on the one hand and with discursive knowledge on the other.

But can so ancient, not to say so unscientific a writer as Augustine advance the study of sensation? The answer to this insinuation is that, if modern writers offer so little hope, help from any source ought to be welcome. And while Augustine and the Neoplatonism from which he drew inspiration fall far short of answering all questions, they may possibly start us on the right road instead of leaving us in a blind alley.

First of all, instead of attempting to explain sensation by an action of the sense object on the soul, these early writers prefer to think of the action as passing from the soul to the sense object. Given a sense object, a healthy retina and nervous system, and given light rays passing through the lens of the eye, it does not follow, as some modern, mechanical views would lead one to expect, it does not follow that a sensation of color is produced. It can be made fairly obvious that the physical conditions do not explain the distinguishing of colors. Most people look at the sky and see blue. They fail to see green, purple, and pink. Trees are seen as green, and for some people even spruce trees are green. But if these people are forced to compare colors, or to duplicate them in oils, they will soon see many colors which previously they had only been looking at. This illustrates Augustine's point that sensation depends on attention and volition, that it is more our grasping the object than it is the object's affecting us.

But still further, it is not merely the distinguishing of colors, it is the seeing of any object at all and the hearing of any sound that requires attention. In studying the problems of sensation one may become so engrossed that sensation vanishes. The open eyes may see nothing before them, and the call for dinner, ordinarily awaited with impatience, goes unheard. Sensation, therefore, seems to require voluntary action, and it may be sound philosophy as well as orthodox theology and crisp English to say, there are none so blind as those who will not see.

Granted, this theory faces a little difficulty with a loud clap of thunder, or a blinding light; these seem to be involuntary perceptions, but these difficulties are so slight when compared with the difficulties of opposing theories that one may confidently hope to dispose of them.

This Augustinian stress on vital action outward rather than mechanical action inward seems to provide a better basis for dealing with the details of epistemology.

In the first place, it would remove the chasm which Kant dug between sensation and intellection. And it would remove it, not by going backward to the expedient of British empiricists in reducing mind to a complex of sensations, but on the contrary by recognizing intellectual activity in the simplest stage of consciousness.

Even those thinkers who have been powerfully influenced by empiricism are beginning to recognize that the old notion of a pure sensation is an hallucination. No one, perhaps, would accuse F. R. Tennant of being an Augustinian, and yet in his *Philosophical Theology* (Volume 1, page 41) he writes, "The purer we conceive our sensa to be, and the more passive we suppose their reception, the further we remove the possibility of a natural explanation of knowledge."

The language of Professor Blanshard of Swarthmore in his recent opus *The Nature of Thought* (Volume 1, page 57) will no doubt be more clearly understood. "We must so construe the world we first live in as to make escape from it conceivable. It is true that we must not read into the earlier what comes later, but it is also true that we must see it in the light of the later, if our account is ever to reach the later at all. Herbert Spencer once suggested that the qualities of sensation could be explained as rapid tatoos of nervous shocks differing in their frequency. If such shocks are taken as units of consciousness, the theory is instructive and interesting; if they are taken as nervous impulses we should be placing the beginning of thought in something from which its escape in *aliud genus* would be unintelligible." And this thought he summarizes admirably in a later phrase: "We do not explain how one thing arises by saying that it was preceded by something radically different."

Obviously, then, thought and knowledge cannot be obtained from pure sensation; or, in other words, to preserve a connection between sense experience and rational knowledge, sensation must be understood as an incipient form of reason. The two types of mental action must somehow be united, and if empiricism in philosophy results in skepticism while in theology it removes revelation, the only possible expedient is to explain sensation in terms of thought rather than thought in terms of sensation.

But perhaps these elementary observations run the risk of becoming technical, and it may not be out of place to conclude the address with a few remarks to the graduation class. After all, it is their commencement. Advice given to young men on such occasions as this can soar grandiloquently into the clouds of cosmic truth, or it can restrict its horizon so as to see one object clearly. In consonance with what has already been said about substituting the shapeless repetition of a universal principle for its detailed application, the latter course of definite detail will be followed.

You who graduate today are passing from a school in which it has been necessary to work with application and diligence. You are passing to another school in which the assignments are considerably more onerous, less explicitly stated, and in which the examinations and grades come at unexpected times and in unfamiliar forms. There are problems of church finance and congregational organization; of shepherding, multiplying, and edifying the saints; and of combatting a satanic opposition that threatens to increase in force. In view of this, should a comfortably fixed guest speaker lay any further burdens upon you?

Or perhaps it is not an added burden; it may rather be a means of lightening the common load of us all.

The power we exert under God is reasonably calculated to vary directly with our mental ability. God has frequently used obscure instruments and has granted them temporary prominence; but the lives of Paul, Augustine, Calvin, and Machen, whose contributions have, or will, exert force over the centuries, prevent us from placing a premium on ignorance. Therefore, graduates of the class of '41, unless you are completely disappointed by the tenor of these words, make it the aim of your life to contribute something of genuine scholarly value to the propagation of the Reformed faith. To be sure, the daily duties of the ministry are heavy, and yet. . .

There was a minister, not conspicuous above his fellows, who for forty-five years served one congregation. He prepared two sermons and a prayer meeting talk every week. He visited the people, he kept in touch with the various organizations; he had his full share of ill-health and adversity. Yet with it all he managed to publish a few articles and two books, one of which was quite a solid volume. Compared with the literary remains of a Hodge or a Warfield, this record may seem barren; but it may also set a commendable and not too distant goal for the average pastor.

Run over in your mind, therefore, the fields in which the need of scholarship is great; select the subject that interests you most—theology, epistemology, literature, or economics;—reject courageously an encyclopedic inquiry of the whole matter, but, rather, decide tentatively upon some manageable detail, and ask whether you could not produce a worthwhile paper within the next ten years. Is it not reasonable to suppose that even a busy pastor can write twenty or twenty-five pages in ten years? Perhaps, on the contrary, some optimistic soul thinks that ten years is too long an estimate. But why discuss it? Five years or fifteen—it is not the speed but the quality that is essential. It is not volume but technical proficiency that is needed. And the second article will require less time and will be of more value than the first. To aid each individual in the preparation of such articles, mutual criticism could be obtained by developing, not just a Calvinistic Philosophical Society, but a research society of Calvinistic scholars. There would thus be provision for the study of subjects beyond the narrow range of the epistemological illustration of this address. Such a society, if it can produce technical proficiency, could hope eventually to publish proceedings. But to save our money for more pressing needs, why should we not make the devil pay our publication expenses? There are numerous technical periodicals that will accept offerings of value. Meeting their standards will test our ability, and after having practiced on them, the best articles could be collected, and . . . and . . . and appropriate plans can be put into effect after we have achieved genuine recognition.

Lord, lift thou up the light
of thy countenance upon us.
Oh, send out thy light and thy
truth; let them lead me.

Appendix C
Art and the Gospel*

In the United States, both within and without the churches, Christianity has many enemies. There are the scientific and not-so-scientific atheists who have tremendous influence in public education. There are the murderous abortionists, and criminals of all types. But none of these is the subject of this article. Within the churches, neo-orthodoxy, more neo than orthodox, reduces the Bible to the level of Aesop's fables. Also within the churches is another group, some of whom have been influenced by Herman Dooyeweerd and H. R. Rookmaaker, some whose background is too diverse to trace, who wish to substitute art for the Gospel. Perhaps they are not technically existentialists, but they dislike intellect and truth just as much. The exact views of these people vary considerably. Some see further into the implications than others. Since this diversity makes it awkward to speak of the group as a whole, the present article will select one particular member. The selection is defensible because the gentleman, Leland Ryken, has edited and written a preface for an anthology entitled *The Christian Imagination* (Baker Book House, 1981). Consider now this quotation from the Preface:

---

*Reprinted from *The Trinity Review*, copyright 1982, The Trinity Foundation.

. . . the imagination is what enables us to produce and enjoy the arts. . . . The imagination is one way we know the truth. For truth, including religious truth, is not solely the province of the reason or intellect. For example, one can experience the truth about God and salvation while listening to Handel's *Messiah*. But how? Not primarily through reason, but through the senses (hearing), emotions that I call the imagination.

A pastor friend of mine . . . first knew that Jesus rose from the grave . . . not during the sermon, but with the sound of the trumpets that concluded the service [one Easter morning]. . . . Not surely with the intellect, but with the senses. . . . Truth, I repeat, does not come to us solely through the reason and intellect.

Consider the way truth comes to us in the Bible. If you asked an adult Sunday School class what topics are covered in the Old Testament Psalms, the list would look something like this: God, providence, guilt. . . . Such a list leans decidedly toward the abstract. . . . But consider an equally valid list of topics . . . dogs, honey, grass, thunder . . . It touches our emotions far more vividly than the first list does. In the Bible truth does not address only the rational intellect. . . . Handel's *Messiah* is as important to us as a Christmas sermon.

Because the ideas expressed in these paragraphs attract the adherence of many who profess Christianity, they should be scrutinized with care. One good thing can be said: The author tries to define his term *imagination*: It is what enables us to enjoy the arts. Later he more explicitly defines it as the combination of mind, senses, and emotions. That no major philosopher had ever used the term in that sense is irrelevant, for every author has the right to define his terms as he pleases. He must however, adhere to his own definition, and the definition must be suitable to the development of the subject. Yet, though the stated definition includes mind, the general tenor of the passage is inimical to mind. Furthermore, if imagination is the complex of all these factors, including the mind, what can the author mean by saying that the imagination is one way to know the truth. What other way could there be? The definition as given includes one's entire consciousness. It fails to distinguish imagination from any other conscious action. Without using one's mind, senses, or emotions, what truths could possibly be learned, and what would the learning process be? The definition is so all inclusive that it is utterly useless in distinguishing between any two methods of learning. Because of this vacuity, because the author obviously wants to find at least two ways to truth, one without the intellect, and because of the next to last sentence in the quotation, it seems that the author wishes to learn some things through the emotions alone.

One must ask whether or not even the enjoyment of the arts depends more on the mind than on the emotions. Critics of painting examine the brush work, they evaluate the relation between light and dark areas (*e.g.* Rembrandt's drawing of the beggar, his daughter, her baby son, and the householder), and they analyze the composition. Composition requires careful thought on the part of both artist and critic. Such analyses are intellectual, not emotional; and I can hardly *imagine* that Rembrandt's drawing arouses much emotion in anyone. If the biographer of Leonardo da Vinci had his facts right, it would seem that this prince of painters was completely non-emotional; or if not completely, his emotion was one of continuing anger. Then too, Milton Nahm's book on *The Aesthetic Response* sharply distinguishes it from emotion.

However, aesthetics is neither the main difficulty with the quoted passage nor of much importance to Christianity. A more, a much more serious difficulty is the author's view of truth. Maybe he has no view of truth, at least no clear view; but he certainly seems to be talking about two kinds of truth. He says, "Religious truth is not solely the province of reason."

Presumably the truths of physics and zoology are truths of reason. Even this is doubtful, for he says that truth, presumably all truth, and therefore religious truth as well, but also the laws of physics, is not solely intellectual. I doubt that many physicists would agree; and it would be interesting to see how Ryken would answer their disclaimer. Our trouble here is to discover what he means by truth. Statements, propositions, predicates attached to subjects, are true (or false). But how could a nocturne or one of Rodin's sculptures be true? The sculpture might resemble its model, and the proposition "the sculpture resembles its model" would be a truth; but how could a bronze or marble statue be a *truth*? Only propositions can be true. If I merely pronounce a word—cat, college, collage—it is neither true nor false: It does not say anything. Buy if I say "the cat is black" or "the collage is abominable, " I speak the truth (or falsehood as the case may be). But *cat*, all by itself and without previous context, is neither true nor false. Note that the Psalms, which the author tries to use as a support, do not simply say, dogs, honey, grass, and thunder: They say that the grass withers, the honey is sweet, and so on, all of which are propositions. And if the words *grass* and *thunder* touch one's emotions "far more vividly" than the words *God* and *guilt*, there is something radically wrong with that person's emotions. Better to have no emotions at all. Emotions are hard to control; they are not only distressing to the one who has them, they are also disconcerting to his friends.

If the author's peculiar aesthetics is relatively unimportant, and if his undefined view of truth is a more serious flaw, the implications of such a defective view of truth are disastrous for the preaching of the Gospel.

It is undoubtedly true that "one can experience the truth about God and salvation *while* listening to Handel's *Messiah*." The reason is that *The Messiah* gives the words of Scripture. Of course, one can have the experience of boredom, or a bright idea on investment policy, or a decision as to which restaurant one will take his girl friend afterward, *while* listening to *The Messiah*. But if one has thoughts of God and salvation *while* and *because* of the oratorio, they come by reason of the Scriptural words. The music adds little or nothing. In fact, the reason why many people do not have thoughts about God while listening is that the music distracts them.

The use of the word *while* is a propaganda device: Literally the sentence is true, but the writer means something else. Fortunately, after inducing a favorable response on the part of the reader by the word *while*, he actually says what he means, twice. First, a pastor first believed Jesus rose from the dead, not during a sermon which told him so, but with (of course *with* is ambiguous too) the sound of the concluding fanfare. At any rate, the pastor did not believe in the resurrection with his mind or intellect: He *sensed* it. One might grant that he sensed the noise of the trumpets; but how can anyone today sense Christ's Resurrection? This is utter nonsense, and the final line of the quotation shows how anti-Christian the whole viewpoint is.

He says, "Handel's *Messiah* is as important to us as a Christmas sermon." Naturally, if the Christmas sermon in a liberal church centers on Santa Claus, and not on the Incarnation of the Second Person of the Trinity, Handel's music might be as important, the equal importance being about zero. But of course the writer means that the music is as important as the words. If this were so, there would be no necessity to preach the Gospel and ask people to believe the good news.

But art is no substitute for Gospel information. In Clowes Hall at Butler University in Indianapolis there hangs a gigantic tapestry which depicts the miraculous draft of fishes. It is supposed to be a great work of art. Now, on one occasion, I accompanied a group of Japanese professors through the place, and one of them asked me, "What is the story?" No amount of art appreciation could give him the information the Bible gives. That Christ was God and that He worked miracles during his Incarnation is understood only through the intellectual understanding of words. Nor would a blast of trumpets help.

If the writer's views were true, the work of missionaries would be enormously easier. They would not have to learn a difficult language: They could just put on a recording of Handel and conversions would follow. Why didn't Paul think of that? Don't preach the Gospel, don't give information, just play some music! Poor Paul: He said, Faith cometh by hearing the word of God. No tapestry, no sculpture, no fanfare. But it is Paul who defines what Christianity is. Anything else is something else.

Scripture Index

8:7 *133-134*
10:17 *228*
13:1 *82*
13:4 *85*
13:9 *105*

2 Thessalonians
1:6 *119*

2 Timothy
3:16-17 *205*

Index

The Crisis of Our Time

Historians have christened the thirteenth century the Age of Faith and termed the eighteenth century the Age of Reason. The twentieth century has been called many things: the Atomic Age, the Age of Inflation, the Age of the Tyrant, the Age of Aquarius. But it deserves one name more than the others: the Age of Irrationalism. Contemporary secular intellectuals are anti-intellectual. Contemporary philosophers are anti-philosophy. Contemporary theologians are anti-theology.

In past centuries secular philosophers have generally believed that knowledge is possible to man. Consequently they expended a great deal of thought and effort trying to justify knowledge. In the twentieth century, however, the optimism of the secular philosophers has all but disappeared. They despair of knowledge.

Like their secular counterparts, the great theologians and doctors of the church taught that knowledge is possible to man. Yet the theologians of the twentieth century have repudiated that belief. They also despair of knowledge. This radical skepticism has filtered down from the philosophers and theologians and penetrated our entire culture, from television to music to literature. *The Christian in the twentieth century is confronted with an overwhelming cultural consensus—sometimes stated explicitly, but most often implicitly: Man does not and cannot know anything truly.*

What does this have to do with Christianity? Simply this: If man can know nothing truly, man can truly know nothing. We cannot know that the Bible is the Word of God, that Christ died for sin, or that Christ is alive today at the right hand of the Father. Unless knowledge is possible, Christianity is nonsensical, for it claims to be knowledge. What is at stake in the twentieth century is not simply a single doctrine, such as the Virgin Birth, or the existence of hell, as important as those doctrines may be, but the whole of Christianity itself. If knowledge is not possible to man, it is worse than silly to argue points of doctrine—it is insane.

The irrationalism of the present age is so thorough-going and pervasive that even the Remnant—the segment of the professing church that remains faithful—has accepted much of it, frequently without even being aware of what it was accepting. In some circles this irrationalism has become synonymous with piety and humility, and those who oppose it are denounced as rationalists—as though to be logical were a sin. Our contemporary anti-theologians make a contradiction and call it a Mystery. The faithful ask for truth and are given Paradox. If any balk at swallowing the absurdities of the anti-theologians, they are frequently marked as heretics or schismatics who seek to act independently of God.

There is no greater threat facing the true Church of Christ at this moment than the irrationalism that now controls our entire culture. Communism, guilty of tens of millions of murders, including those of millions of Christians, is to be feared, but not nearly so much as the idea that we do not and cannot know the truth. Hedonism, the popular philosophy of America, is not to be feared so much as the belief that logic —that "mere human logic," to use the religious irrationalists' own phrase—is futile. The attacks on truth, on revelation, on the intellect, and on logic are renewed daily. But note well: The misologists—the haters of logic—use logic to demonstrate the futility of using logic. The anti-intellectuals construct intricate intellectual arguments to prove the insufficiency of the intellect. The anti-theologians use the revealed Word of God to show that there can be no revealed Word of God—or that if there could, it would remain impenetrable darkness and Mystery to our finite minds.

Nonsense Has Come

Is it any wonder that the world is grasping at straws—the straws of experientialism, mysticism and drugs? After all, if people are told that the Bible contains insoluble mysteries, then is not a flight into mysticism to be expected? On what grounds can it be condemned? Certainly not on logical grounds or Biblical grounds, if logic is futile and the Bible unintelligible. Moreover, if it cannot be condemned on logical or Biblical grounds, it cannot be condemned at all. If people are going to have a religion of the mysterious, they will not adopt Christianity: They will have a genuine mystery religion. "Those who call for Nonsense," C.S. Lewis once wrote, "will find that it comes." And that is precisely what has happened. The popularity of Eastern mysticism, of drugs, and of religious experience is the logical consequence of the irrationalism of the twentieth century. There can and will be no Christian revival—and no reconstruction of society—unless and until the irrationalism of the age is totally repudiated by Christians.

The Church Defenseless

Yet how shall they do it? The spokesmen for Christianity have been fatally infected with irrationalism. The seminaries, which annually train thousands of men to teach millions of Christians, are the finishing schools of irrationalism, completing the job begun by the government schools and colleges. Some of the pulpits of the most conservative churches (we are not speaking of the apostate churches) are occupied by graduates of the anti-theological schools. These products of modern anti-theological education, when asked to give a reason for the hope that is in them, can generally respond with only the intellectual analogue of a shrug—a mumble about Mystery. They have not grasped—and therefore cannot teach those for whom they are responsible—the first truth: "And ye shall know the truth." Many, in fact, explicitly deny it, saying that, at best, we possess only "pointers" to the truth, or something "similar" to the truth, a mere analogy. Is the impotence of the Christian Church a puzzle? Is the fascination with pentecostalism and faith healing among members of conservative churches an enigma? Not when one understands the sort of studied nonsense that is purveyed in the name of God in the seminaries.

The Trinity Foundation

The creators of The Trinity Foundation firmly believe that theology is too important to be left to the licensed theologians —the graduates of the schools of theology. They have created The Trinity Foundation for the express purpose of teaching the faithful all that the Scriptures contain—not warmed over, baptized, secular philosophies. Each member of the board of directors of The Trinity Foundation has signed this oath: "I believe that the Bible alone and the Bible in its entirety is the Word of God and, therefore, inerrant in the autographs. I believe that the system of truth presented in the Bible is best summarized in the Westminster Confession of Faith. So help me God."

The ministry of The Trinity Foundation is the presentation of the system of truth taught in Scripture as clearly and as completely as possible. We do not regard obscurity as a virtue, nor confusion as a sign of spirituality. Confusion, like all error, is sin, and teaching that confusion is all that Christians can hope for is doubly sin.

The presentation of the truth of Scripture necessarily involves the rejection of error. The Foundation has exposed and will continue to expose the irrationalism of the twentieth century, whether its current spokesman be an existentialist philosopher or a professed Reformed theologian. We oppose anti-intellectualism, whether it be espoused by a neo-orthodox theologian or a fundamentalist evangelist. We reject misology, whether it be on the lips of a neo-evangelical or those of a Roman Catholic charismatic. To each error we bring the brilliant light of Scripture, proving all things, and holding fast to that which is true.

The Primacy of Theory

The ministry of The Trinity Foundation is not a "practical" ministry. If you are a pastor, we will not enlighten you on how to organize an ecumenical prayer meeting in your community or how to double church attendance in a year. If you are a homemaker, you will have to read elsewhere to find out how to become a total woman. If you are a businessman, we will not tell you how to develop a social conscience. The professing church is drowning in such "practical" advice.

The Trinity Foundation is unapologetically theoretical in its outlook, believing that theory without practice is dead, and that practice without theory is blind. The trouble with the professing church is not primarily in its practice, but in its theory. Christians do not know, and many do not even care to know, the doctrines of Scripture. Doctrine is intellectual, and Christians are generally anti-intellectual. Doctrine is ivory tower philosophy, and they scorn ivory towers. The ivory tower, however, is the control tower of a civilization. It is a fundamental, theoretical mistake of the practical men to think that they can be merely practical, for practice is always the practice of some theory. The relationship between theory and practice is the relationship between cause and effect. If a person believes correct theory, his practice will tend to be correct. The practice of contemporary Christians is immoral because it is the practice of false theories. It is a major theoretical mistake of the practical men to think that they can ignore the ivory towers of the philosophers and theologians as irrelevant to their lives. Every action that the "practical"men take is governed by the thinking that has occurred in some ivory tower—whether that tower be the British Museum, the Academy, a home in Basel, Switzerland, or a tent in Israel.

In Understanding Be Men

It is the first duty of the Christian to understand correct theory—correct doctrine—and thereby implement correct practice. This order—first theory, then practice—is both logical and Biblical. It is, for example, exhibited in Paul's epistle to the Romans, in which he spends the first eleven chapters expounding theory and the last five discussing practice. The contemporary teachers of Christians have not only reversed the order, they have inverted the Pauline emphasis on theory and practice. The virtually complete failure of the teachers of the professing church to instruct the faithful in correct doctrine is the cause of the misconduct and cultural impotence of Christians. The Church's lack of power is the result of its lack of truth. The

Gospel is the power of God, not religious experience or personal relationship. The Church has no power because it has abandoned the Gospel, the good news, for a religion of experientialism. Twentieth century American Christians are children carried about by every wind of doctrine, not knowing what they believe, or even if they believe anything for certain.

The chief purpose of The Trinity Foundation is to counteract the irrationalism of the age and to expose the errors of the teachers of the church. Our emphasis—on the Bible as the sole source of truth, on the primacy of the intellect, on the supreme importance of correct doctrine, and on the necessity for systematic and logical thinking—is almost unique in Christendom. To the extent that the church survives—and she will survive and flourish—it will be because of her increasing acceptance of these basic ideas and their logical implications.

We believe that the Trinity Foundation is filling a vacuum in Christendom. We are saying that Christianity is intellectually defensible—that, in fact, it is the only intellectually defensible system of thought. We are saying that God has made the wisdom of this world—whether that wisdom be called science, religion, philosophy, or common sense—foolishness. We are appealing to all Christians who have not conceded defeat in the intellectual battle with the world to join us in our efforts to raise a standard to which all men of sound mind can repair.

The love of truth, of God's Word, has all but disappeared in our time. We are committed to and pray for a great instauration. But though we may not see this reformation of Christendom in our lifetimes, we believe it is our duty to present the whole counsel of God because Christ has commanded it. The results of our teaching are in God's hands, not ours. Whatever those results, His Word is never taught in vain, but always accomplishes the result that he intended it to accomplish. Professor Gordon H. Clark has stated our view well:

There have been times in the history of God's people, for example, in the days of Jeremiah, when refreshing grace and widespread revival were not to be expected: the time was one of chastisement. If this twentieth century is of a similar nature, individual Christians here and there can find comfort and strength in a study of God's Word. But if God has decreed happier days for us and if we may expect a world-shaking and genuine spiritual awakening, then it is the author's belief that a zeal for souls, however necessary, is not the sufficient condition. Have there not been devout saints in every age, numerous enough to carry on a revival? Twelve such persons are plenty. What distinguishes the arid ages from the period of the Reformation, when nations were moved as they had not been since Paul preached in Ephesus, Corinth, and Rome, is the latter's fullness of knowledge of God's Word. To echo an early Reformation thought, when the ploughman and the garage attendant know the Bible as well as the theologian does, and know it better than some contemporary theologians, then the desired awakening shall have already occurred.

In addition to publishing books, of which *A Christian Philosophy of Education* is the twentieth, the Foundation publishes a bimonthly newsletter, *The Trinity Review*. Subscriptions to *The Review* are free; please write to the address below to become a subscriber. If you would like further information or would like to join us in our work, please let us know.

The Trinity Foundation is a non-profit foundation tax-exempt under section 501 (c)(3) of the Internal Revenue Code of 1954. You can help us disseminate the Word of God through your tax-deductible contributions to the Foundation.

And we know that the Son of God is come, and hath given us an understanding, that we may know him that is true, and we are in him that is true, in his Son Jesus Christ. This is the true God, and eternal life.

John W. Robbins
President

Intellectual Ammunition

The Trinity Foundation is committed to the reconstruction of philosophy and theology along Biblical lines. We regard God's command to bring all our thoughts into conformity with Christ very seriously, and the books listed below are designed to accomplish that goal. They are written with two subordinate purposes: (1) to demolish all secular claims to knowledge; and (2) to build a system of truth based upon the Bible alone.

Works of Philosophy

Answer to Ayn Rand, John W. Robbins $4.95
   The only analysis and criticism of the views of novelist-philosopher Ayn Rand from a consistently Christian perspective.

Behaviorism and Christianity, Gordon H. Clark $5.95
   Behaviorism *is a critique of both secular and religious behaviorists. It includes chapters on John Watson, Edgar S. Singer Jr., Gilbert Ryle, B.F. Skinner, and Donald MacKay. Clark's refutation of behaviorism and his argument for a Christian doctrine of man are unanswerable.*

A Christian Philosophy of Education, Gordon H. Clark $8.95
   The first edition of this book was published in 1946. It sparked the

contemporary interest in Christian schools. Dr. Clark has thoroughly revised and updated it, and it is needed now more than ever. Its chapters include: The Need for a World-View, The Christian World-View, The Alternative to Christian Theism, Neutrality, Ethics, The Christian Philosophy of Education, Academic Matters, Kindergarten to University. Three appendices are included as well: The Relationship of Public Education to Christianity, A Protestant World-View, and Art and the Gospel.

A Christian View of Men and Things, Gordon H. Clark $8.95

No other book achieves what A Christian View *does: the presentation of Christianity as it applies to history, politics, ethics, science, religion, and epistemology. Clark's command of both worldly philosophy and Scripture is evident on every page, and the result is a breathtaking and invigorating challenge to the wisdom of this world.*

Clark Speaks From The Grave, Gordon H. Clark $3.95

Dr. Clark chides some of his critics for their failure to defend Christianity competently. Clark Speaks is a stimulating and illuminating discussion of the errors of contemporary apologists.

Education, Christianity, and the State $7.95
J. Gresham Machen

Machen was one of the foremost educators, theologians, and defenders of Christianity in the twentieth century. The author of numerous scholarly books, Machen saw clearly that if Christianity is to survive and flourish, a system of Christian grade schools must be established. This collection of essays captures his thought on education over nearly three decades.

Logic, Gordon H. Clark $8.95

Written as a textbook for Christian schools, Logic is another unique book from Clark's pen. His presentation of the laws of thought, which must be followed if Scripture is to be understood correctly, and which are found in Scripture itself, is both clear and thorough. Logic is an indispensable book for the thinking Christian.

The Philosophy of Science and Belief in God $5.95
Gordon H. Clark
  In opposing the contemporary idolatry of science, Clark analyzes three major aspects of science: the problem of motion, Newtonian science, and modern theories of physics. His conclusion is that science, while it may be useful, is always false; and he demonstrates its falsity in numerous ways. Since science is always false, it can offer no objection to the Bible and Christianity.

Religion, Reason and Revelation, Gordon H. Clark $7.95
  One of Clark's apologetical masterpieces, Religion, Reason and Revelation *has been praised for the clarity of its thought and language. It includes chapters on Is Christianity a Religion? Faith and Reason, Inspiration and Language, Revelation and Morality, and God and Evil. It is must reading for all serious Christians.*

Selections from Hellenistic Philosophy, Gordon H. Clark $10.95
  This is one of Clark's early works in which he translates, edits, and comments upon works by the Epicureans, the Stoics, Plutarch, Philo Judaeus, Hermes Trismegistus, and Plotinus. First published in 1940, it has been a standard college text for more than four decades.

William James, Gordon H. Clark $2.00
  America has not produced many philosophers, but William James has been extremely influential. Clark examines his philosophy of Pragmatism.

Works of Theology

The Atonement, Gordon H. Clark $8.95
  This is a major addition to Clark's multi-volume systematic theology. In The Atonement, *Clark discusses the Covenants, the Virgin Birth and Incarnation, federal headship and representation, the rela-*

tionship between God's sovereignty and justice, and much more. He analyzes traditional views of the Atonement and criticizes them in the light of Scripture alone.

The Biblical Doctrine of Man, Gordon H. Clark $5.95
   Is man soul and body or soul, spirit, and body? What is the image of God? Is Adam's sin imputed to his children? Is evolution true? Are men totally depraved? What is the heart? These are some to the questions discussed and answered from Scripture in this book.

Cornelius Van Til: The Man and The Myth $2.45
John W. Robbins
   The actual teachings of this eminent Philadelphia theologian have been obscured by the myths that surround him. This book penetrates those myths and criticizes Van Til's surprisingly unorthodox views of God and the Bible.

Faith and Saving Faith, Gordon H. Clark $5.95
   The views of the Roman Catholic church, John Calvin, Thomas Manton, John Owen, Charles Hodge, and B.B. Warfield are discussed in this book. Is the object of faith a person or a proposition? Is faith more than belief? Is belief more than thinking with assent, as Augustine said? In a world chaotic with differing views of faith, Clark clearly explains the Biblical view of faith and saving faith.

God's Hammer: The Bible and Its Critics, Gordon H. Clark $6.95
   The starting point of Christianity, the doctrine on which all other doctrines depend, is "The Bible alone is the Word of God written, and therefore inerrant in the autographs." Over the centuries the opponents of Christianity, with Satanic shrewdness, have concentrated their attacks on the truthfulness and completeness of the Bible. In the twentieth century the attack is not so much in the fields of history and archaeology as in philosophy. Clark's brilliant defense of the complete truthfulness of the Bible is captured in this collection of eleven major essays.

In Defense of Theology, Gordon H. Clark $12.95
There are four groups to whom Clark addresses this book: the average Christians who are uninterested in theology, the atheists and agnostics, the religious experientalists, and the serious Christians. The vindication of the knowledge of God against the objections of three of these groups is the first step in theology.

Logical Criticisms of Textual Criticism, Gordon H. Clark $2.95
In this critique of the science of textual criticism, Dr. Clark exposes the fallacious argumentation of the modern textual critics and defends the view that the early Christians knew better than the modern critics which manuscripts of the New Testament were more accurate.

Pat Robertson: A Warning to America, John W. Robbins $6.95
The Protestant Reformation was based on the Biblical principle that the Bible is the only revelation from God, yet a growing political-religious movement, led by Pat Robertson, asserts that God speaks to them directly. This book addresses the serious issue of religious fanaticism in America by examining the theological and political views of Presidential candidate Pat Robertson.

Predestination, Gordon H. Clark $7.95
Clark thoroughly discusses one of the most controversial and pervasive doctrines of the Bible: that God is, quite literally, Almighty. Free will, the origin of evil, God's omniscience, creation, and the new birth are all presented within a Scriptural framework. The objections of those who do not believe in the Almighty God are considered and refuted. This edition also contains the text of the booklet, Predestination in the Old Testament.

Scripture Twisting in the Seminaries. Part 1: Feminism $5.95
John W. Robbins
An analysis of the views of three graduates of Westminster Seminary on the role of women in the church.

The Trinity, Gordon H. Clark $8.95
   Apart from the doctrine of Scripture, no teaching of the Bible is more important than the doctrine of God. Clark's defense of the orthodox doctrine of the Trinity is a principal portion of a major new work of Systematic Theology now in progress. There are chapters on the deity of Christ, Augustine, the incomprehensibility of God, Bavinck and Van Til, and the Holy Spirit, among others.

What Do Presbyterians Believe? Gordon H. Clark $6.95
   This classic introduction to Christian doctrine has been republished. It is the best commentary on the Westminster Confession of Faith that has ever been written.

Commentaries on the New Testament

Ephesians, Gordon H. Clark $8.95
First and Second Thessalonians, Gordon H. Clark $5.95
The Pastoral Epistles (I and II Timothy and Titus) $9.95
   Gordon H. Clark
   All of Clark's commentaries are expository, not technical, and are written for the Christian layman. His purpose is to explain the text clearly and accurately so that the Word of God will be thoroughly known by every Christian. Revivals of Christianity come only through the spread of God's truth. The sound exposition of the Bible, through preaching and through commentaries on Scripture, is the only method of spreading that truth.

The Trinity Library

We will send you one copy of each of the 26 books listed above for the low price of $125. The regular price of these books is $178. Or you may order the books you want individually on the order blank on the next page. Because some of the books are in short supply, we must reserve the right to substitute others of equal or greater value in The Trinity Library.

Thank you for your attention. We hope to hear from you soon. This special offer expires June 30, 1989.

Order Form

Name _____

Address _____

_____

Please: □ add my name to the mailing list for *The Trinity Review*. I understand that there is no charge for the *Review*.

□ accept my tax deductible contribution of $ _____ for the work of the Foundation.

□ send me _____ copies of *A Christian Philosophy of Education*. I enclose as payment $ _____.

□ send me the Trinity Library of 26 books. I enclose $125 as full payment for it.

□ send me the following books. I enclose full payment in the amount of $ _____ for them.

_____

_____

_____

_____

_____

_____

Mail to: The Trinity Foundation
                Post Office Box 169
                Jefferson, MD 21755

Please add $1.00 for postage on orders less than $10. Thank you.
For quantity discounts, please write to the Foundation.